Building SOA-Based Composite Applications Using NetBeans IDE 6

Design, build, test, and debug service-oriented applications with ease using XML, BPEL, and Java web services

David Salter

Frank Jennings

PUBLISHING

BIRMINGHAM - MUMBAI

D0814034

Building SOA-Based Composite Applications Using NetBeans IDE 6

Copyright © 2008 Packt Publishing

All rights reserved. No part of this book may be reproduced, stored in a retrieval system, or transmitted in any form or by any means, without the prior written permission of the publisher, except in the case of brief quotations embedded in critical articles or reviews.

Every effort has been made in the preparation of this book to ensure the accuracy of the information presented. However, the information contained in this book is sold without warranty, either express or implied. Neither the authors, Packt Publishing, nor its dealers or distributors will be held liable for any damages caused or alleged to be caused directly or indirectly by this book.

Packt Publishing has endeavored to provide trademark information about all the companies and products mentioned in this book by the appropriate use of capitals. However, Packt Publishing cannot guarantee the accuracy of this information.

First published: February 2008

Production Reference: 1010208

Published by Packt Publishing Ltd.
32 Lincoln Road
Olton
Birmingham, B27 6PA, UK.

ISBN 978-1-847192-62-2

www.packtpub.com

Cover Image by Nilesh R. Mohite (nilpreet2000@yahoo.co.in)

Credits

Authors

David Salter

Frank Jennings

Reviewer

Mario Pérez Madueño

Acquisition Editor

Priyanka Baruah

Development Editor

Nikhil Bangera

Technical Editor

Bhupali Khule

Editorial Team Leader

Mithil Kulkarni

Project Manager

Abhijeet Deobhakta

Indexers

Hemangini Bari

Monica Ajmera

Proofreader

Angie Butcher

Production Coordinator

Shantanu Zagade

Cover Work

Shantanu Zagade

About the Authors

David Salter is an enterprise software architect who has been developing software professionally since 1991. His relationship with Java goes right back to the beginning, using Java 1.0 for writing desktop applications and applets for interactive web sites. David has been developing Enterprise Java Applications using both the J2EE standards and open source solutions for the last five years. David runs the Java community web site Develop In Java (http://www.developinjava.com), a web site for all levels of Java developers.

Foremost, I would like to thank my wife and family for putting up with my many hours at the computer whilst writing this book. Special thanks go to my wife for all her encouragement and support.

I'd also like to say thank you to all the people at Packt Publishing, especially Priyanka, Abhijeet, Bhupali, and Patricia. Thanks also go to the NetBeans Enterprise Developer community, who have provided help and assistance throughout the writing of this book.

Frank Jennings works in the Information Products Group of Sun Microsystems Inc. He has more than 9 years of experience in Java, SOA and System Design. He is an Electronics Engineer from Madras University and has worked for several open source projects. Frank has written regular columns for leading Java journals including Java Developer's Journal and Linux Developer's Week. Frank is also the co-author of the book *SOA Approach to Integration* focusing on SOA design pattern for enterprises. Frank also is involved in the technical publication of Sun Microsystems in the fields of Solaris and Developer AMP Stack. His blog can be read at `http://blogs.sun.com/phantom` and he can be reached at `theghost@sun.com`. He also holds a Post Graduate Diploma in Computer Science and an Advance Diploma in Computer Integrated Management from University of Indianapolis.

It is just amazing how the guys at Packt Publishing put up with me inspite of my late drafts. I would like to thank Abhijeet and Bhupali for all their hardwork in making me work to complete this book. I also thank the NetBeans Documentation team for providing an extensive set of tutorials on the SOA capabilities of NetBeans.

About the Reviewer

Mario Pérez Madueño was born in 1975 in Turin and lives in Barcelona. He graduated in ETIS from the Open University of Catalonia (UOC) in 2006 and is currently finishing studies for the EI degree. He is a foundation member of ARUOC robotics group in the same University. Mario is a Java SE, ME and EE enthusiast and a fan of NetBeans IDE, he is currently contributing with the Spanish translation team for NetBeans 6.

Acknowledgements goes for my wife María, for her unconditional help and support in all the projects I get involved, and to Martín for giving me the force for going ahead.

Table of Contents

Preface

Composite applications aid businesses by stitching together various componented business capabilities. In the current enterprise scenario, empowering business users to react quickly to the rapidly changing business environment is the top most priority. With the advent of composite applications the 'reuse' paradigm has moved from the technical aspect to the business aspect. You no longer re-use a service but re-use a business process. Now, enterprises can define their own behaviors optimized for their businesses through metadata and flows. This business process composition has become increasingly important for constructing business logic.

The ability of composite applications to share components between them nullifies the distinction between actual applications. Business users should be able to move between the activities they need to do without any actual awareness that they are moving from one domain to another.

The composite application design enables your company to combine multiple heterogeneous technologies into a single application, bringing key application capability within reach of your business user. Enterprises creating richer composite applications by leveraging existing interoperable components increase the development organization's ability to respond quickly and cost-effectively to emerging business requirements. While there are many vendors offering various graphical tools to create composite applications, this book will focus on OpenESB and NetBeans IDE for designing and building composite applications.

This book introduces basic SOA concepts and shows how you can use NetBeans and OpenESB tools to design and deploy a composite application. After introducing the SOA concepts, you are introduced to various NetBeans Editors and aids that you need to understand and work with to design a composite application. The last part of the book deals with a full fledged incremental example on how you can build a complex composite application with necessary screen shots accompanied by the source code available on the website.

What This Book Covers

Chapter 1 introduces SOA and BPEL to the readers with simple examples and gives an overview of the JBI components and runtime required to build composite applications. This chapter also gives you an overview of the need for SOA-based applications in companies by depicting an example of an imaginary AirlinesAlliance system.

Chapter 2 shows you how you can quickly setup NetBeans IDE and other runtime environments including OpenESB runtime and BPEL engine. There are many software/tools mentioned in this chapter that you need to download and configure to get started building composite applications using NetBeans.

Chapter 3 provides an overview of Java Business Integration (JBI) and the Enterprise Service Bus (ESB). You will learn about JBI Service Engines and how they are supported within the NetBeans IDE.

Chapter 4 introduces JBI Binding Components and how they provide protocol independent communication between JBI components. You will also learn about the support that the NetBeans IDE provides for Binding Components.

Chapter 5 introduces the NetBeans BPEL Designer that comes bundled with the NetBeans IDE. You will also be introduced to the graphical tools/wizards and palettes available for creating BPEL files.

Chapter 6 provides an overview of WSDL and how WSDL documents are formed. You will learn about the use of WSDL in enterprise applications and the WSDL editor within the NetBeans IDE

Chapter 7 covers the XML schema designer and shows how it aids rapid development and testing of XML schema documents.

Chapter 8 provides you an overview of the Intelligent Event Processor (IEP) module and the IEP Service Engine that can be acquired from the OpenESB software bundle. This chapter also shows the need for an event processing tool through simple composite application examples.

Chapter 9 provides details of fault handling within a BPEL process and shows how these can be managed within the NetBeans IDE by using graphical tools.

Chapter 10 shows you how you can build simple to complex composite applications and BPEL processes using the NetBeans IDE. The examples in this chapter are divided into several parts and the source code for all parts is available in the code bundle.

Chapter 11 gives you the overall picture of the composite application and the need for a composite application to deploy your BPEL processes. The composite application support provided in NetBeans IDE comes with a visual editor for adding and configuring WSDL ports and JBI modules.

What You Need for This Book

- Java SE 5 or higher
- OpenESB Components
- NetBeans 6 + OpenESB Addons Bundle

Who is This Book for

This book is for enterprise developers and architects interested in using NetBeans IDE and OpenESB tools to build their SOA-based applications.

Conventions

In this book, you will find a number of styles of text that distinguish between different kinds of information. Here are some examples of these styles, and an explanation of their meaning.

There are three styles for code. Code words in text are shown as follows: "message `sayHelloRequest` has been defined"

A block of code will be set as follows:

```
<?xml version="1.0" encoding="UTF-8"?>
<definitions name="HelloWSDL"
    targetNamespace="http://j2ee.netbeans.org/wsdl/HelloWSDL"
    xmlns="http://schemas.xmlsoap.org/wsdl/"
```

When we wish to draw your attention to a particular part of a code block, the relevant lines or items will be made bold:

```
<message name="sayHelloReply">
    <part name="outputMessage" type="xsd:string"/>
</message>
<message name="sayHelloFault">
    <part name="faultMessage" type="xsd:string"/>
</message>
```

New terms and **important words** are introduced in a bold-type font. Words that you see on the screen, in menus or dialog boxes for example, appear in our text like this: "From the **New Project** wizard, select **SOA | BPEL Module**".

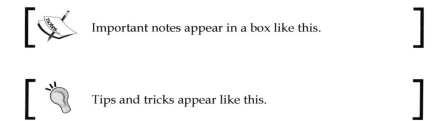

Important notes appear in a box like this.

Tips and tricks appear like this.

Reader Feedback

Feedback from our readers is always welcome. Let us know what you think about this book, what you liked or may have disliked. Reader feedback is important for us to develop titles that you really get the most out of.

To send us general feedback, simply drop an email to feedback@packtpub.com, making sure to mention the book title in the subject of your message.

If there is a book that you need and would like to see us publish, please send us a note in the **SUGGEST A TITLE** form on www.packtpub.com or email suggest@packtpub.com.

If there is a topic that you have expertise in and you are interested in either writing or contributing to a book, see our author guide on www.packtpub.com/authors.

Customer Support

Now that you are the proud owner of a Packt book, we have a number of things to help you to get the most from your purchase.

Downloading the Example Code for the Book

Visit http://www.packtpub.com/files/code/2622_Code.zip, and select this book from the list of titles to download any example code or extra resources for this book. The files available for download will then be displayed.

The downloadable files contain instructions on how to use them.

Errata

Although we have taken every care to ensure the accuracy of our contents, mistakes do happen. If you find a mistake in one of our books—maybe a mistake in text or code—we would be grateful if you would report this to us. By doing this you can save other readers from frustration, and help to improve subsequent versions of this book. If you find any errata, report them by visiting http://www.packtpub.com/support, selecting your book, clicking on the **Submit Errata** link, and entering the details of your errata. Once your errata are verified, your submission will be accepted and the errata added to the list of existing errata. The existing errata can be viewed by selecting your title from http://www.packtpub.com/support.

Questions

You can contact us at questions@packtpub.com if you are having a problem with some aspect of the book, and we will do our best to address it.

1
Enterprise Application Development

Organizations are rapidly moving towards an information-driven business model that exerts a lot of pressure on the response time. Response time is the primary issue for organizations adopting new technologies. Any Business process model designed by an organization should be flexible, extensible, and reliable primarily to tackle the "information burst" experienced by most enterprises.

The objective of this book is to help enterprise application architects and developers understand various **Service Oriented Architecture** (SOA) tools available as part of the NetBeans IDE thus, enabling them to build an enterprise grade, scalable application in a short period using a single development interface.

In this chapter, we will be discussing the following topics:

- SOA concepts
- Introduction to various BPEL Processes
- Composite Applications and JBI
- AirAlliance—our sample application

According to Gartner Inc., enterprises will eventually adopt SOA for their business critical processes, sooner or later. Although architects have been discussing and implementing SOA for the past several years, practicing SOA is still new, and generally requires the utmost care in application design when compared to other similar architectures. SOA always emphasizes on distributed architecture spanning multiple web services and applications that are part of a different heterogeneous category of applications. This in turn adds additional complexity to the whole system. If you do not carefully connect your various business applications through a set of well defined processes, it will lead to data chaos and breakdowns.

Not all SOA implementations you see today are tuned for maximum performance. In fact performance was always a key issue when considering SOA for business integration. When SOA principles are applied too rigidly, you can expect some run-time issues. Hence it is better not to go by any book or guidelines and instead, to adopt your own SOA-based system that is scalable and reliable for your needs. The primary factor that you need to understand is that SOA is a paradigm shift in doing business and requires a complete comprehension of the events, processes, and fault endpoints that occur in your enterprise.

Developing enterprise applications is much more than just building a system that can process and share data between web services and various clients. Consider, for example, an airlines reservation web service that processes the guest itinerary. If a reservation cannot be made, it should have the capability of contacting a partner airline's web service and then process the itinerary. If the itinerary processing is successful, it should confirm the booking to the client. Now, there is more than one type of enterprise system involved. Which part of your enterprise system will orchestrate the transaction? Who will set the guidelines for fail-safe communication? There is a clear need for a "middle man" or a "centralized web service" to orchestrate these disparate web services to make the reservation process successful and fail-safe. BPEL (Business Process Execution Language) is widely accepted as an industry standard for orchestrating web services to perform meaningful business processes.

This book focuses on using a particular BPEL implementation for solving business integration problems. This implementation is the BPEL Service Engine from the OpenESB project at `https://open-esb.dev.java.net/`.

Project OpenESB implements an Enterprise Service Bus runtime using Java Business Integration (JBI) as the base. This allows easy integration of web services to create loosely coupled enterprise class composite applications.

SOA and POA

Today, most companies are considering SOA and web services as a viable business process model to address the integration needs for building a robust enterprise application. While SOA has become a model to implement and solve integration problems, many companies are still confused about implementing SOA as there appear to be a myriad of ways to implement an SOA-based model. Also there are companies that already have a time tested solution implemented and would like to move to the much extensible SOA model. SOA and POA based applications enable businesses by leveraging existing web services and by minimizing the cost of deploying new services.

The primary objective of designing an enterprise application is to glue together different services to suit a particular business need. However, there is a bigger challenge involved in designing this whole system wherein introducing new services or modifying existing services should not affect the system to a larger extent. This can only be achieved when you have a set of business processes that can orchestrate the system, making the services communicate with each other at the right time. Hence, orchestrating services through BPEL has become a much acclaimed solution for designing enterprise applications. BPEL is emerging as the clear standard for composing multiple synchronous and asynchronous services into collaborative and transactional process flows.

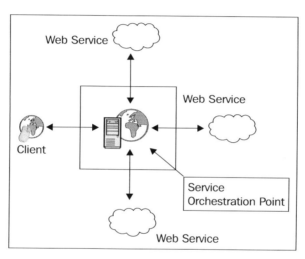

Well designed SOA-based applications reduce the cost and complexity of implementing business processes that cater to all the connected partners including customers, suppliers, and other clients. Prior to the SOA-based model, many businesses found this objective almost unattainable, because technical roadblocks made it difficult to offer a business process as a service that could be universally shared by its target community of users. The Web has demonstrated that universal access is not only possible but is now a fact of business life, and has proven that a combination of open protocols, tools, and infrastructure can create great value for the business community. The SOA extends this value to cover the creation and sharing of business processes, utilizing web protocols, tools, and infrastructure to meet this new objective. The challenge is to find the **Service Orchestration Point** for hosting the business processes that interact with heterogeneous services and provide a seamless and quick solution to the customers.

Introduction to Various BPEL Processes

A business process is the procedure that an organization uses to achieve a larger business goal. A business process is actually a series of individual tasks, and each task is executed in a specific order. Business Processes are synchronous or asynchronous, depending on the method you choose to invoke your business process. A synchronous business process can contain asynchronous operations, but they must be added after the starting event in the process flow. That is, at runtime the processes are executed after the synchronous starting event is complete.

As an integral part of the NetBeans SOA tools, business processes provide the primary means through which enterprise services are integrated. NetBeans SOA tools features the BPEL Designer, which has been formulated so that architects can easily create complex composite applications involving web services without much programming effort. To this end, you can easily create and develop a business process in an intuitive graphical programming environment called the BPEL Designer and deploy it to a separate runtime environment for execution. This runtime is the OpenESB runtime that is integrated with the GlassFish application server.

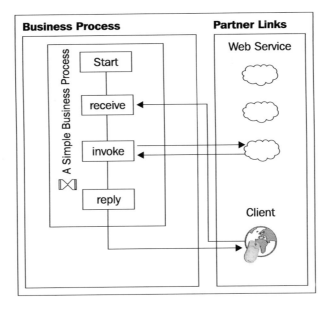

The BPEL Process starts with a **receive** activity, proceeds with **invoking** external services and finishes by replying back to the **Client**. A BPEL process typically interacts with one or more external **Web Services** (the BPEL process is also a web service). These external web services are called partner services.

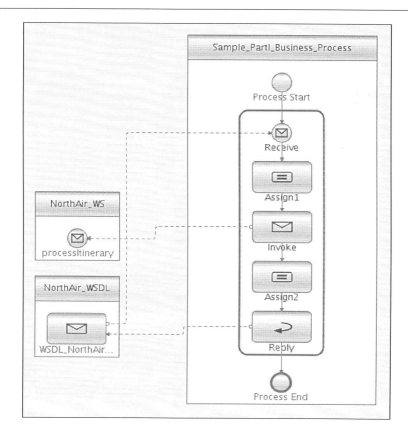

The above figure shows a preview of how a simple BPEL process can be designed using the NetBeans BPEL Designer. In the above example, there are two partner services, one is the BPEL client implementation and the other one is the web service EJB implementation which has one operation **processItinerary**.

In order to understand the simple BPEL process, let us define some of the terms most commonly used while designing a BPEL process.

Partner Services

Any external service or client that interacts with the BPEL process is called a partner service. A process starts and ends somewhere, and involves the interaction of at least one other outside partner. In the above example, the partner is the web service that has the ability to process the client's request. The customer sends the guest itinerary for processing. The BPEL process receives the itinerary, invokes a web service that processes the itinerary, and returns the itinerary back to the customer. This simple process helps us understand the BPEL activities that we will focus on later in this book.

Refer to Chapter 10 to learn how partner services can be designed and created using NetBeans.

Activities

Activities are the individual business tasks within the process that compose the larger business goal. In the previous screenshot, activities represent each step in the process. Thus the most common activities are **Receive, Invoke, Assign,** and **Reply**. For more information on the BPEL activities supported in the BPEL Designer, refer to Chapter 5.

Variables

In the previous example, between the **Receive** and the **Invoke** activity, we are assigning the guest itinerary elements to a new variable. (Assigning Guest name, travel date, preferred class.) This is basically a copying process (creates an XPath expression in the BPEL file) and it can be done visually using the NetBeans BPEL Mapper (explained in Chapter 5). Variables store the data that are used by the business process.

As we discussed earlier, the partner service interacts with the business process for the purpose of receiving a message in response to a request.

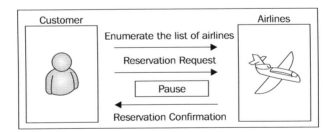

The above figure depicts a typical asynchronous and synchronous business process. An asynchronous process is used when the BPEL process is long-running. The results are returned to the client by performing an invocation on the client. Thus the customer asks for reservation and disconnects. The business process processes the requests and gets back to the customer. It is more like a "Leave a message and we will get back to you" kind of setup. This pause does not happen with a synchronous business process, wherein the customer waits indefinitely to get the response. A classic example is the reservation process.

However, there is a caveat here. The BPEL process is shared and is not a singleton. Many customers work with the same business process. There should be a way for the business process to identify its customers.

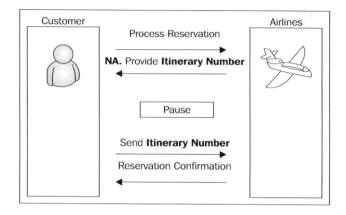

The above figure depicts an example wherein the customer sends a reservation request for a particular airlines' destination on a particular date. The business process, after communicating with the airlines' web service, finds out the reservation cannot be processed. Hence it updates the customer itinerary with an itinerary number that the customer can use later to send the reservation request.

This is how a correlation is used by the business process, to distinguish the customer in their initial interaction so that they can recognize each other in the future. A correlation is the record that the business process uses to keep track of multiple partners in the same business process. NetBeans BPEL Designer lets you set correlations for **Invoke** activities through a visual interface as discussed later in this book. Note that the business process is able to manage multiple tasks, and does not hang in a single business process waiting for it to conclude at the expense of all other activities. Instead, while they are waiting for the itinerary number to arrive, the process conducts similar business, using the same business process with other customers.

Since multiple clients can use the same business process, it is possible that each application implementation may desire slight variations of the same business process. Therefore, it is important that business processes have points-of-variability. Thus giving the user of the composite application the ability to configure the business process to their specific requirements.

A Business process can also be abstract in the sense that the appropriate business logic to make decisions is defined, but the sensitive information needed to choose a course of action is hidden from the process partners. An abstract process is basically a description of a business process, and cannot be run on the server, unlike an executable business process. We will discuss these processes in the coming chapters.

Consider the following guidelines for creating BPEL processes:

- Support multiple clients—your business process should be able to process multiple clients simultaneously. So make sure that you have correlations set on messages.

- Intelligent event processing—you need a real-time business event collection and processing mechanism to create an efficient process.

- Secure your business processes—we are talking about enterprise systems. You had better secure your business processes. This is quite easy using the Identity enabled web services support in NetBeans.

- Create re-usable partner services—make sure that partner services are reusable and can be used across different business processes. For example, the *getItinerary* operation of an airlines web service will be used by multiple business processes.

Why do you need to consider BPEL for orchestration? In a complex business transaction, just developing web services and exposing their functionalities over WSDL is not enough. Sequence of execution and branching in case of failures and other events are critical to business transactions. Sequencing and conditional behavior are the strengths of BPEL.

BPEL does the following for your business transactions:

1. Coordinates asynchronous communication between different web services. A client requests for a flight reservation and the BPEL process interacts with various partner services to process the reservation.

2. Manipulates data before exchanging between different services. The BPEL process can check, verify, and modify data from the client before sending requests to partner services. A classic example of data manipulation is an intelligent event processing mechanism.

3. Conditional and parallel processing is possible with BPEL services. If a reservation with one airline is not available, the BPEL process can send the reservation request to another partner airlines web service.

4. BPEL process can undo or compensate at any state in its life cycle.

5. Support long running business processes.

Composite Applications and JBI

A composite application is an accepted solution that addresses a specific business problem by bringing together business logic and data sources from multiple underlying systems. Typically a composite application will be associated with one or many business processes, and may bring together several process steps, presenting them to the client through a single interface that is customized to the requirements of the business need.

SOA describes a category of composite applications composed of service provider and service consumer components that segregates business logic and offers location transparency for the service providers and consumers. The SOA approach lets you replace or upgrade individual components in the application without affecting other components or the process as a whole. Moreover, you can independently specify alternative paths through which the components in the application exchange messages. The next couple of chapters in this book provide concepts and constructs needed for building a composite application using the NetBeans SOA tools.

Our example application that we will be creating in this book is finally deployed as a Java Business Integration (JBI) module in the **JBI Runtime Environment** provided by GlassFish application server.

JBI runtime is integrated with Sun Java System Application Server and the open-source GlassFish application server. This is the same JBI runtime that was available as part of OpenESB project. OpenESB is also available as an add-on in the Java Application Platform SDK.

The OpenJBI Components project on java.net is an incubator project started to foster community-based development of JBI components that conform to the Java Business Integration specification (JSR 208).

JBI is integrated with Sun Java System Application Server as a pre-configured lifecycle module, which means that whenever the application server's instance starts up, the JBI runtime will be available.

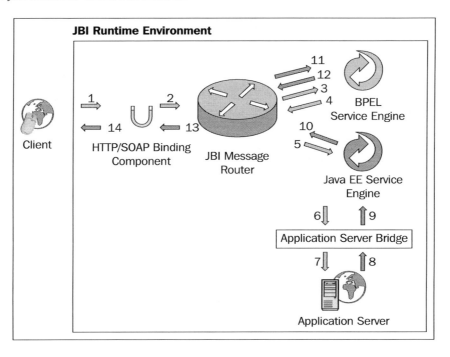

There is no user interaction required to configure or start the JBI runtime. It is just like any other service of the application server. **Java EE Service Engine** acts as the bridge between Java EE applications and JBI. A Java EE application archive (ear/war/jar) can be packaged in a JBI composite application and deployed as one single entity. Service units belonging to other JBI components and Java EE applications can share the same transaction and security contexts. JBI is built on a web services model, and provides a pluggable architecture for a container that hosts service producer and consumer components. Client and services connect to the container via binding components or can be hosted inside the container as part of a service engine.

Java Business Integration (JBI) is a Java standard (JSR 208) for structuring business integration systems along SOA lines. It defines an environment for plug-in components that interact using a services model based directly on WSDL 2.0.

Project OpenESB is an open-source implementation of JBI. It extends the JBI specification by creating an enterprise service bus (ESB) from multiple JBI instances. The instances are linked by a proxy-binding based on JMS. This allows components in separate JBI instances to inter-operate in the same fashion as local ones.

JBI defines standard packaging for composite applications that are composed of service consumers and providers. Individual service units are deployable to components; groups of components are gathered together into a service assembly. The service assembly includes metadata for bonding the service units together, as well as bonding service units to external services. This provides a simple mechanism for performing composite application assembly using services.

AirAlliance Company

All that we have discussed so far is the general principles of SOA and BPEL based business processes. To make things a little easier, we will attempt to discuss various concepts covered in this book in the context of an imaginary airline called AirAlliance.

The Problem

AirAlliance is the largest airline with 64 partner airlines working across 124 countries. AirAlliance attempts to build an enterprise application wrapper on top of the 64 partner airlines web services so that travel reservation can be made across airlines from a single web interface. The challenge is to build BPEL processes that orchestrate different partner services to provide a seamless travel experience to the customers.

The problem is how to build a global airline alliance enterprise system that offers customers worldwide reach and a smooth travel experience. For the customer querying on the flight status, baggage transfer, connection information and other itinerary related information is through a single interface that connects to the AirAlliance Web Service (BPEL Process). The itinerary processing and airlines querying happens transparently.

Look at the following figure that depicts a simple business process:

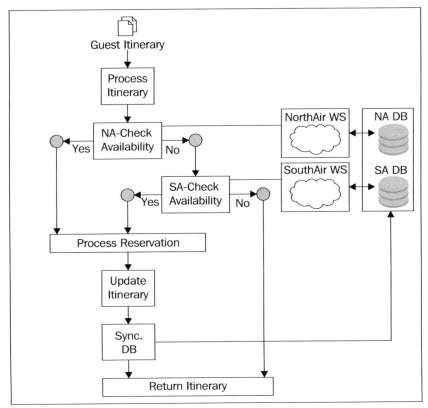

The client sends the **Guest Itinerary** for reservation processing. The business process enumerates the travel preferences. These include the travel date, food preference, seating preference, and information like maximum travel stop overs. It then finds a suitable airline that matches the customer's preference. The above business process does an availability check on partner airlines based on the travel preference. It then updates the itinerary and sends it back to the client. Finally the airline's DBs are synced to reflect the current seat status.

Note that **NorthAir** Web Service and **SouthAir** Web Service work independently of each other and need not know that they are part of a business process or that they are being orchestrated. This kind of process can be implemented in BPEL easily. Throughout Chapter 10, we will discuss various business processes examples.

In all the chapters of this book, we will use the same company as an example (AirAlliance) and will design solutions to improve the architecture of our company.

The Enterprise Stack

Before proceeding with a solution for the AirAlliance problem, you need to understand the tools stack that will be used in this book. Let us briefly discuss the enterprise tools. In the following figure, the left side shows the tasks that you are most likely to perform and the right side shows the tools that you use to perform those tasks. The AirAlliance company collaborates with many partner airlines through their web services. For designing and building web services, we'll be using the NetBeans IDE's web service creation methods. For simplicity, all our airlines web services are deployed as a stateless session beans.

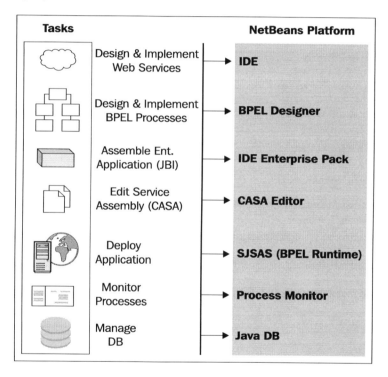

Once you have the partner services ready, you will build the business processes that interact with the partner services. Our business processes are implemented as BPEL processes. There could be BPEL processes for each operation like Reservation BPEL Process, Flight Information Business Process and Baggage Information Business Process. We use the NetBeans IDE's BPEL Designer that comes with the NetBeans Enterprise Pack for designing these processes.

When we have the business processes ready, we create JBI Modules so that they can be deployed as a service assembly in the BPEL Engine. We use NetBeans's Composite Application Module to build these deployable applications. Based on the need, we might use the CASA Editor to edit the Composite Applications' deployment descriptors. When we have the deployable enterprise application, we deploy them to the Glassfish's BPEL Engine as a Service Assembly.

There is a robust visual tool for monitoring the business processes, message transaction and status through a BPEL Process Monitor. You can also use the Java DB for storing airline information. NetBeans has very good support for managing the Java DB from the IDE.

So these are the required tools to get you started with building your enterprise applications.

Summary

This chapter provided an overview of SOA and the need for SOA in enterprise applications. SOA will mean different integration patterns to different companies. There is not a single implementation of SOA that can be termed the best. Implementing SOA in your enterprise applications depends mostly on your business requirements.

BPEL is widely accepted as the means to orchestrate disparate web services to conceive meaningful business processes. What BPEL does to your business transaction is explained in this chapter with an imaginary airline. This chapter also dealt with the need for SOA tools for rapidly building and deploying enterprise grade applications. The tools used in this book are shipped with the NetBeans IDE and the OpenESB 2.0 bundle.

The next couple of chapters introduce the NetBeans SOA Tools and the NetBeans IDE and highlight various features and functionalities of the SOA Tools. Some of these are the BPEL Designer, Activities Palette, BPEL Mapper, and XML Schema Editors. All of them are available as part of the OpenESB-NetBeans bundle. Chapter 2 deals with the information that you need to quickly get started with these tools.

2
Getting Started

In Chapter 1, we discussed some general SOA concepts related to building scalable enterprise applications. As we discussed earlier, there could be different ways of implementing enterprise applications using different tools available in the market. In this book, we will restrict our views on SOA to designing web services and focus on the BPEL orchestration to perform complex business processes. We will build Java EE-based web services and BPEL-based processes using the NetBeans IDE and SOA tools available with NetBeans. Any detailed discussion on any tool, apart from the SOA tools, could be considered as out of the scope for this book and is left to the reader to compare and understand the differences.

In this chapter, we will discuss:

- Getting the software
- Setting up the environment
- NetBeans projects
- Enterprise tools and editors

Getting the Software

For enterprise application development using Java EE and web services, the most commonly used IDE is the NetBeans IDE. We can obtain the NetBeans IDE as a built-in feature in the following software:

- NetBeans IDE 6.0
- OpenESB

NetBeans IDE 6.0

You need to install NetBeans IDE 6.0 or higher to have the base IDE for creating Java EE-based web services. The software can be obtained from `http://www.netbeans.org`. Just follow the links specific to a version. NetBeans IDE 6.0 comes with SOA capabilities and includes the GlassFish Application Server. NetBeans SOA tools contains open-sourced features from Sun's Java Studio Enterprise and Java CAPS products, as well as new features for creating composite applications, BPEL-based web services, secure Java EE web services, and XML artifacts like XML schema and WSDL. With these tools, you should be able to:

- **Visually Design:** You will be able to visually design an XML schema and visualize BPEL-based orchestration of web services using a flowchart-like interface. Here you can concentrate on the design part while the IDE bothers with the syntax and specification compliance.

- **Test:** You should be able to test your composite applications without leaving your design and development environment. In other words, a single interface for building, testing, and deploying enterprise applications.

- **Secure Applications:** You should be able to secure your enterprise application using available identity solutions and built-in IDE tools.

- **Integrated BPEL Engine:** You don't need a standalone application server for deploying your web services. Most popular applications servers, including GlassFish Application Server and the Sun Java System Application Server, can be integrated and managed from the IDE. BPEL Engine is available as a JBI Service Engine on both the servers.

OpenESB

You can also download the OpenESB bundle from the OpenESB project site: `https://open-esb.dev.java.net`. The OpenESB bundle includes NetBeans IDE 6.0 along with GlassFish Application Server, SOA tools, and JBI components.

The following table compares the NetBeans 6.0 bundle and the OpenESB 2.0 bundle:

Functionality	NetBeans 6.0 bundle	OpenESB 2.0 bundle
BPEL–Support for BPEL-based business processes — you can use the BPEL Designer to design and implement processes that can orchestrate Java EE-based web services.	Yes	Yes

Functionality	NetBeans 6.0 bundle	OpenESB 2.0 bundle
Composite Applications Support—BPEL Modules can be combined into a composite application and can be deployed as a composite application to a JBI runtime.	Yes	Yes. Support for editing composite applications.
Intelligent Event Processing—real-time business event collection and processing.	No	Yes
Editing XSLT	Yes	Yes
Editing WSDL	Yes	Yes

[We recommend that you go with OpenESB 2.0 bundle   ]

Setting up the Environment

In this book, we will assume that you have already installed the NetBeans IDE. If you need help installing the NetBeans IDE, visit the NetBeans site at `http://www.netbeans.org/`.

When you configure your environment successfully as per the installation document, clicking on **Servers** in the **Services** tab will show you a list of available servers. Right-click on **GlassFish** and select the **Start** option. This will initiate the GlassFish startup process, which you will be able to see in the output screen. After GlassFish Server is started, expand **JBI | Service Engines** and verify **sun-bpel-engine** and other engines shown as follows:

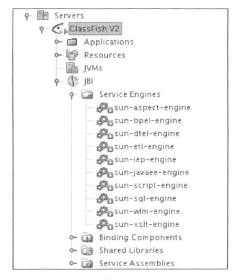

NetBeans SOA bundle installs and configures the bundled GlassFish Application Server and Sun Java System Access Manager. You need Sun Java System Access Manager for managing identities.

When GlassFish Application Server is started, the BPEL Service Engine may not be started automatically. However, when you deploy your first composite application, the BPEL service engine starts automatically.

```
Started BPEL service engine in-out thread
BPEL service engine started with following configurations
        Persistence Enabled : false
        Monitor Enabled : false
        Persistence Database NonXA JNDI Resource Name : jdbc/bpelseNonXA
        Persistence Database XA JNDI Resource Name : jdbc/bpelseXA
        Engine Expiry Interval (failover setting) : 60 seconds
        Debug Enabled : false
        Debug Port : 3,343
        Thread Count 10
        Engine Installed on Application Server Cluster : false
JBIFW1146: Engine sun-bpel-engine has been started.
```

If you experience problems while installing or running the software, see the list of issues for workarounds and known issues in the Release Notes at http://www.netbeans.org/community/releases/60/relnotes.html.

Now that we have both the GlassFish Application Server and the IDE environment setup, we need to start the Java DB database and check to see if we can connect to any default DB. Use **Tools | Java DB Database | Start Java DB Server** to start the integrated Java DB Server.

Some of the examples we build in this book use the Java DB as the data store. You can use any JDBC-compliant DB for your projects. Starting from NetBeans 6.0, you can also connect to PostgreSQL DB, which is most widely used by the community. Java DB has an advantage of being completely managed from the NetBeans run-time environment.

NetBeans Projects

NetBeans add-ons are pieces of software that extend the functionality of the base IDE. When NetBeans is installed with the SOA options, **New Project** types are created that allow you to work with a specific enterprise artifact. The general categories of NetBeans projects include **Web, Enterprise, SOA, NetBeans Modules, Java, JBI Components**.

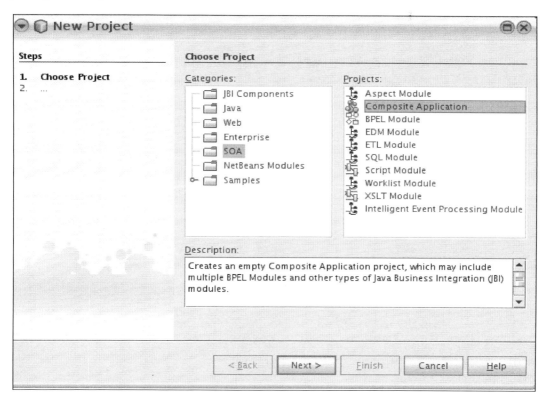

The NetBeans IDE offers comprehensive GUI support for building enterprise applications and rich client applications on the NetBeans platform. Throughout this book, we will be creating projects that belong to the **Web, Enterprise,** and **SOA** categories. Starting from NetBeans 6.0, the following project types are supported:

1. **BPEL Module:** This project lets you create a **BPEL Module** that can hold one or more BPEL processes. Refer to Chapter 5 on BPEL Designer for more information.

2. **IEP Module:** This project lets you create an **Intelligent Event Processing Module**, which may contain one or more intelligent event processors. The IEP Module Projects works with Service Oriented Architecture or Composite Application projects to generate service engine deployment assembly for event processor deployment. Refer to Chapter 8 on IEP for more information.

3. **Composite Application:** This project lets you create a **Composite Application** project, which may include one or more **BPEL Modules,** and other types of Java Business Integration (JBI) modules.

4. **SQL Module:** You can create a CAPS **SQL Module** project from this option.

5. **XSLT Module:** Creates an empty **XSLT Module** project, which may contain multiple XSLT services.

We will not be exploring other project types in order to restrict the focus of this book to BPEL.

Summary

This chapter gave a detailed explanation about the software required for working with this book along with the installation instructions. The next chapter describes the Service Engines and other JBI components supported by OpenESB NetBeans bundle.

3
Service Engines

In Chapter 1, we introduced the concept of SOA applications, and introduced BPEL processes and JBI applications. To gain a greater understanding of these concepts and to enable us to develop enterprise level SOA applications, we need to understand JBI in further depth, and how JBI components can be linked together. This chapter will introduce the JBI Service Engine and how it is supported within the NetBeans Enterprise Pack.

In this chapter, we will discuss the following topics:

- Need for Java Business Integration (JBI)
- Enterprise Service Bus
- Normalized Message Router
- Introduction to Service Engines
- NetBeans Support for Service Engines
- BPEL Service Engine
- Java EE Service Engine
- SQL Service Engine
- IEP Service Engine
- XSLT Service Engine

Need for Java Business Integration (JBI)

To have a good understanding of Service Engines (a specific type of JBI component), we need to first understand the reason for Java Business Integration.

In the business world, not all systems talk the same language. They use different protocols and different forms of communications. Legacy systems in particular can use proprietary protocols for external communication. The advent and acceptance of XML has been greatly beneficial in allowing systems to be easily integrated, but XML itself is not the complete solution.

When some systems were first developed, they were not envisioned to be able to communicate with many other systems; they were developed with closed interfaces using closed protocols. This, of course, is fine for the system developer, but makes system integration very difficult. This closed and proprietary nature of enterprise systems makes integration between enterprise applications very difficult. To allow enterprise systems to effectively communicate between each other, system integrators would use vendor-supplied APIs and data formats or agree on common exchange mechanisms between their systems. This is fine for small short term integration, but quickly becomes unproductive as the number of enterprise applications to integrate gets larger. The following figure shows the problems with traditional integration.

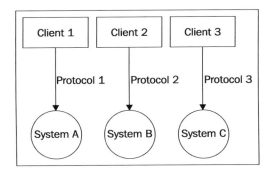

As we can see in the figure, each third party system that we want to integrate with uses a different protocol. As a system integrator, we potentially have to learn new technologies and new APIs for each system we wish to integrate with. If there are only two or three systems to integrate with, this is not really too much of a problem. However, the more systems we wish to integrate with, the more proprietary code we have to learn and integration with other systems quickly becomes a large problem.

To try and overcome these problems, the Enterprise Application Integration (EAI) server was introduced. This concept has an integration server acting as a central hub. The EAI server traditionally has proprietary links to third party systems, so the application integrator only has to learn one API (the EAI server vendors). With this architecture however, there are still several drawbacks. The central hub can quickly become a bottleneck, and because of the **hub-and-spoke** architecture, any problems at the hub are rapidly manifested at all the clients.

Enterprise Service Bus

To help solve this problem, leading companies in the integration community (led by Sun Microsystems) proposed the Java Business Integration Specification Request (JSR 208) (Full details of the JSR can be found at `http://jcp.org/en/jsr/detail?id=208`). JSR 208 proposed a standard framework for business integration by providing a standard set of service provider interfaces (SPIs) to help alleviate the problems experienced with Enterprise Application Integration.

The standard framework described in JSR 208 allows pluggable components to be added into a standard architecture and provides a standard common mechanism for each of these components to communicate with each other based upon WSDL. The pluggable nature of the framework described by JSR 208 is depicted in the following figure. It shows us the concept of an Enterprise Service Bus and introduces us to the Service Engine (SE) component:

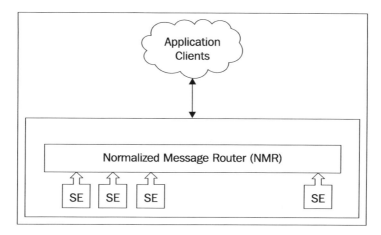

JSR 208 describes a service engine as a component, which provides business logic and transformation services to other components, as well as consuming such services. SEs can integrate Java-based applications (and other resources), or applications with available Java APIs.

Service Engine is a component which provides (and consumes) business logic and transformation services to other components. There are various Service Engines available, such as the BPEL service engine for orchestrating business processes, or the Java EE service engine for consuming Java EE Web Services. We will discuss some of the more common Service Engines later in this chapter.

The Normalized Message Router

As we can see from the previous figure, SE's don't communicate directly with each other or with the clients, instead they communicate via the NMR. This is one of the key concepts of JBI, in that it promotes loose coupling of services.

So, what is NMR and what is its purpose? NMR is responsible for taking messages from clients and routing them to the appropriate Service Engines for processing. (This is not strictly true as there is another standard JBI component called the Binding Component responsible for receiving client messages. Binding Components are discussed in Chapter 4. Again, this further enhances the support for loose coupling within JBI, as Service Engines are decoupled from their transport infrastructure).

NMR is responsible for passing normalized (that is based upon WSDL) messages between JBI components. Messages typically consist of a payload and a message header which contains any other message data required for the Service Engine to understand and process the message (for example, security information). Again, we can see that this provides a loosely coupled model in which Service Engines have no prior knowledge of other Service Engines. This therefore allows the JBI architecture to be flexible, and allows different component vendors to develop standard based components.

 Normalized Message Router enables technology for allowing messages to be passed between loosely coupled services such as Service Engines.

The figure below gives an overview of the message routing between a client application and two service engines, in this case the EE and SQL service engines.

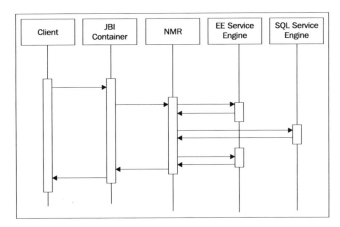

In this figure, a request is made from the client to the JBI Container. This request is passed via NMR to the EE Service Engine. The EE Service Engine then makes a request to the SQL Service Engine via NMR. The SQL Service Engine returns a message to the EE Service Engine again via NMR. Finally, the message is routed back to the client through NMR and JBI framework. The important concept here is that NMR is a message routing hub not only between clients and service engines, but also for intra-communication between different service engines.

The entire architecture we have discussed is typically referred to as an Enterprise Service Bus.

 Enterprise Service Bus (ESB) is a standard-based middleware architecture that allows pluggable components to communicate with each other via a messaging subsystem.

Now that we have a basic understanding of what a Service Engine is, how communication is made between application clients and Service Engines, and between Service Engines themselves, let's take a look at what support the NetBeans IDE gives us for interacting with Service Engines.

Service Engine Life Cycle

Each Service Engine can exist in one of a set of predefined states. This is called the Service Engine life cycle.

- Started
- Stopped
- Shutdown
- Uninstalled

The figure below gives an overview of the life cycle of Service Engines:

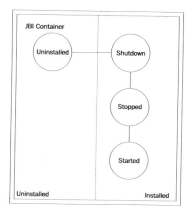

Service Engines can be managed from the command line utility, `asadmin`, that is supplied as part of the Sun Java System Application Server. The table below shows some of the common commands that can be used to manage Service Engines:

`asadmin list-jbi-service-engines`	Obtains a list of installed Service Engines
	
	`$>./asadmin list-jbi-service-engines`
	
	`sun-aspect-engine`
	
	`sun-bpel-engine`
	
	`sun-dtel-engine`
	
	`sun-etl-engine`
	
	`sun-iep-engine`
	
	`sun-javaee-engine`
	
	`sun-script-engine`
	
	`sun-sql-engine`
	
	`sun-wlm-engine`
	
	`sun-xslt-engine`
	
	`Command list-jbi-service-engines executed successfully.`

`asadmin show-jbi-service-engine`	Shows the status of an installed Service Engine
	
	`$>./asadmin show-jbi-service-engine sun-bpel-engine`
	
	`Component Information`
	
	`--------------------`
	
	`Name       : sun-bpel-engine`
	
	`State      : Shutdown`
	
	`Description : This is a bpel service engine.`

`asadmin start-jbi-component`	Starts a Service Engine
	
	`$>./asadmin start-jbi-component sun-bpel-engine`
	
	`Started component sun-bpel-engine.`

`asadmin stop-jbi-component`	Stops a Service Engine
	
	`$>./asadmin stop-jbi-component sun-bpel-engine`
	
	`Stopped component sun-bpel-engine.`

Service Engines can also be managed from within the NetBeans IDE instead of using the `asadmin` application. We will look at that in the next section.

Service Engines in NetBeans

As we discussed in Chapter 2, the NetBeans Enterprise Pack provides a version of the Sun Java System Application Server 9.0 which includes several Service Engines from the Open ESB project.

All of these Service Engines can be administered from within the NetBeans IDE from the **Services** explorer panel. Within this panel, expand the **Servers | Sun Java System Application Server 9 | JBI | Service Engines** node to get a complete list of Service Engines deployed to the server.

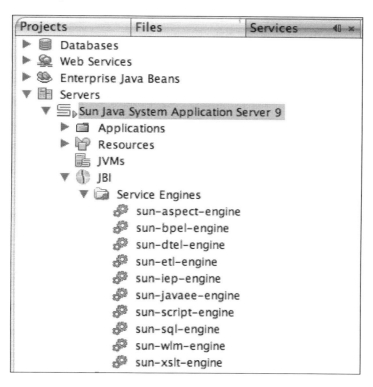

The NetBeans Enterprise Pack 5.5 and the NetBeans 6.0 IDE have different **Service Engines** installed. The following table lists which Service Engines are installed in which version of the NetBeans Enterprise Pack:

Service Engine Name	Description	NetBeans 6.0	NetBeans 5.5
sun-aspect-engine	Aspect Service Engine	Yes	No
sun-bpel-engine	BPEL Service Engine	Yes	Yes
sun-dtel-engine	DTEL Service Engine	Yes	No
sun-etl-engine	ETL (Extract, Transform and Load) Service Engine	Yes	No
sun-iep-engine	IEP (Intelligent Event Processor) Service Engine	No	No
sun-javaee-engine	Java EE Service Engine	Yes	Yes
sun-script-engine	Scripting Service Engine	Yes	No
sun-sql-engine	SQL Service Engine	Yes	No
sun-wlm-engine	WLM (Work List Manager) Service Engine	Yes	No
sun-xslt-engine	XSLT Service Engine	Yes	No

In the previous section, we discussed the life cycle of Service Engines and how this can be managed using the `asadmin` application. Using the NetBeans IDE, it is easy to manage the state of a Service Engine. Right-clicking on any of the **Service Engines** within the **Services** explorer shows a menu allowing the life cycle to be managed as shown in the figure below:

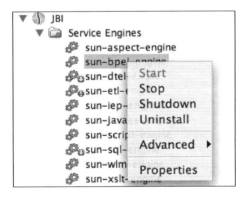

To illustrate the different states in a Service Engine life cycle, a different icon is displayed:

Start	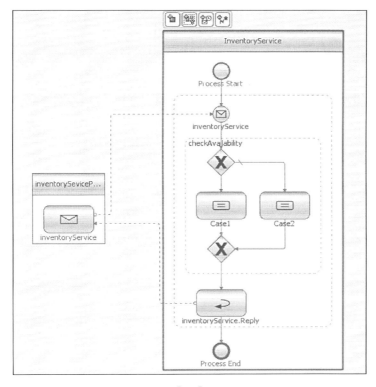
Stop	
Shutdown	
Uninstalled	The service engine is not displayed in the list.

Now that we have a good understanding of what Service Engines are, and what support the NetBeans IDE provides, let's take a closer look at some of the more common Service Engines provided with the NetBeans Enterprise Pack.

BPEL Service Engine

Similar to all the other Service Engines deployed to the JBI Container within the Sun Java System Application Server and accessible through NetBeans, the BPEL Service Engine is a standard JBI Compliant component as defined by JSR 208.

The BPEL Service Engine enables orchestration of WS-BPEL 2.0 business processes. This enables a work flow of different business services to be built as shown in the following figure:

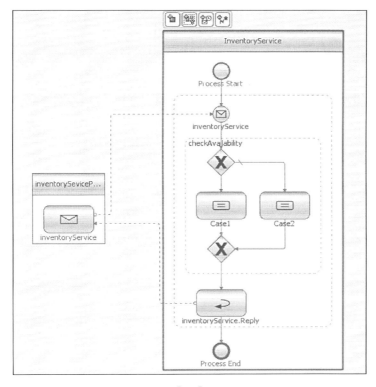

Within NetBeans, we can create BPEL modules which consist of one or more BPEL processes. BPEL modules are built into standard JBI component, and then deployed to the JBI container where the BPEL Service Engine allows the processes within the module to be executed. In JBI terms, this is called a Service Unit.

 A *Service Unit* is a deployable component (jar file) that can be deployed to a Service Engine.

New BPEL modules are created in NetBeans by selecting the **File | New Project** menu option and then selecting **BPEL Module** from the **SOA** category as shown in the following figure:

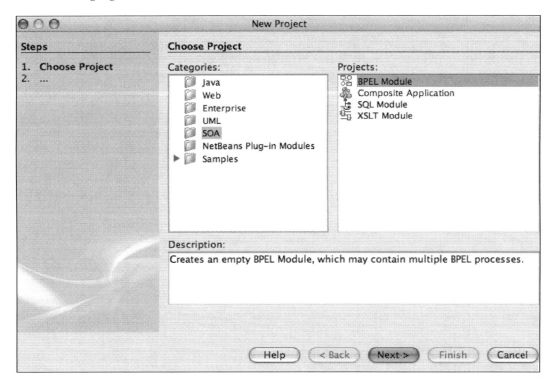

Within a BPEL module project, we add **BPEL Processes**. These processes describe the orchestration of different services.

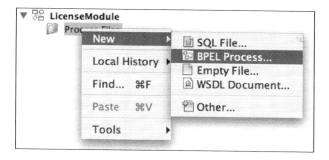

All the standard operations specified by WS-BPEL 2.0 Specification (like Providing and Consuming Web Services, Structuring the processing logic, and performing basic activities such as assignments and waiting) are available within the BPEL Service Engine. The NetBeans designer provides simple drag-and-drop support for all of these activities.

Consider, for example, a service for generating license keys for a piece of software. In a Service Oriented Architecture, our system may consist of two services:

1. A Customer Service: this service would be responsible for ensuring that license requests are only made by valid customers.
2. A License Generation Service: this service would be responsible for generating valid license keys.

Within NetBeans, we can create a BPEL process that ties these services together allowing us to return valid license keys to our customers and details of purchasing options to non-customers.

Java EE Service Engine

The Java EE service engine acts as a bridge between the JBI container allowing Java EE web services to be consumed from within JBI components. Without the Java EE service Engine, JBI components would have to execute Java EE Web Services via remote calls instead of via in-process communication. The Java EE Service Engine allows both servlet and EJB-based web services to be consumed from within JBI components.

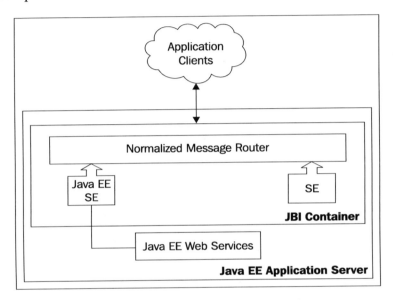

The Java EE Service Engine provides several benefits when executing Java EE Web Services.

- Increased performance
- Transaction support
- Security support

These are explained in the following subsections.

Increased Performance

Using the Java EE service engine enables Java EE web services to be invoked in process within the same JVM, as the services are running. This eliminates the need for any wire-based transmission protocols and provides increased performance.

Transaction Support

Using an in-process Communication Model between Java EE Application Server and JBI container allows both web services and JBI modules to use the same transaction model. Through multiple web service calls and calls to other JBI modules. For example, BPEL processes can all use the same transaction.

Security Support

When executing Java EE Web Services from within the JBI container, the Java EE Service Engine allows security contexts to propagate between components. This removes the need to authenticate against each service.

SQL Service Engine

SQL service engine allows SQL statements to be executed against relational databases and allows the results of SQL statements to be returned to the client application or other Service Engines for further processing.

SQL service engine allows SQL DDL (Data Definition Language), SQL DML (Data Manipulation Language), and stored procedures to be executed against a database. This, therefore, allows different scenarios to be executed against the database. For example, obtaining a customer's address or the number of outstanding invoices a customer may have.

Within NetBeans, the SQL module is used to interact with the SQL Service Engine. The SQL module project consists of three artifacts as follows:

- configuration xml file (`connectivityInfo.xml`)
- one or more SQL files containing distinct SQL statements
- WSDL file describing the SQL operations.

SQL Modules are created by choosing **File | New Project** and then selecting the **SQL Module** option from within the **SOA** projects category.

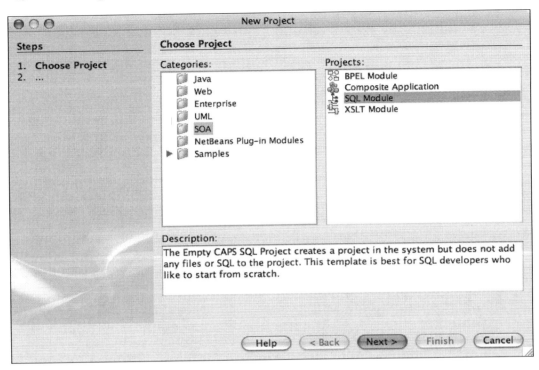

Within a **SQL Module**, there is a configuration file called `connectivityInfo.xml` which contains connection details for the database. This can either be specified as a driver connection or as a JNDI name for a data source.

```xml
<?xml version="1.0" encoding="UTF-8"?>
<connection>
    <database-url value='jdbc:derby://localhost:1527/db_name'/>
    <jndi-name value=''/>
</connection>
```

Each SQL statement that is to be presented to client applications as a new operation must be stored in a separate SQL file. Using the example scenarios above, we would have two SQL files with contents shown in the following table:

`customer_address.sql`	`select address1, address2, zip from customer where customer_id=?`
`outstanding_invoices.sql`	`select count(*) from invoices where customer_id=? and isPayed='n'`

In order for other JBI components to be able to access our SQL module, we must have a WSDL file which describes the operations we have defined (`customer_address.sql` and `outstanding_invoices.sql`). NetBeans will generate this file for us when we select the **Generate WSDL** option from right-clicking on the project in the **Projects** explorer.

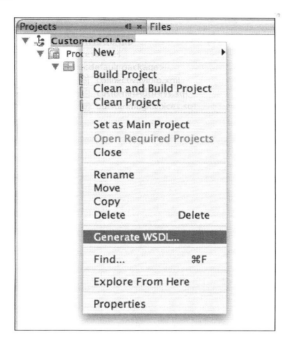

SQL Service assembly units cannot be executed directly from within the JBI container. To execute the SQL Service Unit, it needs to be added as part of a composite application. This is then called a Service Assembly. Composite applications are further discussed in Chapter 4.

 Service Assembly: a deployable component (jar file) that consists of a collection of Service Units.

IEP Service Engine

The Intelligent Event Processing service engine allows data to be read from an input source and then processed into a format that can be used for a variety of different purposes such as reporting or business intelligence information.

For example, an IEP project could be created that takes sales information from a retail system, collects all information made over the last hour, and then outputs it to a database table for reporting purposes. This would enable fast reporting based upon a periodically updated subset of the business data. Any reporting queries performed would therefore be "off-line" to the business database. This way different reporting queries could be performed as and when necessary without any performance impact on the business database.

Depending on the version of NetBeans that you have installed, you may not automatically have support for creating and editing IEP projects. If you do not have IEP project support within NetBeans, both the IEP service engine and NetBeans editor support for IEP projects can be downloaded from http://www. glassfishwiki.org/jbiwiki/attach/IEPSE/InstallationGuide.zip.

New IEP modules can be created within NetBeans by selecting the **File | New Project** menu option and then selecting the **Intelligent Event Processing Module** option within the **SOA** category as shown in the following figure:

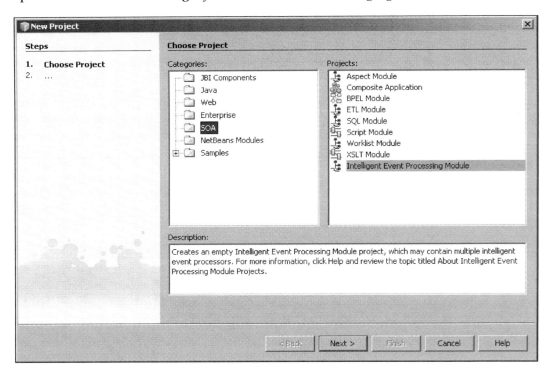

After making the above selections, the second stage of the **New Project** wizard allows the **Project Name** and the **Project Location** to be specified.

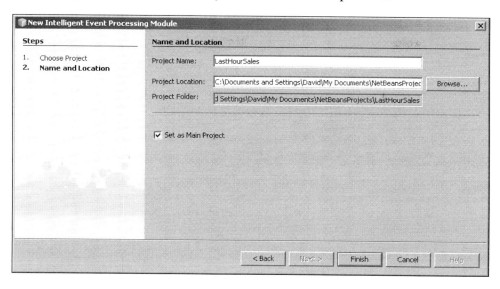

Finally, after creating the new IEP module, new Intelligent Event Processors can be added to the project. This is achieved by right-clicking on the newly created IEP project within the NetBeans **Project** pane and selecting the **New | Intelligent Event Processor** menu option. Selecting this option displays the **New Intelligent Event Processor** wizard which includes one page allowing the IEP **File Name** and **Folder** to be specified.

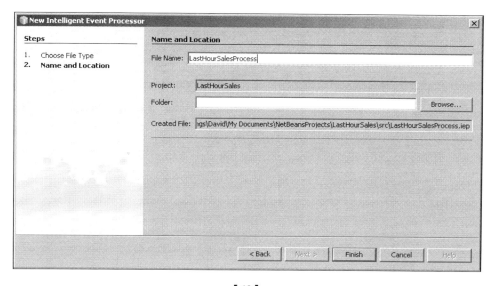

The IEP Process Editor within NetBeans allows many different processing actions to be performed on data. IEP Processes are defined using a drag-and-drop editor. The **Palette**, which shows all of the operations that can be performed on data, is shown in the following figure:

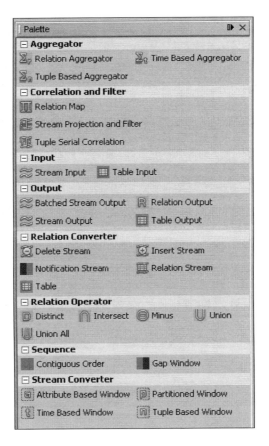

IEP Processes (Service Assemblies) cannot be executed directly from within the JBI container. To execute IEP Processes, they need to be deployed into a Service Assembly and added as part of a composite application. Composite applications are further discussed in Chapter 4.

XSLT Service Engine

XSLT Service Engine enables transformations of XML documents from one format to another using XSL stylesheets. The service engine allows XSL transformations to be deployed as web services which can then be used by external clients.

New XSLT modules can be built to run against the XSLT service engine by selecting the **File | New Project** menu option and then selecting the **XSLT Module** option from within the **SOA** category as shown in the following figure:

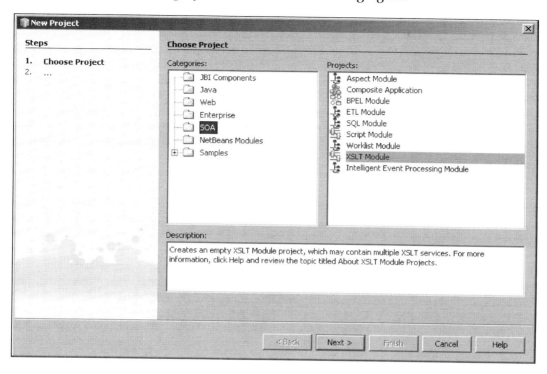

Several different types of files can be created within an **XSLT Module** to allow the service engine to transform XML files from one format to another. XML Schema files can be used to define XML within the transformation process. WSDL files are used to define the operations that are transformed within the service engine. We won't discuss how WSDL files and XML Schema files are created and maintained in this chapter, however, we will discuss them in full detail later in this book.

The final type of file that can be specified within an **XSLT Module** is an XSLT Service. These types of files can be created by right-clicking on the **XSLT Module** within the **Project** explorer in NetBeans and selecting the **New | XSLT Service** menu option. The result is shown in the next screenshot.

When creating an XSLT Service Unit, two different processing modes (**Service type**) are available:

- Request-Reply Service
- Service Bridge

The **Request-Reply Service** mode enables an XML message to be received from a client, transformed, and then sent back to the original client.

The **Service Bridge** mode enables an XML message to be received from a client and transformed into a different format. The transformed message is then used as an input for invoking a service. The output of this service is then transformed using a second **XSL** stylesheet and returned to the original caller. The **Service Bridge** mode is therefore acting as a bridge between two services. This is an implementation of the Adapter Pattern as defined in Design Patterns—Elements of Reusable Object-Oriented Software by Erich Gamma, Richard Helm, Ralph Johnson, and John Vlissides.

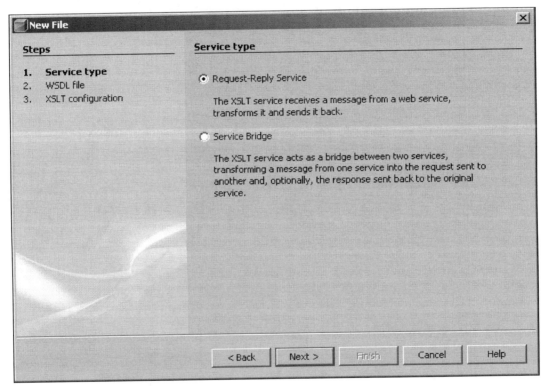

When creating a **Request-Reply Service**, the **New XSLT Service** wizard allows the web service for the XSLT transformation to be specified including details of the port, the operation being executed and the input and output types of the operation as shown in the following two screenshots:

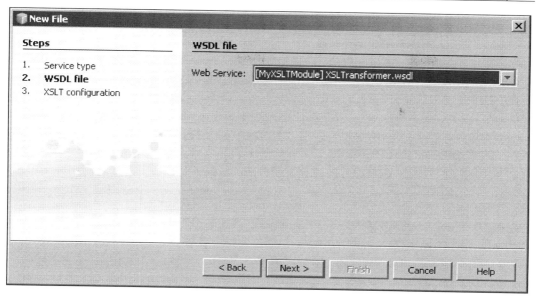

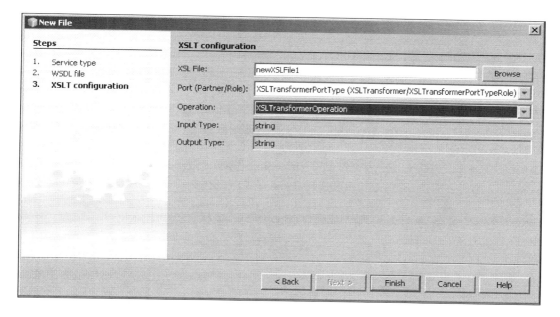

When creating a **Service Bridge** service, the two web services to be bridged are specified by first selecting the WSDL for the implemented web service and then for the invoked web service.

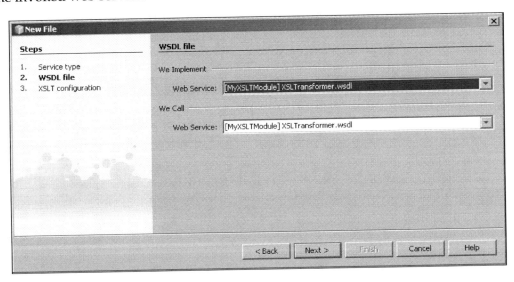

Having selected the web services to bridge, the wizard allows the implemented and invoked web services to be fully specified. Here we need to specify the operation from our implemented service and the operation to call on the invoked service.

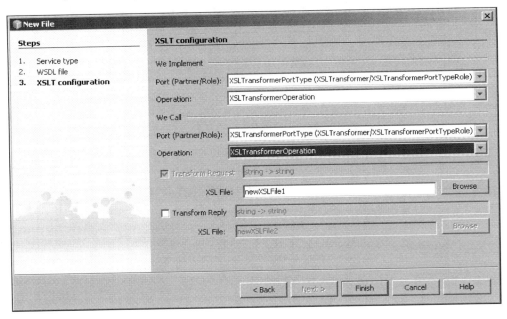

Summary

In this chapter, we have introduced the concept of a Service Engine and given an overview of the Service Engines installed with the NetBeans Enterprise Pack (the BPEL, Java EE, SQL, IEP, and XSLT Service Engines). We've learned that Service Engines:

- provide business logic functionality to their clients
- can be consumers and/or providers
- run within a Java Business Integration (JBI) Server
- expose their interfaces via WSDL
- communicate within an Enterprise Service Bus via messaging

We've also discussed some basic concepts about JBI such as the Normalized Message Router, Service Assemblies, and Service Units. We have a good understanding of JBI, some of the problems with Enterprise Application integration and why JBI is useful. In the next chapter, we extend our knowledge of JBI and SOA application development with NetBeans by describing another standard JBI component—the binding component.

4
Binding Components

In Chapter 3, we introduced the need for JBI and discussed JBI concepts and components—Service Engines. In this chapter, we will take a closer look at JBI components, discuss binding component (BC), and look at the support that NetBeans Enterprise Pack provides for these components.

In this chapter, we will discuss:

- The role of binding components in JBI Container
- NetBeans Support for binding components
- File BC
- SMTP BC
- SOAP BC
- JDBC BC
- JMS BC
- FTP BC

Binding Components

In Chapter 3, we discussed how Service Engines are pluggable components which connect to the Normalized Message Router (NMR) to perform business logic for clients. Binding components are also standard JSR 208 components that plug in to NMR and provide transport independence to NMR and Service Engines. The role of binding components is to isolate communication protocols from JBI container so that Service Engines are completely decoupled from the communication infrastructure. For example, BPEL Service Engine can receive requests to initiate BPEL process while reading files on the local file system. It can receive these requests from SOAP messages, from a JMS message, or from any of the other binding components installed into JBI container.

[*Binding Component* is a JSR 208 component that provides protocol independent transport services to other JBI components.]

The following figure shows how binding components fit into the JBI Container architecture:

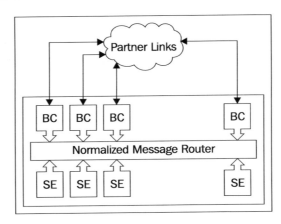

In this figure, we can see that the role of **BC** is to send and receive messages both internally and externally from **Normalized Message Router** using protocols, specific to the binding component. We can also see that any number of binding components can be installed into the JBI container. This figure shows that like Service Engines (**SE**), binding components do not communicate directly with other binding components or with Service Engines. All communication between individual binding components and between binding components and Service Engines is performed via sending standard messages through the **Normalized Message Router**.

NetBeans Support for Binding Components

The following table lists which binding components are installed into the JBI container with NetBeans 5.5 and NetBeans 6.0:

Binding Component	NetBeans 5.5	NetBeans 6.0
File BC	No	Yes
HTTP BC	No	Yes
JDBC BC	No	No
JMS BC	No	Yes
SOAP BC	Yes	No
SMTP	No	No

As is the case with Service Engines, binding components can be managed within the NetBeans IDE. The list of **Binding Components** installed into the **JBI** container can be displayed by expanding the **Servers | Sun Java System Application Server 9 | JBI | Binding Components** node within the **Services** explorer.

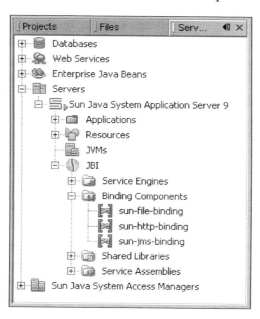

The lifecycle of binding components can be managed by right-clicking on a binding component and selecting a lifecycle process — **Start**, **Stop**, **Shutdown**, or **Uninstall**.

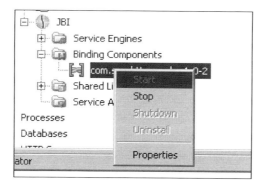

The properties of an individual binding component can also be obtained by selecting the **Properties** menu option from the context menu as shown in the following figure.

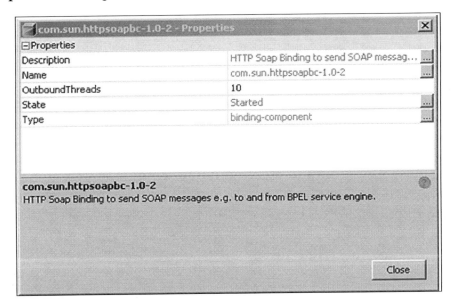

Now that we've discussed what binding components are, and how they communicate both internally and externally to the Normalized Message Router, let's take a closer look at some of the more common binding components and how they are accessed and managed from within the NetBeans IDE.

File Binding Component

The file binding component provides a communications mechanism for JBI components to interact with the file system. It can act as both a **Provider** by checking for new files to process, or as a **Consumer** by outputting files for other processes or components.

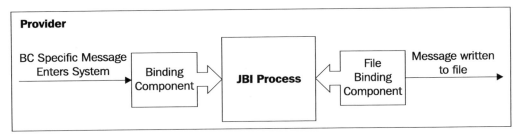

The figure above shows the file binding component acting as a **Provider** of messages. In this scenario, a message has been sent to the JBI container, and picked up by a protocol-specific binding component (for example, a SOAP message has been received). A **JBI Process** then occurs within the JBI container which may include routing the message between many different binding components and Service Engines depending upon the process. Finally, after the **JBI Process** has completed, the results of the process are sent to **File Binding Component** which writes out the result to a **file**.

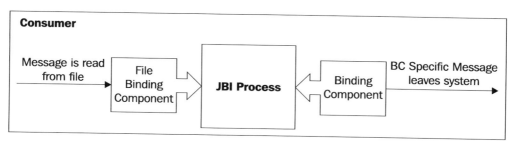

The figure above shows the file binding component acting as a **Consumer** of messages. In this situation, the **File Binding Component** is periodically polling the file system looking for files with a specified filename pattern in a specified directory. When the binding component finds a file that matches its criteria, it reads in the file and starts the **JBI Process**, which may again cause the input message to be routed between many different binding components and Service Engines. Finally, in this example, the results of the **JBI Process** are output via a **Binding Component**.

Of course, it is possible that a binding component can act as both a provider and a consumer within the same JBI process. In this case, the file binding component would be initially responsible for reading an input message from the file system. After any JBI processing has occurred, the file binding component would then write out the results of the process to a file.

Within the NetBeans Enterprise Pack, the entire set of properties for the file binding component can be edited within the **Properties** window. The properties for the binding component are displayed when either the input or output messages are selected from the WSDL in a composite application as shown in the following figure. (Don't worry if you don't understand the WSDL editor and its role in SOA applications yet. In Chapter 6 we'll describe the WSDL editor in depth. Then in Chapter 10, we'll bring all of the SOA concepts learned together, and describe how to use them to build a complete business application.)

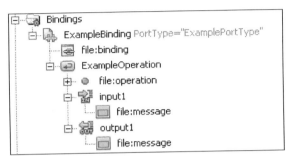

The entire set of properties that are configurable for an instance of a file binding component is shown in the next screenshot. You probably won't need all of the properties within your applications, so we've described some common properties that you will probably need to access in applications where you use file binding components.

- *fileName*: Specifies the input or output filename (depending on whether the binding component is acting as a consumer or a provider). If the **fileNameIsPattern** property is set to true, the markers %d, %u and %t can be specified within the filename to represent numbers, uuid's, and date and times respectively. These file patterns act differently when the file binding component is being used in a consumer or provider capacity.

	Consumer	Provider
%d	Pattern matches any integer number.	Replaced by sequential integer starting at 0.
%u	Pattern matches any string.	Replaced by a generated UUID
%t	Pattern matches any date and time (yyyyMMdd-HH-mm-ss-SSS)	Replaced by current timestamp (yyyyMMdd-HH-mm-ss-SSS)

- *pollingInterval*: Specifies the time in milliseconds between polling the file system when acting as a consumer. The default time is always set to 1s.

- *multipleRecordsPerFile*: When acting as a consumer, the property specifies whether there are multiple messages in the input file. When acting as a provider, this property specifies whether multiple output messages will be stored within the output file by appending messages to the output file every time they are generated.

- *archive*: Specifies whether input messages are archived to the **archiveDirectory** after being processed.

SMTP Binding Component

The SMTP Binding Component provides email services to the JBI Server and can act as either a provider by receiving inbound SMTP messages or as a consumer by sending SMTP email to external email addresses.

Neither NetBeans Enterprise Pack 5.5 nor the NetBeans 6 SOA pack provide inbuilt support for the SMTP binding component. This support can be downloaded from the OpenESB project website (`http://open-esb.dev.java.net/Downloads.html`).

To add support for the SMTP binding component, the following packages need to be downloaded:

- **smtpbc.jar**: The actual SMTP binding component.
- **org-netbeans-modules-wsdlextensions-smtp.nbm**: NetBeans Module Support allowing SMTP binding editing for WSDL files.
- **javax-mail.nbm**: NetBeans Modules Support for email.

`Smtpbc.jar` can be downloaded from the **Components** section of the **OpenESB** project website, whereas the NetBeans modules can be downloaded from the **Developer Tools** section.

Install the binding component (`smtpbc.jar`) into the application server by right-clicking on **Servers | Sun Java System Application Server 9 | JBI | Binding Components** and selecting the **Install New Binding Component** menu option.

After installing the SMTP binding component into the application server, we can install developer support into the NetBeans IDE. This is done by installing the two new NetBeans modules (`org-netbeans-modules-wsdlextensions-smtp.nbm` and `javax-mail.nbm`) through the **NetBeans Update Manager or Plugin Manager**. This developer support allows SMTP to be chosen as the Binding Type for WSDL bindings.

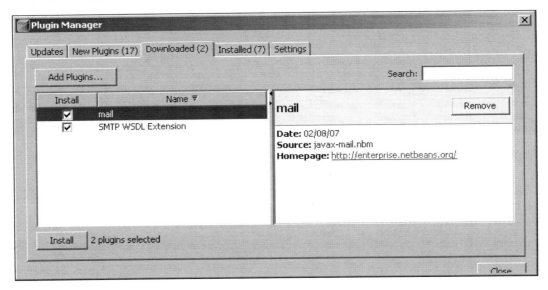

When the binding component is acting as a **Provider**, standard properties (such as who the message is from, who it is addressed to, the subject and body of the message) can be read from the message and converted into a WSDL message. This then allows any of these properties to be used within a JBI process. For example, an input message sent via an email could be processed differently depending on who it is addressed to or what the subject of the email is. If the design time support for the binding component is installed into NetBeans (as discussed earlier in this section), then all of these email properties can be edited as part of the WSDL message structure, shown as follows:

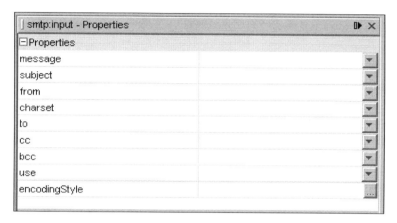

If the binding component is acting as a **Consumer**, it is responsible for sending emails via SMTP. In this situation, the `mailto: protocol (RFC 2368)` is fully supported. This allows emails to be sent to specified email addresses and also sent to **cc** and **bcc** addresses. Support is also provided for SMTP servers that require authentication (in the form of the **username** and **password** parameters). SSL Support is also provided (**useSSL**) for situations where the remote email server requires the secure sockets layer.

When the design time modules for the binding component are installed into NetBeans, then the properties for outgoing SMTP messages can be edited within the WSDL message structure, shown as follows:

FTP Binding Component

The FTP binding component provides FTP transport services to the JBI container allowing messages to be received and sent via the FTP protocol. The component can act as a consumer or a provider and supports the FTP protocol as described by RFC 959.

When the binding component is acting as a consumer, it functions in a similar fashion to the file binding component in that it polls periodically for files based upon a given file name or file name pattern. The difference however, is that the FTP binding component polls specified FTP sites rather than the local file system. After a file is polled by the binding component, the contents of the file are routed as a standard message into the JBI framework. These inbound messages are then routed via the Normalized Message Router to other binding components and/or Service Engines as defined by the JBI process.

The binding component can also act as a provider and in this instance it is responsible for routing JBI messages to a specified FTP address. Depending upon the complexity of your JBI process, the FTP binding component can act as both a consumer and provider all within the same service assembly.

If you are running your SOA application behind a firewall, the FTP binding component can be configured to use a proxy server to allow access outside the firewall. The binding component supports SOCKS4 and SOCKS5 proxy servers. The proxy server support for the binding component is defined at a global level against the binding component itself, rather than defined within the WSDL bindings within a service assembly. The proxy is configured within NetBeans by setting the **Proxy URL**, **Proxy User ID,** and **Proxy User Password** properties on the binding component.

In addition to setting the proxy details, you can specify the maximum number of simultaneous threads the binding component can use. This can be done by using the **Outbound Threads Number** property. The default value for the number of threads is 10, but you will need to configure this value depending on the number of users accessing your SOA application, and the number of times that the FTP binding component is called.

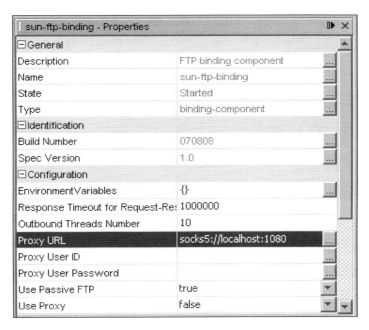

Neither the FTP binding component nor the support for FTP binding within the WSDL editor is provided, by default, within the NetBeans 5.5 Enterprise Pack, or NetBeans 6 SOA pack. To add support for these components, the following files need to be downloaded from the OpenESB project website and installed in the same way that we installed the SMTP binding component earlier in this chapter (that is, to install the binding component into the application server and to install the FTP Binding support into the WSDL editor as a NetBeans plugin).

- `ftpbc.jar`: The actual FTP Binding Component.
- `org-netbeans-modules-wsdlextensions-ftp.nbm`: NetBeans Module Support allowing FTP binding editing for WSDL files.

Once we have installed these components into the Application Server and the NetBeans IDE, we can start using the FTP Binding Component. Within a service assembly, we can specify the WSDL binding to use the FTP binding component. The properties window within the IDE allows us to modify the properties for the FTP binding, enabling the connection details of the FTP connection to be specified, shown as follows. The **url** property allows the address of the FTP server to be specified in the standard `ftp://username:password@host` format. Several other properties are available to control the connection, however, the most common that you will probably need to modify are the **dirListStyle** and **mode** properties which allow the host type and connection mode (**Binary** or **ASCII**) to be set.

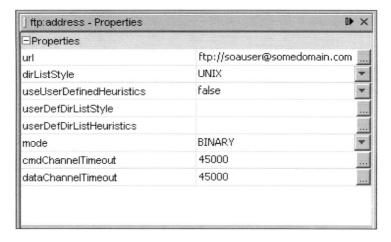

The FTP message properties within a WSDL message are displayed in the IDE properties window by selecting the operation within the WSDL bindings section of the WSDL editor. This property window allows the message properties to be set.

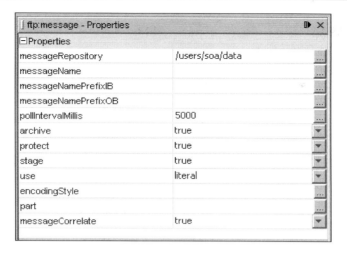

The common properties that you will probably need to set when using the FTP Binding Component are:

- **messageRepository**: directory name where messages are stored within the FTP server. This base directory must have an additional directory structure underneath it to enable the binding component to perform its processing. The following sub-directories must be available:
  - ° **/inbox**: directory where inbound messages are stored.
  - ° **/instage**: directory where inbound messages are stored before they are fully uploaded to the FTP server.
  - ° **/inprotect**: directory where inbound messages are stored to stop them from being overwritten.
  - ° **/inarchive**: directory where inbound messages are stored after they have been processed.
  - ° **/outbox**: directory where outbound messages are stored.
  - ° **/outstage**: directory where outbound messages are stored before they are fully uploaded to the FTP server.
  - ° **/outprotect**: directory where outbound messages are stored to stop them from being overwritten.
  - ° **/outarchive**: directory where outbound messages are stored after they have been processed.

- **messageName**: The name of the message file created within the **messageRepository**. Inbound messages are prefixed by the value held in the **messageNamePrefixIB** property, whilst outbound messages are prefixed by the value held in the **messageNamePrefixOB** directory.

- **pollIntervalMillis**: The time between polls of the FTP server in milliseconds.

- **archive**: Boolean indicating whether messages are archived or removed after being processed.

- **protect**: Boolean indicating whether existing messages are moved to a protected area before the current message is processed hence stopping the existing message from being overwritten.

SOAP Binding Component

The SOAP binding component (also known as the HTTP binding component) allows JBI messages to be sent and received using SOAP over HTTP and HTTPS. The component supports RPC Literal, RPC Encoded, and Document Literal encoding schemes.

The component can act as a consumer providing HTTP SOAP 1.1 Services externally. This is achieved by using the embedded Grizzly HTTP connector.

The component can also act as a provider and in this situation is capable of invoking external web services. The WSDL Editor within NetBeans provides support for editing the WSDL bindings and allows the address of remote SOAP servers to be specified.

In situations where the JBI container is running inside a firewall, the SOAP binding component can be configured to use a proxy server to enable remote web services outside the firewall to be accessed.

Many of the properties of the SOAP binding component are global to all service assemblies within the JBI container that make use of the binding component. NetBeans provides support for editing these properties directly within the IDE.

The most common properties that you will probably need to configure in your applications are:

- **Default HTTP Port Number**: The port number for inbound SOAP requests when the binding component is acting as a consumer of SOAP requests. The default port is **9080**.

- **Default HTTPS Port Number**: The port number for inbound SOAP requests when HTTPS is being used as the transport mechanism instead of HTTP. The default port is **9181**.

- **Non proxy hosts**: This is a pipe | separated list that contains all the hosts that will be contacted directly instead of through a proxy server if a proxy is enabled.

- **Proxy Host**: The specifies the name of the proxy server for outbound SOAP requests. If the proxy server requires authentication, then the **Proxy user name** and **Proxy user password** properties can be specified. The port number of the proxy server can be specified using the **Proxy port** property.

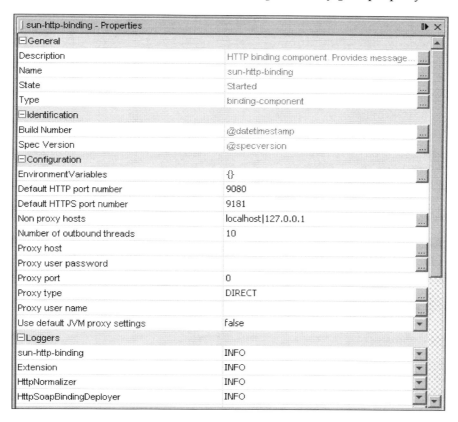

JDBC Binding Component

In some situations, you will find that you need to interact with a database as part of your JBI applications. When interacting with the database, we can use the SQL Service Engine as described in Chapter 3. Alternatively, if you have more limited database needs, you can use the JDBC binding component.

The JDBC binding component can act as a provider or a consumer. When acting as a provider, the component can issue these different DML commands to the database either to select information from the database or to change data:

- Select
- Insert
- Update
- Delete

When acting as a consumer, the component can poll specified tables on the database to find newly inserted data. When new data is identified by the component, this data can be routed into the JBI framework as a standard WSDL message to other components. The JDBC Binding Component can connect to any database that conforms to the JDBC 3.0 specification and can be accessed via a JNDI datasource lookup.

The JDBC Binding Component is not supplied with the NetBeans 5.5 Enterprise Pack or with the NetBeans 6.0 SOA pack, and must be downloaded separately from the Open ESB project (http://open-esb.dev.java.net/Downloads.html). Similarly, WSDL editor support can be downloaded from the open ESB project website. To fully support the JDBC Binding Component, the following files must be downloaded:

- jdbcbc.jar: The actual JDBC binding component.
- org-netbeans-modules-wsdlextensions-jdbc.nbm: NetBeans Module support allowing JDBC binding editing for WSDL files.

These additional components can be installed into NetBeans in the same way we installed the SMTP binding component and WSDL support earlier in this chapter.

After installing the WSDL extensions for the JDBC Binding Component, you will find that visual editing is provided within NetBeans for both consumer and provider instances. The properties of the WSDL binding can be seen in the following figure:

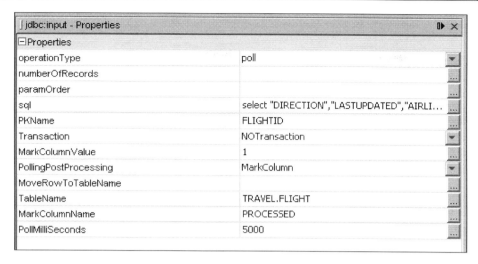

The WSDL editor provides support for editing the different properties that can be specified for the binding component. The major properties that you will probably need to edit when using this component are described as follows:

- **operationType**: specifies what operation the binding component is performing—**poll**, **insert**, **update**, **find**, or **delete**.

- **sql**: sql that will be executed against the database. If the sql is a **select** statement, then the **numberOfRecords** property specifies how many rows are retrieved from the database.

- **PollingPostProcessing**: After the database has been polled for new records, the binding component can be requested to perform post processing on the rows that have been polled. The **PollingPostProcessing** property can be set to several different values:

  - ○ **Delete**: polled rows are deleted after polling.

  - ○ **MarkColumn**: The column specified by the **MarkColumnName** property on the polled rows will be updated to hold the value specified in the **MarkColumnValue** property. This property can be checked when the database is polled to ensure the existing data is not continually re-polled.

  - ○ **MoveRow**: polled rows of data are moved to the table specified by the **MoveRowToTableName** property.

  - ○ **CopyRow**: polled rows of data are copied to the table specified by the **MoveRowToTableName** property.

- **PollMilliSeconds**: time period in milliseconds between individual polls of the database.

- **TableName**: name of the database table that is being accessed in the binding operation.

JMS Binding Component

The final binding component we are going to discuss in detail is the JMS Binding Component.

The JMS Binding Component allows the JBI container to communicate with JMS message queues and topics. The component can act as a provider and/or as a consumer of JMS messages, and as such can subscribe to a topic and wait for JMS messages, or it can send messages to a predefined Queue or Topic.

 A JMS Queue allows messages to be consumed by only one client and is a point to point type of messaging. A JMS Topic allows messages to be consumed by any number of clients and is a publish or subscribe type of messaging.

The binding component can send and receive JMS TextMessage's and MapMessage's.

The NetBeans Enterprise Pack provides design time support for the JMS Binding Component and allows the binding attributes to be defined graphically within the WSDL editor. The connection details of the JMS Message Server can be specified within the *service* of the WSDL file.

- **connectionURL**: This property allows the base address of the message server to be specified. This can be in the format mq:// for the Sun Java Message Queue system, or in the more generic jndi:// format where the message queue is obtained via a JNDI lookup. The **username** and **password** properties enable the connection details to be specified for the message server.

- **connectionFactoryName**: If JNDI is being used to look up the message server, then the **connectionFactoryName** property specifies the JNDI name of the connection factory to use. The **initialContextFactory** and **providerURL** properties provide the standard lookup configuration parameters for JNDI lookups. If access to the message server is secured using JAAS, then the **securityPrincipal** and **securityCredential** properties can be used to specify the caller.

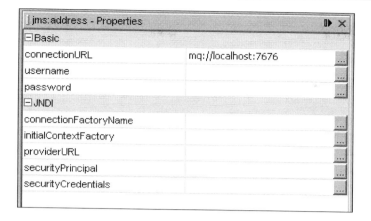

For a specific JMS operation, it is necessary to specify whether the binding component is connecting to a queue or a topic and whether transaction support is to be used for the connection.

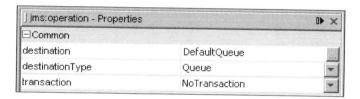

NetBeans provides editor support to enable these properties to be configured:

- **destination**: name of the queue or topic that the binding component is to receive messages from or send messages to.

- **destinationType**: indicates whether the destination is a **Queue** or a **Topic**

- **transaction**: specifies whether the JMS conversation will use **NoTransactions** or whether it will be enrolled in a **XATransaction**. XA transaction support is only enabled when the binding component is acting as a **Consumer** and is receiving inbound messages.

Finally, the payload and type of a JMS message can be configured for a given WSDL operation.

- **messageType**: type of the message being sent or received from the specified **Queue** or **Topic**. The **messageType** can be either **TextMessage** (for `javax.jms.TextMessage` type messages) or **MapMessage** (for `javax.jms.MapMessage` type messages).

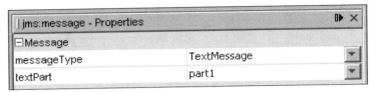

Other Binding Components

Due to the standardized nature of the JBI Framework and JBI components, many other JBI binding components have been written by the developer community, all of which can be deployed to the Sun Java System Application Server or the GlassFish Server. One such source of JBI components can be found in the OpenESB project (`https://open-esb.dev.java.net`). The OpenESB project provides many different binding components such as:

- CICS Binding Component
- MSMQ Binding Component
- LDAP Binding Component

The full list of binding components available from the OpenESB project can be found at `https://open-esb.dev.java.net/Components.html`.

Summary

In this chapter, we've continued our discussion of the JBI framework and discussed Binding Components and their role within the JBI Container. We've seen how the Binding Component provides transport and protocol independence for other JBI components. We've seen how this enables the JBI container to provide a highly decoupled framework allowing developers and integrators to build resilient SOA applications.

We continued to discuss the different binding components (namely file, FTP, SOAP, JDBC, JMS and SMTP) that are either installed into the application server with the NetBeans Enterprise pack or can be downloaded directly from the OpenESB project web site. We also discussed that because binding components are developed to a standard set of interfaces, any JBI compliant binding component can be installed into the Application Server.

In the next chapter, we will expand our knowledge of developing SOA applications with the NetBeans Enterprise Pack by taking a tour of the WSDL editor within NetBeans—a key component for developing SOA applications.

5
BPEL Designer

Over the last couple of years, BPEL has rapidly emerged as the standard for combining a set of services into a number of discrete and long running enterprise processes. I have interacted with IT heads of several companies and found out that they are either using BPEL or planning to use it over their other middleware framework. Before considering BPEL, you need to clearly understand what BPEL is and is not. BPEL, as I understand, deals only with the functional aspects of business processes. It can only define the flow and scope of business transactions. It does not offer any way to measure or manage processes, and there is no abstraction for players or roles involved in the business processes, but different BPEL implementers have extended it by adding these capabilities. For instance, Oracle's BPEL Process Manager is capable of understanding workflow.

BPEL is still the ultimate standard for assembling a set of discrete services into an end-to-end process flow. There are many tools available in the market that can manage the lifecycle of business processes and also offers the support of authoring and testing processes. Out of all of them, a BPEL Designer is a GUI-based tool that lets you create complex business processes using BPEL constructs. One of those tools is the BPEL Designer that comes with the NetBeans Enterprise Pack.

I cannot possibly discuss the merits of various BPEL Designers on the market, but can say that NetBeans BPEL Designer lets you create and manage BPEL-based business processes in a very elegant way.

In this chapter, let us discuss some points which include:

- Why BPEL?
- NetBeans BPEL Designer
- Supported BPEL Elements
- Runtime Integration
- Design and Source Views
- BPEL Palette
- BPEL Mapper

BPEL for Business Process

BPEL is an XML-based execution environment intended to enable simple to complex business process definitions for document-centric business processes. BPEL's goal is to make it possible to write a business process once in BPEL and then run it on any BPEL environment.

Throughout this chapter, we will talk much about 'processes', as the core of BPEL. A BPEL process is just like any other process providing standard facilities such as storage, scope, and fault endpoints. Commands given in a BPEL process are called activities and the definition of a BPEL process consists of exactly one activity.

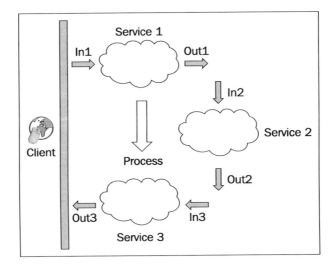

A process usually comprises multiple web services that work sequentially to define a scope. Often, the output from one web service is fed into another web service. Now, a web service can wait for its input from another web service like an Airways Baggage Tracking System that sends a 'Request-for-Information' to all available partner airlines and waits for the baggage information. It may even wait for several hours. We need to understand that enterprise processes are long running and complex. A major benefit of implementing a long-running process as a BPEL process is that the persistence of the process can be provided by BPEL engine, greatly simplifying the business logic.

Once we have a process up to a longer running life cycle, a number of inter-related issues come to the forefront. One is synchronous versus asynchronous messaging. Asynchronous messaging is more appropriate for longer-running processes because it doesn't require connections to be maintained for unreasonable amounts of time using unreasonable amounts of resources.

BPEL, when used for defining business processes, has the following advantages:

1. **Endpoint management:** BPEL introduces the concept of partner links that can be defined during design time. Partner links are a first-class concept in BPEL, and can be manipulated directly in processes. BPEL provides a full solution to endpoint management from the simple static deployment to the dynamic resolution. It may depend on multiple factors, including technical considerations as well as business logic.

2. **High level of abstraction:** BPEL provides such a high level of abstraction that business analysts can compose and run executable business by working with friendly modeling environments.

3. **WSDL centric approach:** The defining technical characteristic of a service from a BPEL standpoint is that it can be described in a WSDL. Every message exchange described in a BPEL process is in terms of `portTypes` and `operations` which are defined in the WSDL. BPEL does not assume that services are accessed via SOAP over HTTP.

4. **Minimizes complexity:** Complexity will remain an unavoidable part of the enterprise technology landscape. Managing and minimizing this complexity is the primary objective of BPEL.

Why is BPEL important for your business? Adopting BPEL is currently the only elegant way to orchestrate existing web services into a meaningful business process.

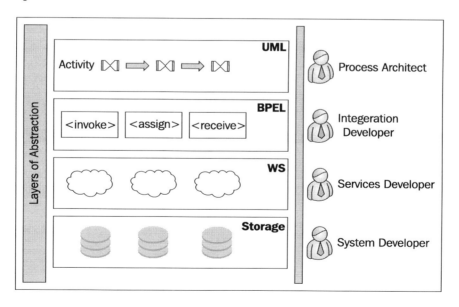

BPEL specification defines the syntax and semantics of the BPEL language, which contains a variety of process flow constructs. Just as today's software development tools include web services in their development capabilities, there also exist easy-to-use tools to create and manage business processes using BPEL, such as the NetBeans BPEL Designer. If your organization has the capability to utilize web services for system integration, then a product to manage and control the resulting business processes is critical. BPEL and web services now provide a standardized integration interface, a language for integration, and process automation. BPEL, in effect, has the potential to commoditize the capabilities provided by proprietary EAI solutions.

By using BPEL to define business processes, companies can select processes and services to incorporate into their operations. This provides flexibility to replace or upgrade certain aspects of a business process without impacting the systems that are working well. For instance, in our Airways application, airlines can participate and opt out of the common reservation system anytime they want, without affecting the customer interface.

BPEL processes specify the order in which participating web services should be invoked. This can be done sequentially or in parallel. With BPEL, we can express conditional behavior, like a web service invocation, that can depend on the result of a previous invocation. We can also construct loops, declare variables, copy and assign values, define fault handlers, and so on.

A BPEL process consists of steps, where each step is called an activity. BPEL supports primitive and structured activities.

For its clients, a BPEL process looks like any other web service. When we define a BPEL process, we actually define a new web service that is a composition of existing services. The interface of the new BPEL composite web service uses a set of port types, through which it provides operations like any other web service. To invoke a business process described in BPEL, we have to invoke the resulting composite web service also known as a composite application, as defined by JBI.

BPEL also supports compensation by undoing steps in the business process that have already completed successfully. The goal of compensation is to reverse the effects of previous activities that have been carried out as part of a business process that is being revoked.

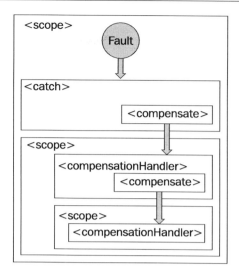

Compensation is required in most business processes, which are long running and use asynchronous communication with heterogeneous partner web services. Business processes are often sensitive in terms of successful completion because the data they manipulate is sensitive and they span multiple partners. So, it is very important to ensure that business processes either fully complete or that the partial results are compensated. BPEL supports the concept of compensation with the ability to define compensation handlers, which are specific to scopes.

 The <compensate> activity can execute the <compensationHandler> of an immediate child <scope> by name or, by default, of all immediate children in reverse order of completion. The execution of a <while> loop creates one <compensationHandler> per iteration. The <compensate> activity can only occur within a <compensationHandler> or during fault handling.

If BPEL heavily depends on web services, what is the differentiator between web services and BPEL? Web services are stateless while business processes require a stateful model. When a client starts a business process, a new instance is created. This instance lives for the duration of the business process. Messages sent to the business process need to be delivered to the correct instance of the business process. BPEL provides a mechanism to use specific business data to maintain references to specific business process instances. This process is termed **correlation.** We will discuss correlation in more detail later in this chapter.

Understanding BPEL Projects

NetBeans' BPEL Designer lets you to create and deploy BPEL processes which are compliant with the WS-BPEL 2.0 specification. To perform these actions you need to create a BPEL module, which is a NetBeans project type. The BPEL Designer provides a complete environment to enable you to quickly and efficiently orchestrate web services.

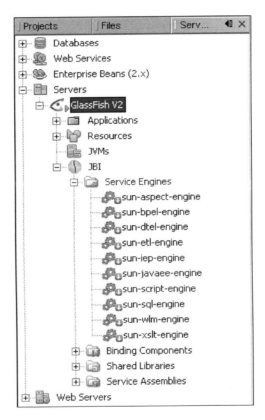

NetBeans IDE provides a BPEL runtime plug-in that provides the standard BPEL runtime capability. The BPEL runtime that the IDE provides is a framework for the execution content of BPEL: specifically, compiling BPEL, validating BPEL, and assembling composite application descriptors. The BPEL runtime runs inside the Sun Java System/GlassFish Application Server, which provides a container for the JBI suite. Runtime services for executing BPEL-based applications are provided by the BPEL **Service Engine**, which is a component of the JBI server. (Refer to Chapter 3 on *Service Engines*). The BPEL Service Engine is started together with the Application Server. Thus, before deploying and test running a Composite Application project, you must make sure that the Application Server is started.

BPEL Views

You can perform source level editing as well as visual designing, through the views provided by the BPEL Designer. The BPEL Designer will perform round-trip two-way engineering to ensure that the Design view and Source view remain synchronized with each other. The IDE will automatically re-parse the BPEL source file and rebuild the diagram every time you edit the BPEL file through the Source view.

 BPEL Design view is the default view and it is the view that gets invoked whenever you create a new BPEL module. To switch to the corresponding place in the Source view, right-click an element in the Design view and select Go to Source (Alt-O).

Source and Design View are always in-sync.

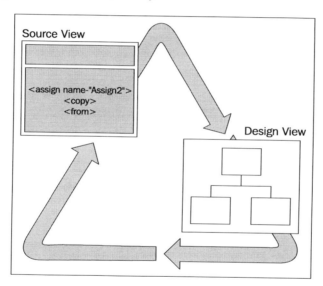

Design View

The **Design** view is the diagram view. The **Design** view and the **Source** view are fully synchronized to do two-way forward and reverse engineering. If you use the **Design** view to author your process, you will be restricted to adding some language constructs that may not be supported by the BPEL runtime.

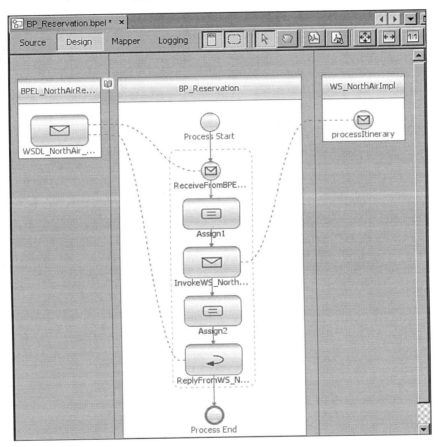

The **Design** view is a business process designer, where you can author a diagram of your business process. In the **Design** view, you add, edit, and delete BPEL activities. The diagram constructed in the **Design** view is automatically generated into BPEL source code which is compliant with the WS-BPEL 2.0 specification. For a list of supported BPEL 2.0 constructs refer to https://open-esb.dev.java.net/kb/ preview3/ep-bpel-se.html#BPEL.

Source View

The **Source** view supports the entire BPEL 2.0 language specification as defined in the BPEL schema. So, you can still add non-supported elements in the **Source** view. When you switch back to **Design** view, the **Design** view renders those constructs in the diagram because it has successfully reverse engineered from the **Source** view. However, this is just a byproduct of the fact that this functionality was already built into the **Design** view. When the validation system runs, it will flag these entries as 'Not supported by the runtime'.

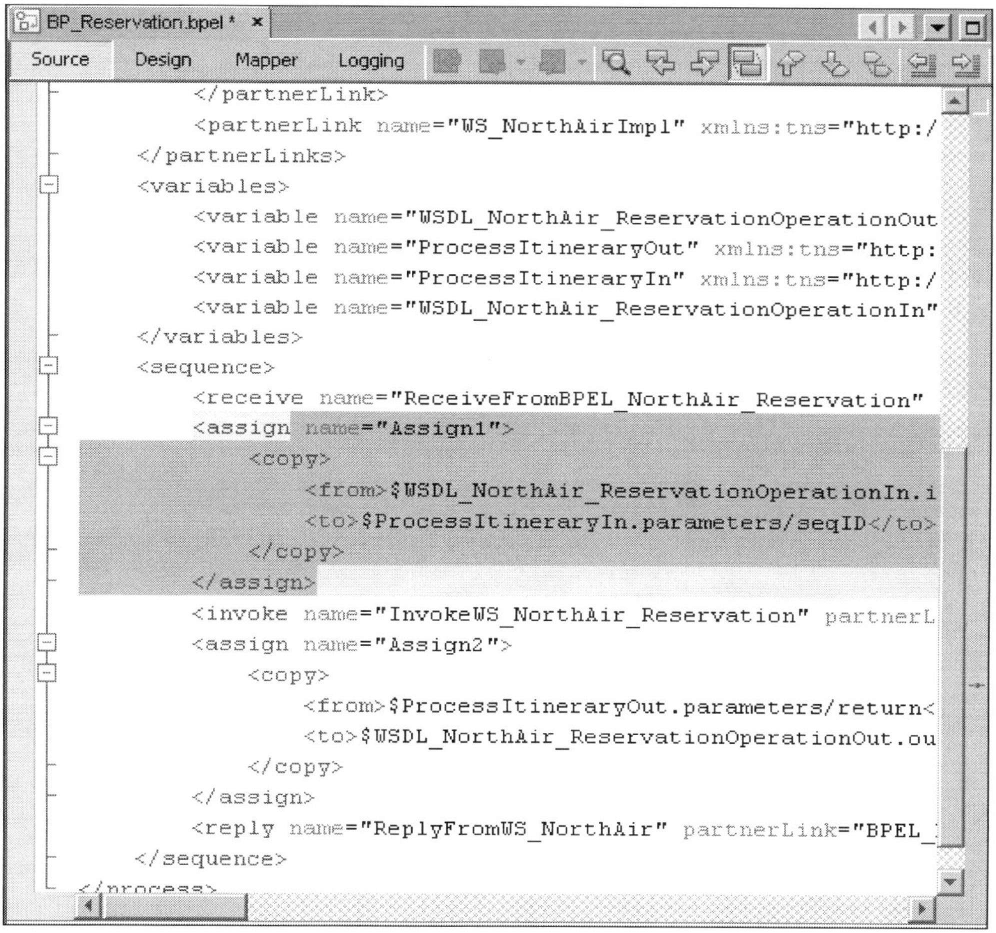

```
            </partnerLink>
            <partnerLink name="WS_NorthAirImpl" xmlns:tns="http:/
        </partnerLinks>
        <variables>
            <variable name="WSDL_NorthAir_ReservationOperationOut
            <variable name="ProcessItineraryOut" xmlns:tns="http:
            <variable name="ProcessItineraryIn" xmlns:tns="http:/
            <variable name="WSDL_NorthAir_ReservationOperationIn"
        </variables>
        <sequence>
            <receive name="ReceiveFromBPEL_NorthAir_Reservation"
            <assign name="Assign1">
                <copy>
                    <from>$WSDL_NorthAir_ReservationOperationIn.i
                    <to>$ProcessItineraryIn.parameters/seqID</to>
                </copy>
            </assign>
            <invoke name="InvokeWS_NorthAir_Reservation" partnerL
            <assign name="Assign2">
                <copy>
                    <from>$ProcessItineraryOut.parameters/return<
                    <to>$WSDL_NorthAir_ReservationOperationOut.ou
                </copy>
            </assign>
            <reply name="ReplyFromWS_NorthAir" partnerLink="BPEL_
        </sequence>
    </process>
```

See the above figure. We are configuring an Assign activity and copying variables. You can either use Source view to type BPEL code (If you are comfortable with BPEL) or use the visual editor to copy variables.

BPEL Mapper

BPEL **Mapper** allows you to add and edit functions that are specific for some business process elements, such as `Assign`, `If`, and `ElseIf`. Each of these elements can have specific expression types, such as copy assignments, condition expressions, and time functions. For example, the If, `ElseIf` element of `If`, and `Repeat Until` activities can have condition expressions, the Assign element includes copying expressions, the Wait element can have duration expressions, and the `ForEach` activity can have expressions with integer values. Using the BPEL Mapper's graphic interface, you can perform calculations by assigning XPath operations and functions to variables and to XSD elements, attributes, and parts. A simple variable copy operation is shown in the following example.

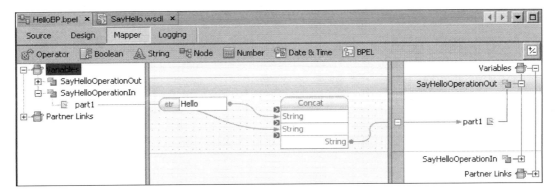

You need to first click on the **Assign** activity in the **Design** view and switch to **Mapper** view using the views button provided as shown in the above figure. For copying values of variables, drag-and-drop from one variable to another.

The BPEL **Mapper** enables you to create a predicate that consists of XPath functions. A predicate applies a condition to a node that can have multiple values. The result is the subset of nodes that satisfy the condition. The BPEL **Mapper** has a menu bar that shows a collection of XPath. These functions are based on the XPath 1.0 specification.

For mapping examples and more information on predicates and XPath function reference, refer to **The BPEL Mapper** section of the **Developers Guide to the BPEL Designer** available at http://www.netbeans.org/kb/60/soa/bpel-guide-mapper.html.

Palette

When you create a new BPEL module, NetBeans IDE automatically shows the **Activities Palette** window. The **Palette** consists of BPEL activities that you can drag-and-drop on the designer (**Design** view). The **Palette** activities are broadly classified into three types, namely **Web Service, Basic Activities,** and **Structured Activities.** The **Palette** will show only the BPEL 2.0 elements that are supported by the **Design** view. However, you are free to go to the **Source** view to manually edit the BPEL files (If you already know BPEL).

As already mentioned earlier in this book, the BPEL elements supported by the Design view may vary from the BPEL support provided by the JBI runtime. Hence most of the time, even if the Design view does not support a particular BPEL 2.0 element, you can still get it working in the process. The following figure shows the BPEL activities palette:

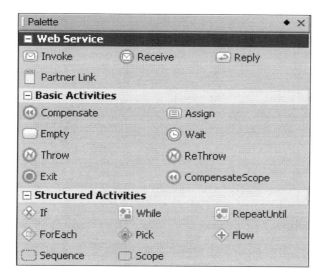

Both the **Basic Activities** and **Structured Activities** nodes are not expanded by default. Click on the [+] icon to expand the node.

When you drag-and-drop a Palette element into the BPEL diagram, it becomes a BPEL activity. Click on any palette element and drag the element over the BPEL diagram. Some point in the BPEL diagram will be highlighted in an **orange** color. You are supposed to drop the elements only in those areas. For instance, you can drag-and-drop an **Invoke** element only after a Receive element.

Web Service Activities

To be instantiated, an executable business process must contain at least one
`<receive>` or `<pick>` activity annotated with a `createInstance="yes"` attribute.
This is a general rule for creating an instance of your process. Most of the time, your
business process interacts with other web services and will exchange data then.
The BPEL process itself acts as a web service. This palette element provides all the
activities that a BPEL process needs while interacting with partner links.

Invoke

The **Invoke** activity enables the business process to invoke a **One-Way** or
Request-Response operation on a `portType` offered by a partner. The `operation` is
defined in the partner's WSDL file.

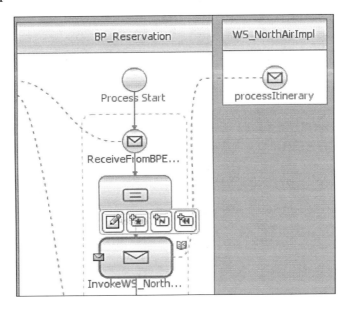

In our AirAlliance example, the business process invokes an operation exposed
by the NorthAir Web Service. The operation is called processItinerary. When you
drag-and-drop the invoke activity from the palette into the designer, you will get a
Property Editor window, where you can set **Correlations,** choose **Partner Link,** and
corresponding operations.

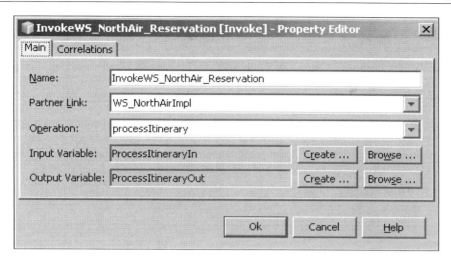

Partner Links should have already been created to use the invoke activity. When you drag-and-drop a web service into the designer, you will be prompted to create a new **Partner Link**. **Invoke** is a web service call addressed to a service endpoint, or URL. If the service is long-running, the calling process waits for a callback message in a **Receive** or **Pick** activity, reporting that the task has completed and is returning result data.

Correlation sets on **Invoke** activities deal with outbound operations. Invoke activities are used to validate that outgoing messages contain data which is consistent with the data contained within specified correlation set instances. Correlation is the means by which the BPEL runtime tracks conversations between a particular process instance and corresponding instances of its partner services. Consider correlation as a primary key that is used by the BPEL runtime to correlate incoming and outgoing messages, and route them accordingly.

Also see Chapter 9 for information on Handling Events where correlation is depicted.

Receive

The **Receive** activity allows the business process to perform a blocking wait for a particular message to arrive. Typically the receive activity is the start of a process instance. It is typically used to receive a message from the client or a callback from a partner web service. Whenever the process receives a message, a new instance of the process is created. To keep track of the right process, you need to set the correlation.

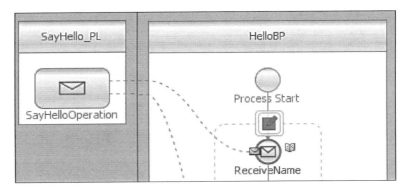

You can add any number of receive activities but they should receive messages from different **Partner Links**. Also, if you do not create an instance from the **Property Editor** window, make sure that you have the **Correlations** set on **Receive** activity. This is because the **Receive** element must have a valid `<correlations>` child if it does not have the `createInstance="yes"` attribute.

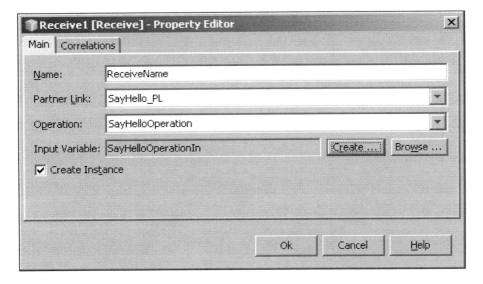

In the example shown above, we have selected the BPEL **Partner Link** that corresponds to a WSDL file. Operations created in the WSDL file are automatically populated. You can select any **Operation** from which the message will be received to the process.

Reply

The **Reply** activity is used to return a message from the process to the same partner that initiated the operation. This activity is used in a synchronous operation, and specifies the same partner, port type, and operation as the **Receive** activity that invoked the process. For example, a web service invoking the Reservation BPEL process gets a reply back from the NorthAir Reservation web service regarding the itinerary status.

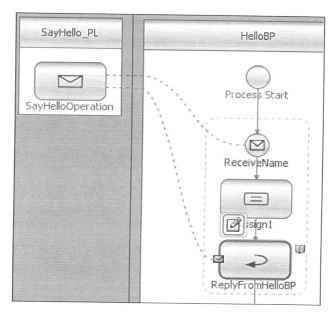

The above figure shows a **HelloBP** BPEL process sending a reply back to the invoked web service. There could be multiple replies from your process depending on the conditions. Each reply activity should be in a sequence. However, you can add `reply` activities on multiple partner links defined for the process. Thus the process can reply to multiple invoke activities from different partner links.

In a `receive-reply` pair, only one outstanding `reply` activity can correspond to an executed `receive`. This means that, at most, one `reply` is executed for a given `receive`. At runtime, only one `reply` activity is executed, because the `reply` activities will most likely be in exclusive branches of execution.

The combination of **Receive** and **Reply** activities creates a **Request-Response** operation. This activity is used in a synchronous (request/response) operation, and specifies the same partner, port type, and operation as the **Receive** activity that invoked the process.

A valid BPEL process can have only one receive activity and one reply activity.

Partner Link

Any web service that communicates with the BPEL process is identified as a **Partner Link**. Each partner link will contain child elements that correspond to the available web service activities supported by that partner link's interface. You do not directly add elements to a partner link container. The **Design** view will query the partner's WSDL and automatically populate the partner link container with the appropriate child elements. If you need to modify a partner link, edit the partner WSDL files which will allow the **Design** view to re-render the partner link, and thereby reflect the modified interface.

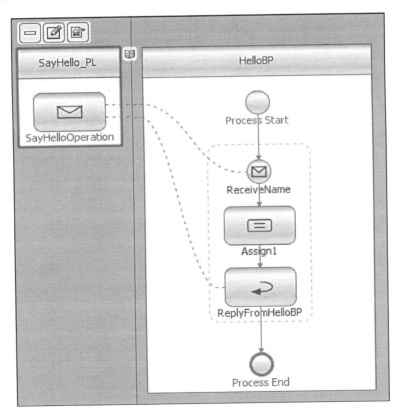

In the above example, we have one partner link. SayHello_PL is the BPEL implementation that invokes the BPEL process. To add a partner link just drag-and-drop any external element, like a web service or a WSDL file, on the highlighted area of the BPEL diagram. When you drag-and-drop an external element, a partner link dialog box is shown where you can configure the partner link by selecting the correct WSDL file.

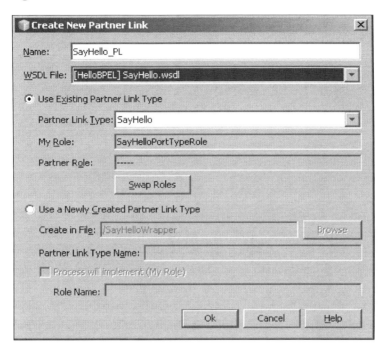

Partner Link elements identify the parties that interact with our business process. Each link is defined by a partner link type and a role name. The **Partner Link Type** determines the relationship between a process and its partners by defining the roles played by each service in a conversation. The relationship is further determined by specifying the port type provided by each service to receive messages. Each role specifies one port type in the WSDL file. You use a single role for a synchronous operation, as the results are returned using the same operation.

When you drag-and-drop a web service into the diagram, the BPEL Designer retrieves the WSDL file from the Application Server. To successfully retrieve the WSDL file, the Application Server should be running and the web service project must be deployed.

In the **Partner Link** editor window, you can choose whether to use the existing partner link type or create a new partner link type. If the WSDL file you selected contains partner link types, the **Use Existing Partner Link Type** option is selected automatically and the **Partner Link Type** drop-down list is populated with the partner link types found in the WSDL file. You can use one of the existing partner link types or select the **Use a Newly Created Partner Link Type** option to create a new partner link type. If the WSDL file does not contain partner link types, the **Use a Newly Created Partner Link Type** option is selected. When in doubt, always accept the default options provided by NetBeans property editors.

Other BPEL Activities

BPEL activities are broadly classified into **Basic Activities** and **Structured Activities** that you frequently use in your project. They are defined in the following table:

BPEL Activity	What For?
<assign>	To copy or manipulate data flowing through the process.
<throw>	To indicate a fault or specific event handling in the process. Refer to Chapter 9 on *Event Handlers*.
<wait>	To hold the process execution for a specific period of time.
	There may be cases where you may need to introduce an intentional delay for a specific duration, or delay execution until a specified time. For instance, you may need to pause to instruct the business process to invoke a web service at a specified time. Or there may be cases where you may need to wait for some time before you can resume execution.
<sequence>	To define a set of activities that will be invoked in a sequence.
<flow>	To define a set of activities that will be invoked simultaneously.
<pick>	To select a path of execution.

Read the Developer Guide to BPEL Designer available at `http://www.netbeans.org/kb/60/soa/bpel-guide.html` for more information on using the palette elements in your BPEL process. The guide offers detailed help on using the BPEL palette elements. So the BPEL palette elements are not explained in this book.

Navigator Window

The BPEL Navigator window lets you quickly navigate through your BPEL process. When the BPEL process gets complicated and becomes huge, you can quickly navigate through the elements using the **BPEL Logical View** offered by the **Navigator**. To enable the BPEL Navigator, press **Ctrl+7** or select **Window | Navigating | Navigator**.

When you right-click on any node, you can see two options:

1. Go to Source – Takes you to the occurence of that element in the
    Source View

2. Go to Design – Takes you to the occurence of the element in the Design view.

A Simple Example

In the previous sections of this chapter, you were introduced to BPEL activities and the different views offered by NetBeans for BPEL editing. Let us use that knowledge to create a simple synchronous BPEL process that gets a name from a web service client and replies with a 'Hello' message. This example has one receive and reply activity.

To create a BPEL process, you need to first create a **BPEL Module** project in NetBeans. Click **File | New Project | BPEL Module** from the **SOA** category. Click **Next** to continue.

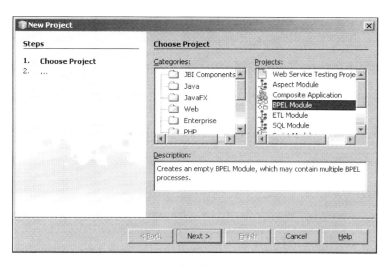

Enter **HelloBPEL** as the **Project Name**. Select your **Project Location** and click **Finish**.

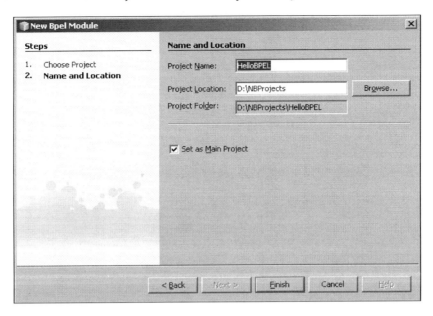

You will see a top node with **HelloBPEL** and an empty **Process** sub folder. Right-click on **HelloBPEL** node and select **New** | **BPEL** Process to create a new BPEL process.

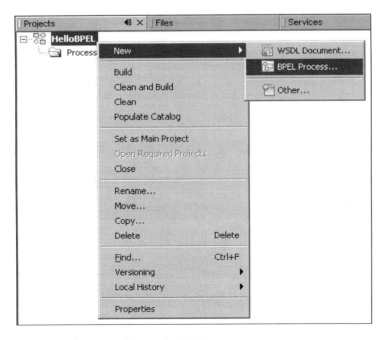

Enter **HelloBP** as the name of the BPEL process. Leave the **Target Namespace** to be the default namespace and click **Finish**.

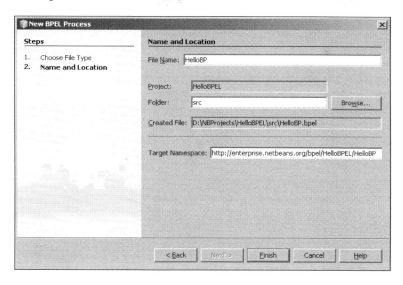

When you finish creating the BPEL process, a file by the name of **HelloBP.bpel** is created and the **Design** view is automatically shown. The BPEL process is empty and does not have any BPEL activity. We know that any BPEL process should have at least one receive activity to receive requests from external clients. So the BPEL process is incomplete and is highlighted in **red** colour.

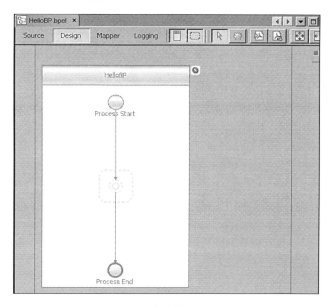

Now, we will create a web service that invokes our business process. To create a web service, we need to create a **WSDL Document**. Right-click on the **Process Files** and select **New | WSDL Document** to create a new WSDL document.

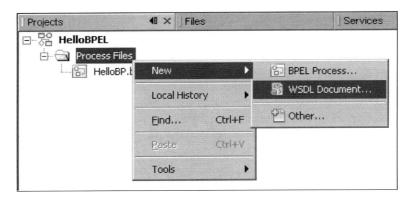

Enter **SayHello** as the **File Name** and leave the other fields as default.

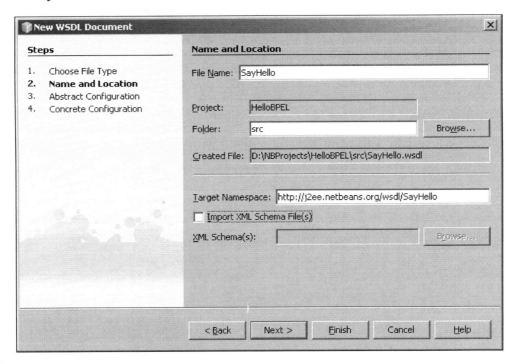

You will be shown the **Abstract Configuration** window. Leave the **Port Type Name,** **Operation name,** and **Operation Type** as default. The **Operation Type** is **Request-Response Operation** as our web service sends a string to the BPEL process and receives a string back from the process.

Our **Input** and **Output** variables are both strings. So leave the **Element or Type** value of both **Input** and **Output** at xsd:string.

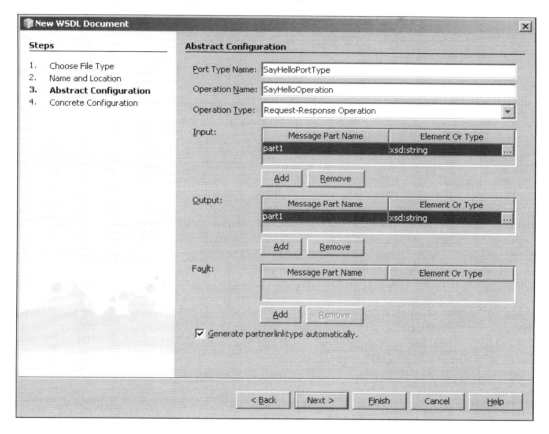

If you are using an older version of NetBeans IDE, partnerLinkType will be automatically generated. In the newer versions, you have the option to disallow NetBeans from generating **partnerLinkType**.

In the **Concrete Configuration** page, set the **Binding Type** to **SOAP**. A Later part of this book shows how you can use other WSDL binding types. Leave the default values for the other fields and click **Finish**.

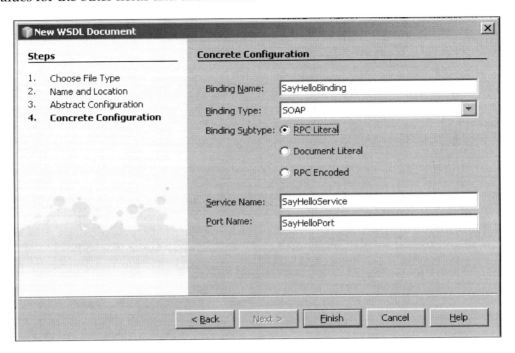

Now, notice that the `SayHello.wsdl` file shows up in the **Process Files** sub-folder. You can double-click the file to edit the file. You can edit the WSDL file manually or use the graphical view to edit. For more information on editing WSDL files, refer to Chapter 6 on WSDL Editor.

Look at the generated WSDL file that has a port configured with SOAP binding.

```xml
<?xml version="1.0" encoding="UTF-8"?>
<definitions name="SayHello" targetNamespace=
                        "http://j2ee.netbeans.org/wsdl/SayHello"
    xmlns="http://schemas.xmlsoap.org/wsdl/"
    xmlns:wsdl="http://schemas.xmlsoap.org/wsdl/"
    xmlns:xsd="http://www.w3.org/2001/XMLSchema"
    xmlns:tns="http://j2ee.netbeans.org/wsdl/SayHello"
    xmlns:plnk="http://docs.oasis-open.org/wsbpel/2.0/plnktype"
    xmlns:soap="http://schemas.xmlsoap.org/wsdl/soap/">
    <types/>
    <message name="SayHelloOperationRequest">
        <part name="part1" type="xsd:string"/>
```

```
        </message>
        <message name="SayHelloOperationResponse">
            <part name="part1" type="xsd:string"/>
        </message>
        <portType name="SayHelloPortType">
            <operation name="SayHelloOperation">
                <input name="input1" message=
                                    "tns:SayHelloOperationRequest"/>
                <output name="output1" message=
                                    "tns:SayHelloOperationResponse"/>
            </operation>
        </portType>
        <binding name="SayHelloBinding" type="tns:SayHelloPortType">
            <soap:binding style="rpc" transport=
                                "http://schemas.xmlsoap.org/soap/http"/>
            <operation name="SayHelloOperation">
                <soap:operation/>
                <input name="input1">
                    <soap:body use="literal"
                        namespace="http://j2ee.netbeans.org/wsdl/SayHello"/>
                </input>
                <output name="output1">
                    <soap:body use="literal"
                        namespace="http://j2ee.netbeans.org/wsdl/SayHello"/>
                </output>
            </operation>
        </binding>
        <service name="SayHelloService">
            <port name="SayHelloPort" binding="tns:SayHelloBinding">
                <soap:address location=
                    "http://localhost:18181/SayHelloService/SayHelloPort"/>
            </port>
        </service>
        <plnk:partnerLinkType name="SayHello">
            <plnk:role name="SayHelloPortTypeRole" portType=
                                        "tns:SayHelloPortType"/>
        </plnk:partnerLinkType>
</definitions>
```

Now, drag `SayHello.wsdl` to the highlighted circle on the BPEL diagram to create a new partner link.

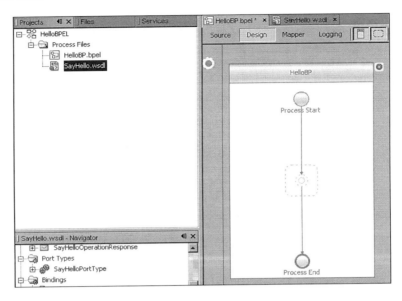

When you drag-and-drop any external component into the **Design** view of the BPEL file, you will be prompted to create a new **Partner Link**. When the **Create New Partner Link** dialog box appears, enter `SayHello_PL` as the partner link name and click **OK**.

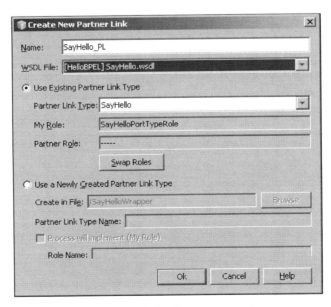

The **Design** view of the BPEL process shows the newly created partner link with one operation **SayHelloOperation**.

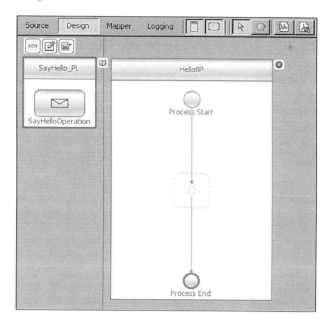

Our BPEL process needs at least one receive activity. From the BPEL **Palette**, drag-and-drop a **Receive** activity into the highlighted area in the diagram.

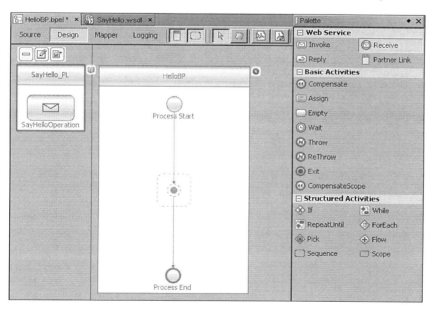

Now, double-click on the **Receive** activity to open the **Property Editor**.
Type **ReceiveName** as the name of the **Receive** activity. Select the **Partner Link**
SayHello_PL and select the only **Operation** available: **SayHelloOperation**. Now,
click the **Create** button, accept the defaults, and click **OK**. Now, you can see an **Input**
Variable by the name of **SayHelloOperationIn** configured. Click **OK**.

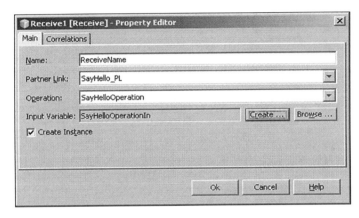

Now, our BPEL diagram shows our BPEL processing by receiving a request through
the **SayHello_PL Partner Link**. You can switch to the **Source** view and take a look
at the generated BPEL code. If you already know BPEL, you can directly edit the
code. However, it is advisable to perform all operations through the **Design** view
because whatever is valid in **Source** view may not be supported in **Design** view. The
NetBeans SOA tools are still evolving at the time of writing this book.

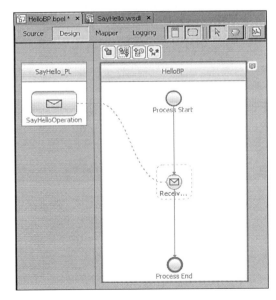

Now that you have configured a **Receive** activity, your BPEL should return some result back to the caller. For that, our process should have a **Reply** activity. Drag-and-drop the **Reply** activity from the **Palette** into the highlighted area after the **Receive** activity.

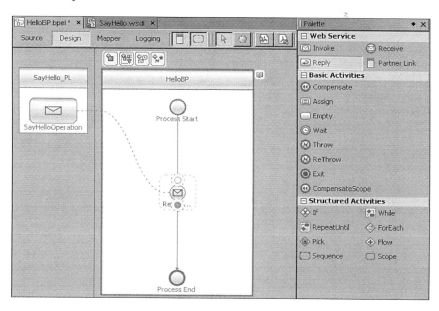

Once you have added the **Reply** activity, double-click on the activity and configure its properties. Enter **ReplyFromHelloBP** as the **Name**. Select **SayHello_PL** for the **Partner Link** and select the operation from the drop down box (If there is only one operation, it will be automatically selected.). Click the **Create** button, accept the default name for the variable, and click **OK**.

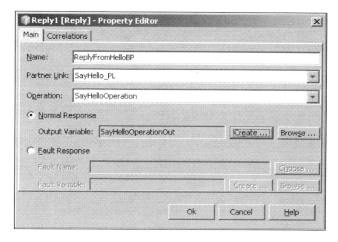

After adding a **Reply** activity, take a look at our BPEL process. It doesn't do anything yet, but at least looks semantically complete. You can't try to execute this business process yet, as the variables in the BPEL are not initialized.

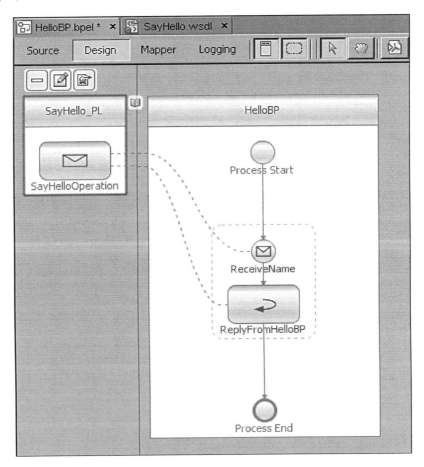

The objective of this BPEL process is to get a name from an external client and greet the client. The name obtained from the client is the input variable of the **Receive** activity. This variable should be copied to the output variable of the **Reply** activity with a string literal 'Hello' concatenated to it.

For this reason, let us add an **Assign** activity for performing this copy operation. Drag-and-drop an **Assign** activity between **Receive** and **Reply** activity on the highlighted area.

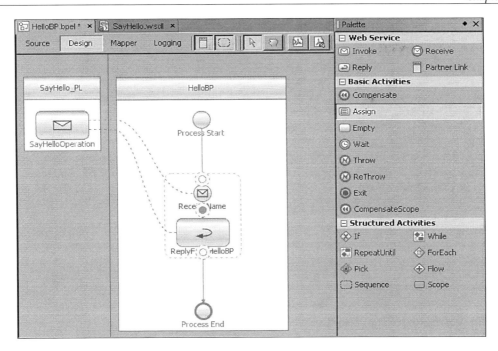

Now, click on the **Assign** activity and switch to **Mapper** view. From the **String** menu, select **Concat** and add it to the middle pane of the BPEL **Mapper.** From the same **String** menu, select **String Literal** and add it to the middle pane. Now, expand **Variables** in the left pane, navigate to **SayHelloOperationIn,** and click on **part1** variable. Drag-and-drop this **part1** variable into the **String Literal.** Add **Hello** as the String literal. Now connect the other end of the String literal to the first String entry in **Concat** box. Connect the last **String** entry of the **Concat** box to the variable, **SayHelloOperationOut | Part1** as shown in the following screenshot:

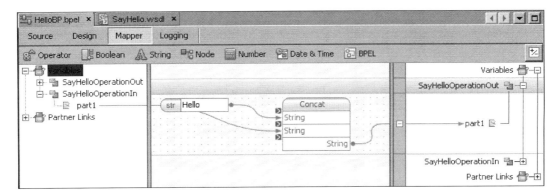

If you find the GUI complex to use, switch to **Source** view and edit your **Assign1** activity to look something like the following code:

```
<assign name="Assign1">
    <copy>
        <from>concat('Hello ', $SayHelloOperationIn.part1)</from>
        <to variable="SayHelloOperationOut" part="part1"/>
    </copy>
</assign>
```

After making changes in the **Source** view, click on **Design** view to see if you can see the graphical representation.

Now, our BPEL process is complete. Whenever the SOAP client sends a text message, for example 'BPEL', the process returns 'Hello BPEL' to the client. For deploying our BPEL process, we need a **Composite Application**. Our BPEL process should be deployed as a JBI module, in a **Composite Application** to be processed by the BPEL Service Engine.

So, create a new **Composite Application** by clicking **File | New Project** and selecting **Composite Application** from the **SOA** category.

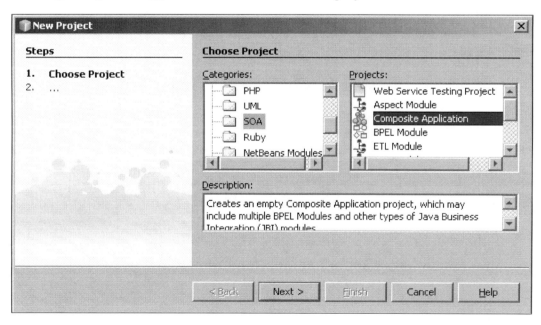

Enter **HelloBPELCA** as the name of our **Composite Application**. Provide a valid path for the **Project Location** field and click **Finish**.

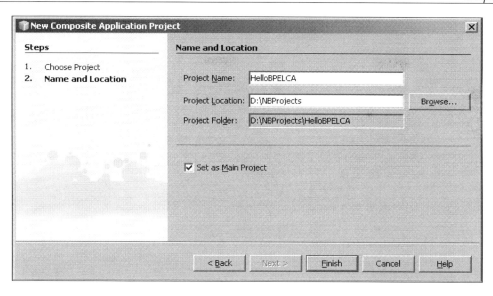

Now, right-click on **HelloBPELCA** node and select **Add JBI Module,** to add a new JBI Module.

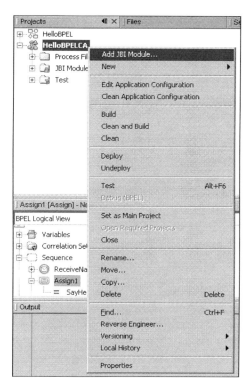

In the **Select Project** window, select the **HelloBPEL** NetBeans project file you created earlier. Note that the Service Engine deployment jar is selected automatically from the project. Click **Add Project Jar Files** to continue.

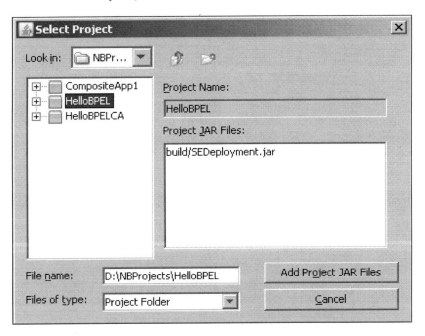

Now, if you notice the folder structure of the composite application, **HelloBPEL.jar** is copied to the **JBI Modules** folder so that it can be deployed to a BPEL Service Engine.

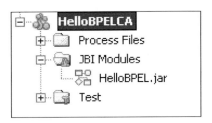

Right-click on the composite application and select **Clean and Build,** to build the composite application as shown in the following screenshot:

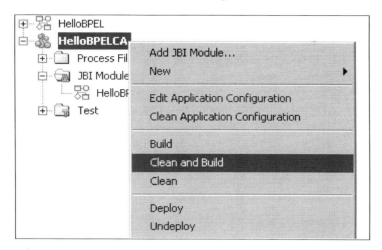

After building the composite application, right-click on the composite application and select **Deploy** to deploy the project.

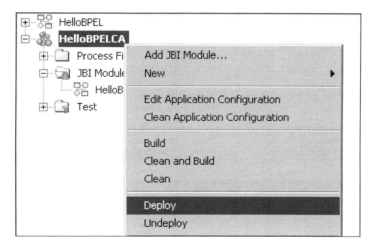

Now, we need to test if our BPEL is working fine. To test the BPEL process, we create a new test case. The test involves sending a SOAP request to the BPEL process and getting the correct SOAP response back from the process.

The composite application we created will have an empty **Test** folder. Right-click on the **Test** folder and select **New Test Case**.

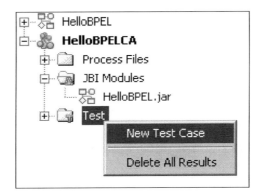

Enter **TestHello** as the name of our test case and click **Next** to continue.

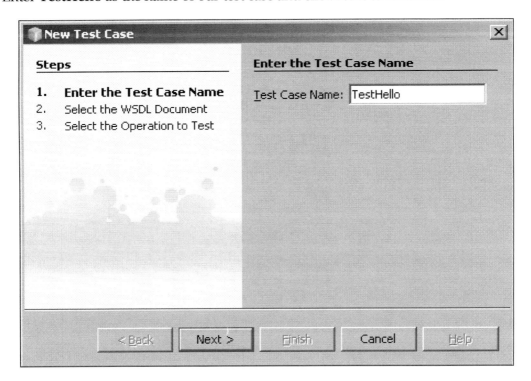

You need to select the web service to which the SOAP request has to be sent. Select **SayHello.wsdl** under **HelloBPEL – Source Packages**.

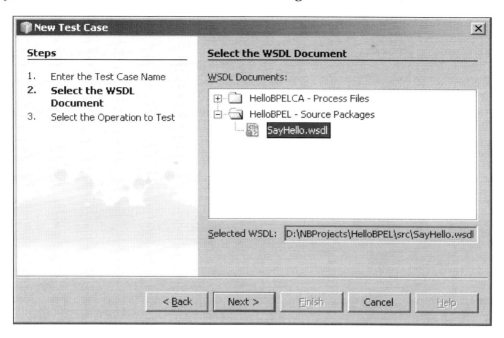

Our WSDL has only one operation by the name of **SayHelloOperation**. Select that operation and click **Finish**.

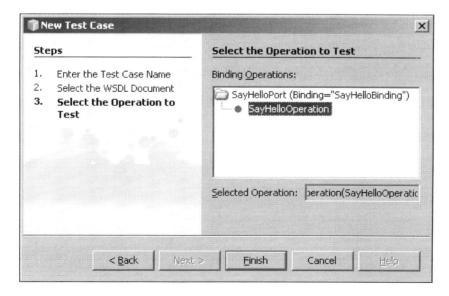

Once the test case is created, double-click on the **Input** node to edit `Input.xml`. Make changes to the `Input.xml` as shown in the following code:

```
<soapenv:Envelope xsi:schemaLocation=
                "http://schemas.xmlsoap.org/soap/envelope/
                http://schemas.xmlsoap.org/soap/envelope/"
   xmlns:xsi="http://www.w3.org/2001/XMLSchema-instance"
   xmlns:xsd="http://www.w3.org/2001/XMLSchema"
   xmlns:soapenv="http://schemas.xmlsoap.org/soap/envelope/"
   xmlns:say="http://j2ee.netbeans.org/wsdl/SayHello">
   <soapenv:Body>
     <say:SayHelloOperation>
       <part1>BPEL</part1>
     </say:SayHelloOperation>
   </soapenv:Body>
</soapenv:Envelope>
```

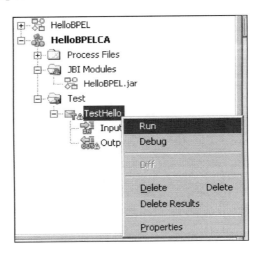

Now, right-click on **TestHello** test case and select **Run** to run the test case. On the first try, the test will fail and the `Output.xml` file will be created. You need to click Yes when you are prompted with a dialog box showing 'Overwrite Empty Output?' message **Run** the test case for the second time. The test case will pass. Double-click on **Output** node to open `Output.xml`. Here is how the output should look:

```
<?xml version="1.0" encoding="UTF-8"?>
<SOAP-ENV:Envelope xmlns:SOAP-ENV=
                        "http://schemas.xmlsoap.org/soap/envelope/"
   xmlns:xsd="http://www.w3.org/2001/XMLSchema"
   xmlns:xsi="http://www.w3.org/2001/XMLSchema-instance"
```

```
xsi:schemaLocation="http://schemas.xmlsoap.org/soap/envelope/
                    http://schemas.xmlsoap.org/soap/envelope/">
<SOAP-ENV:Body>
  <m:SayHelloOperationResponse xmlns:m=
                              "http://j2ee.netbeans.org/wsdl/SayHello">
      <part1 xmlns:msgns="http://j2ee.netbeans.org/wsdl/
                          SayHello" xmlns="">Hello BPEL</part1>
  </m:SayHelloOperationResponse>
</SOAP-ENV:Body>
</SOAP-ENV:Envelope>
```

This is just a simple business process illustrating how BPEL processes should be built and executed through NetBeans SOA tools and runtime. For a more complex example, refer to Chapter 10 – *Building a Sample Application*.

BPEL 2.0 Elements

Some of the common errors that might occur while validating your BPEL file—endpoint conflict, unsupported BPEL elements, and other BPEL Service Engine issues. For troubleshooting validation errors in your BPEL document, refer to `https://open-esb.dev.java.net/kb/60/ep-bpel-guide-troubleshoot.html`.

> The BPEL Designer that gets bundled with NetBeans supports the BPEL 2.0 final specification and does not support any previous specifications. This means that, when you open the BPEL files that comply with the previous versions of the specification, the BPEL Designer shows the Unable to Show the Diagram message.

The following BPEL 2.0 elements and attributes are not present in the 5.5 release of the BPEL Designer.

Element	Parent Element
Validate, Rethrow, Compensate, ExtensionActivity, FromPart, CompensationHandler	NA
CompensationHandler, Catch, CatchAll	Invoke
From	Variable
Targets, Sources	Activity
FromPart	Receive, Invoke, OnEvent, OnAlarm
ToPart	Reply, Invoke
ExtensibleAssign	Assign
Documentation, Namespace	From, To in Assign

Element	Parent Element
Links	Flow
PartnerLinks, CorrelationSets, CompensationHandler, TerminationHandler	Scope
MessageExchange	Scope, Process
Attribute	Element
QueryLanguage, ExpressionLanguage, SuppressJoinFailure, AbstractProcess, ExitOnStandardFault	Process
InitializePartnerRole	PartnerLink
SuppressJoinFailure	Activity
Validate	Assign
ExpressionLanguage, Property, PartnerLink, EndPointReference, Opaque	From
QueryLanguage, Property, PartnerLink	To
Isolated, ExitOnStandardFault	Scope
Parallel	ForEach
MessageExchange	Receive, Reply, OnMessage, OnEvent

It is possible that some of the above BPEL elements are supported in the newer release at the time of publishing this book. For the latest list of supported BPEL constructs, always refer to the BPEL Service Engine User Guide available at https://open-esb.dev.java.net/kb/60/ep-bpel-se.html.

BPEL Products and Vendors

The BPEL product vendors can be classified into two types. The one that offers the BPEL Engine or the BPEL Server, and the other that offers the designer capabilities for authoring BPEL-based processes. The following is a list of BPEL server and designer vendors:

- Oracle BPEL Process Manager (http://www.oracle.com/technology/products/ias/bpel/index.html)

- IBM WebSphere Business Integration Server Foundation (http://www.ibm.com/software/integration/wbisf)

- IBM alphaWorks BPWS4J (http://www.alphaworks.ibm.com/tech/bpws4j)

- OpenStorm Service Orchestrator (http://www.openstorm.com)

- Vergil VCAB Server (http://www.vergiltech.com/products_VCAB.php)

- Active Endpoints ActiveWebflow Server
  (`http://www.active-endpoints.com/products/index.html`)

- ActiveBPEL engine (`http://www.activebpel.org/`)

- Fivesight Process eXecution Engine

- Microsoft BizTalk 2004 (`http://www.microsoft.com/biztalk/`)

- Oracle BPEL Designer

- IBM WebSphere Studio Application Developer, Integration Edition

- IBM BPWS4J Editor

- Vergil VCAB Composer

- Active Endpoints ActiveWebflow Designer

Summary

SOA will simplify the building, managing, and maintaining of distributed systems because the technologies you use to build these systems are often standard-based like BPEL. BPEL is one of the technologies that provides a rich web service-based infrastructure and an orchestration language that has widespread industry support. BPEL's promise is that the creation of abstract and executable schemes can be defined as a business process and run in any compliant engine.

NetBeans' BPEL Designer allows you to create simple to complex BPEL-based processes that can run on application servers like GlassFish Application Server.

In this chapter, we learned the usage of NetBeans' BPEL Designer and how it can be used to create simple processes visually. You were also introduced to the graphical tools and palette available for creating BPEL files and composite applications.

6
WSDL Editor

In Chapter 5, we discussed the need for BPEL and BPEL Designer within NetBeans Enterprise Pack. In this chapter, we will give a brief overview of what WSDL is, and how WSDL documents are formed. This chapter is not intended as a complete introduction to WSDL but as an overview of what WSDL is. We will continue and concentrate on the use of WSDL in enterprise applications and in particular, discuss the WSDL editor within NetBeans Enterprise Pack. Finally, we will show how NetBeans Enterprise Pack assists in the development of web services based upon WSDL documents.

The following topics will be discussed in this chapter:

- What is WSDL?
- Why WSDL?
- How are WSDL documents formed?
- Managing WSDL documents in NetBeans
- Different Views of WSDL documents
- Abstract and Concrete WSDL configurations
- Creating Web Services from WSDL documents

At the end of this chapter, you will have a better understanding of WSDL and what support the NetBeans Enterprise Pack provides for developers using WSDL.

What is WSDL?

In Chapter 3, we discussed the need for standards when developing and integrating enterprise applications. The Web Services Definition Language (WSDL) provides a standard for describing services, the location of services, and what operations these services provide, all in a platform and language independent way. This allows the enterprise application developer to build and consume loosely coupled services, which is one of the key tenets of building successful SOA applications.

WSDL documents provide both an abstract and a concrete view of the services they are describing. The abstract view describes the operations of the services whereas the concrete view describes how those operations are mapped onto a specific protocol, for example SOAP. We will discuss these abstract and concrete views later in this chapter.

WSDL documents are correctly formed XML documents, which again aids in developing enterprise applications in a Service Oriented Architecture. Correctly formed XML documents can be read and parsed automatically by computers, which allows clients to look up and consume web services automatically (for example, by using a **uddi** registry) or allows the Normalized Message Router (see Chapter 3) to pass standardized messages between the different JBI components (for example, Service Engines and Binding Components).

WSDL was first proposed in March 2001 as a note to the W3C (http://www.w3.org/wsdl) by Ariba, IBM, and Microsoft. In their W3C note, they describe WSDL as:

> ...an XML format for describing network services as a set of endpoints operating on messages containing either document-oriented or procedure-oriented information. The operations and messages are described abstractly, and then bound to a concrete network protocol and message format to define an endpoint. Related concrete endpoints are combined into abstract endpoints (services). WSDL is extensible to allow description of endpoints and their messages regardless of what message formats or network protocols are used to communicate.

Why WSDL?

The key benefits of using WSDL are:

- **WSDL is XML-based:** being XML-based means any system that can read and interpret XML, can read and interpret WSDL documents.
- **WSDL is platform and language independent:** WSDL is not tied into one programming language and platform. WSDL-based web services could be developed and deployed in Microsoft's .NET environment and consumed via Java GUI applications. Alternately, WSDL-based web services could be developed and deployed in a Java environment and consumed via PHP-based web applications.
- **WSDL describes services in an abstract fashion:** services are described in an abstract fashion as they help to promote loose coupling and aid in developing against interfaces, promoting good design.

- **WSDL binds services to concrete protocols:** the specific binding for a service is separated from the description of the service because loose coupling between services and their transports is enabled.

- **WSDL is extensible:** WSDL does not tie communications to one specific protocol, for example SOAP over HTTP. As new transport mechanisms are required, additional bindings can be specified. Today, we may only need to access our WSDL described services via SOAP, but in the future we may need JMS or SMTP bindings. WSDL format allows us to extend WSDL documents to add additional bindings as and when necessary.

The Format of WSDL Documents

Now that we've described what WSDL is and the benefits that it gives, lets take a look at what WSDL documents look like.

In the previous section, we stated that WSDL documents are correctly formed XML documents. The basic structure of a WSDL document is shown as follows:

```
<?xml version="1.0" encoding="UTF-8"?>
<definitions name="myService" targetNamespace=
                        "http://j2ee.netbeans.org/wsdl/myService"
  xmlns="http://schemas.xmlsoap.org/wsdl/"
  xmlns:wsdl="http://schemas.xmlsoap.org/wsdl/"
  xmlns:soap="http://schemas.xmlsoap.org/wsdl/soap/"
  xmlns:xsd="http://www.w3.org/2001/XMLSchema"
  xmlns:tns="http://j2ee.netbeans.org/wsdl/myService"
  xmlns:ns="http://xml.netbeans.org/schema/myService"
  xmlns:plnk="http://docs.oasis-open.org/wsbpel/2.0/plnktype">
    <types>
    </types>
    <message name="myMessageRequest">
    </message>
    <message name="myMessageReply">
    </message>
    <portType name="myPortType">
      <wsdl:operation name="myOperation">
        <wsdl:input name="input1" message="tns:myMessageRequest"/>
        <wsdl:output name="output1" message="tns:myMessageReply"/>
      </wsdl:operation>
    </portType>
```

```
<binding name="myBinding" type="tns:myPortType">

</binding>
<service name="myService">
  <wsdl:port name="myPort" binding="tns:myBinding">

  </wsdl:port>
</service>
</definitions>
```

The WSDL file is broken down into 5 main elements all below the main `<definitions>` element:

\<types/\>	abstract	Describes the data types used by the operations; described for the service. These data types are defined using XML Schema Definitions. We will learn more about the XML Schema Designer in NetBeans in Chapter 7.
\<message/\>	abstract	Describes the messages that are used within the service.
\<portType/\>	abstract	Describes the operations that are available within the service.
\<binding/\>	concrete	Describes what binding the service is using (e.g. SOAP, JMS)
\<service/\>	concrete	Describes connection details for the specific bindings.

WSDL Types

The `<types/>` element of WSDL document allows the different data types used by operations in the service to be defined using XML schema language. In the following code, types are imported from XSD file `hello.xsd` located in the same directory as the WSDL file.

```
<types>
    <xsd:schema targetNamespace="http://j2ee.netbeans.org/wsdl/hello">
        <xsd:import namespace="http://xml.netbeans.org/schema/hello"
          schemaLocation="hello.xsd"/>
    </xsd:schema>
</types>
```

WSDL Messages

Within the `<message/>` section of WSDL document, we define different messages that can be used from the operations within the service. Each message defined describes the names and types of its parameters. In the following example, we have defined two messages (`sayHelloRequest` and `sayHelloReply`) for a simple `Hello World` type service.

```
<message name="sayHelloRequest">
    <part name="request" element="ns:stringElement"/>
</message>
<message name="sayHelloReply">
    <part name="response" element="ns:stringElement"/>
</message>
```

WSDL Port Types

The `<portType/>` element within WSDL document describes the operations that are available from the service. For each operation described by WSDL, we describe the `name` of the operation, and the names and types of the parameters (`message`) used by the operation. A sample code for the `<portType/>` element looks like, shown as follows:

```
<portType name="helloPortType">
    <wsdl:operation name="sayHello">
        <wsdl:input name="input1" message="tns:sayHelloRequest"/>
        <wsdl:output name="output1" message="tns:sayHelloReply"/>
    </wsdl:operation>
</portType>
```

WSDL allows four different types of operations to be defined as follows:

- **One-Way:** the service endpoint receives a message and processes it without returning a response to the client.
- **Request / Response:** The service endpoint receives a message, processes it and then returns a response to the client.
- **Notification:** The endpoint sends a message to a client without first receiving a message from the client.
- **Solicit / Response:** The endpoint sends a message to a client and then receives a response back from the client.

These different operation types are defined within WSDL by specifying which different message types are used by a specific operation.

 Notification or **Solicit/Response** type messages have to be added manually within WSDL editor.

One-Way	`<portType ...>`
	`  <wsdl:operation ...>`
	`    <wsdl:input name="input1" ... />`
	`  </wsdl:operation>`
	`</portType>`

Request / Response	`<portType ...>`
	`  <wsdl:operation ...>`
	`    <wsdl:input name="input1" ... />`
	`    <wsdl:output name="output1" ... />`
	`  </wsdl:operation>`
	`</portType>`

Notification	`<portType ...>`
	`  <wsdl:operation ...>`
	`    <wsdl:output name="output1" ... />`
	`  </wsdl:operation>`
	`</portType>`

Solicit / Response	`<portType ...>`
	`  <wsdl:operation ...>`
	`    <wsdl:output name="output1" ... />`
	`    <wsdl:input name="input1" ... />`
	`  </wsdl:operation>`
	`</portType>`

WSDL Binding

The `<binding/>` elements of the WSDL document describe concrete protocols for the operations (portType's) described by WSDL. In the following code sample, the operation from the `tns:helloPortType` is bound to a `soap transport` using a `document` encoding `style`.

```
<binding name="helloBinding" type="tns:helloPortType">
  <soap:binding style="document" transport=
                    "http://schemas.xmlsoap.org/soap/http"/>
      <wsdl:operation name="sayHello">
          <soap:operation/>
          <wsdl:input name="input1">
              <soap:body use="literal"/>
          </wsdl:input>
          <wsdl:output name="output1">
              <soap:body use="literal"/>
          </wsdl:output>
      </wsdl:operation>
</binding>
```

WSDL Service

The `<service/>` section of the WSDL document describes concrete endpoint ports for the binding, specified in the `<binding/>` section. In the following code, we can see that the `binding` is for a SOAP-based `service` with a URL endpoint (`http://localhost:18181/helloService/helloPort`).

```
<service name="helloService">
  <wsdl:port name="helloPort" binding="tns:helloBinding">
    <soap:address
      location="http://localhost:18181/helloService/helloPort"/>
  </wsdl:port>
</service>
```

Now that we've had a brief of into WSDL, lets take a look at what support NetBeans provide for creating and editing WSDL documents.

NetBeans Support for Creating WSDL Documents

Within the NetBeans IDE, new WSDL documents can be created by selecting the **File | New File** menu option. Under the **XML** category in the **New File** dialog we can select to create a new **WSDL Document** shown as follows:

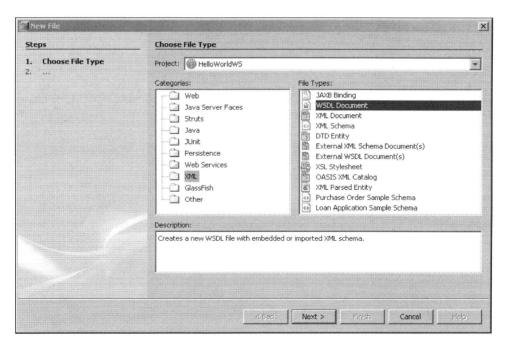

Upon starting the **New File** wizard and selecting a new **WSDL Document**, NetBeans displays a wizard allowing the configuration of the **New WSDL Document** to be specified. After selecting a **New WSDL Document**, the second step is to specify the **Name and Location** of the new WSDL document. This dialog allows us to specify the **File Name** and location of the new file together with the **Target Namespace** for the file. The namespace defaults to `http://j2ee.netbeans.org/wsdl/fileName`, where **File Name** is the name of the file being created, but this can be overridden with any application specific values.

This stage in the wizard also provides facilities to import an XML schema file into the WSDL document. Importing XML schema files into the WSDL document saves having to re-specify any custom data types in your WSDL file that may be in use elsewhere within your application. The WSDL creation wizard only allows one XML schema file to be imported, however additional XML schema files can be imported once the WSDL file is created — we'll see how to do that in the next section.

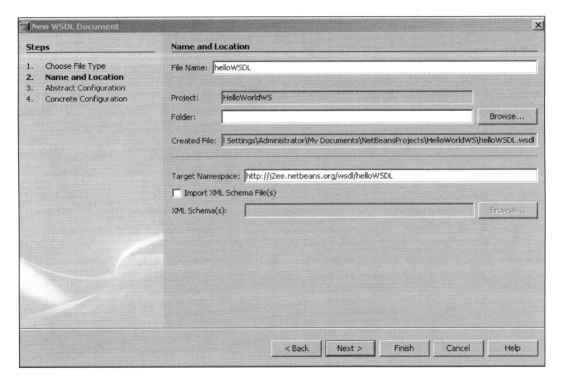

The following screenshot shows the NetBeans dialog that allows XML schema files to be imported into the WSDL document. This dialog allows files to be imported based upon either the **File Name** or the **Namespace** of the file. To use this feature therefore, the XML schema file must already be a part of the current NetBeans project—it is not possible to import XML schema files that are hosted on remote servers, without first adding them to the current NetBeans project.

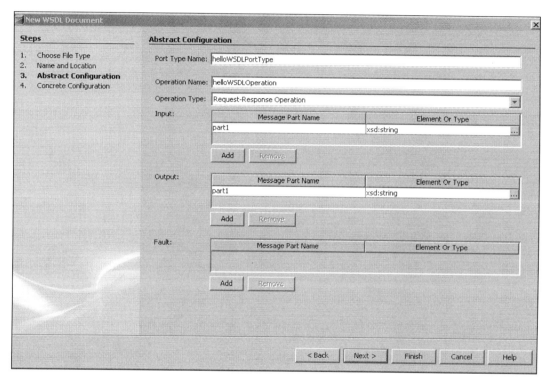

After specifying the file and namespace details for the new WSDL document, the wizard continues to the **Abstract Configuration** page for the WSDL file. You will remember that we discussed the abstract configuration previously—this contains details of the methods, parameters, and faults that are described in the WSDL document. This page in the dialog allows us to specify one operation only within the WSDL file—further operations can be specified once the file has been created.

After specifying the **Port Type Name** and the **Operation Name**, the **Operation Type** must be specified. This field allows only **One-Way Operation** and **Request-Response Operation** to be specified. If we wish to create either a **Notification** or **Solicit/Response** type message, then the ordering of the messages needs to be manually edited within the WSDL document.

Within this page in the wizard, we can specify the names of message part names by editing the appropriate **Message Part Name**. To select a type for the message part, press the "**...**" button under the **Element or Type** column. This displays the following dialog, within which all the built-in schema types (**xsd:string, xsd:boolean**) and the custom types that are available (in the current NetBeans project) are displayed.

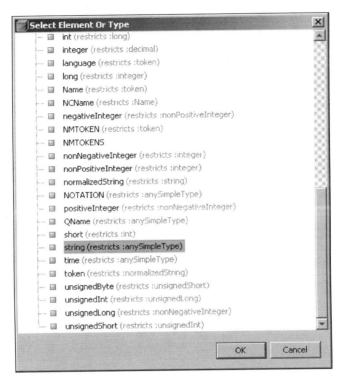

The final page of the new WSDL document wizard displays the **Concrete Configuration** page for the WSDL document. This page allows a **Binding Name** and **Binding Type** to be specified. The NetBeans enterprise pack installs support for the following binding types:

- File
- FTP
- HTTP
- JDBC
- JMS
- SMTP
- SOAP

Depending upon the binding type selected, different options are displayed allowing binding type specific details to be configured. For example, selecting the **SOAP** binding type allows us to specify whether we want to use **RPC Literal**, **Document Literal** or **RPC Encoding** for the **SOAP** message.

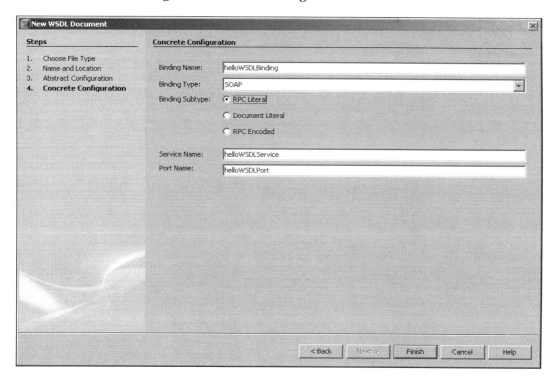

NetBeans Support for Editing WSDL Documents

The NetBeans editor provides raw XML, graphical and partner views of WSDL documents. These are chosen by selecting either **Source**, **WSDL** or **Partner** buttons at the top of the WSDL window.

The **Source** window displays the raw XML for the WSDL document. Similar to other code windows within the NetBeans editor, this code window is color coded and supports code folds for XML elements within the file.

Any changes made to the WSDL file in the **Source** view is also displayed in the **WSDL** and **Partner** view. If the XML is not well formed however, NetBeans cannot display the **WSDL** or **Partner** views and will display a message indicating this (*The WSDL is not well-formed.* message box). To help ensure that your WSDL remains valid whilst editing the XML, two buttons are provided on the editor toolbar to check the XML and to validate the XML.

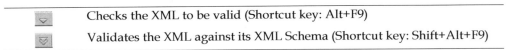

	Checks the XML to be valid (Shortcut key: Alt+F9)
	Validates the XML against its XML Schema (Shortcut key: Shift+Alt+F9)

The first of these buttons checks whether the WSDL document is a valid XML document. This performs basic XML checks such as ensuring that each start tag has a corresponding end tag or that elements do not have multiple attributes with the same name.

The second of these checks, validates the WSDL document against the WSDL XML schema, and reports errors such as invalid tags or attributes.

If you are familiar with WSDL, then the **Source** editor provides a powerful way of manually editing WSDL documents. If you prefer editing WSDL files graphically, then the **WSDL** view provides both a hierarchical tree view and a column based view of the WSDL file.

	Hierarchical Tree Based View
	Column Based View

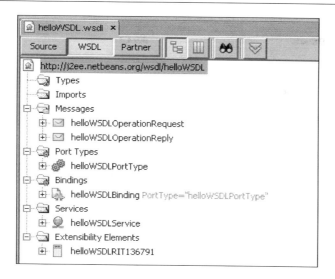

Clicking on any of the top level elements in the WSDL file (**Types, Import, Messages, Port Types, Bindings, Services, Extensibility Elements**) displays a popup-menu from which new entities can be added into the WSDL document. For example, to add a new port type into the WSDL document is simply a matter of right-clicking on **Port Types** in either the tree or column views and selecting the **Add Port Type...** menu option. This then displays a dialog similar to the **Abstract Configuration** page within the **New WSDL Document** wizard allowing all of the details of the new port type to be specified.

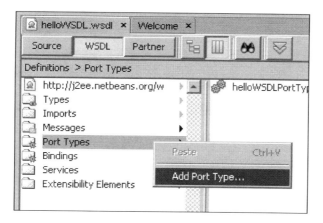

The final view in the WSDL editor is the **Partner** view. This view allows messages and the interactions between different partners to be graphically modeled. From within this view, we can add new operations by right-clicking on a port type within a partner view and selecting the **New operation...** menu option. All operations are displayed in the partner view window in a UML style showing the external partner, the operations that are available and the port type supporting the operations.

New Port Types and **Messages** can be added to the WSDL document by selecting the appropriate component from the palette and dragging it into the **Partner** view.

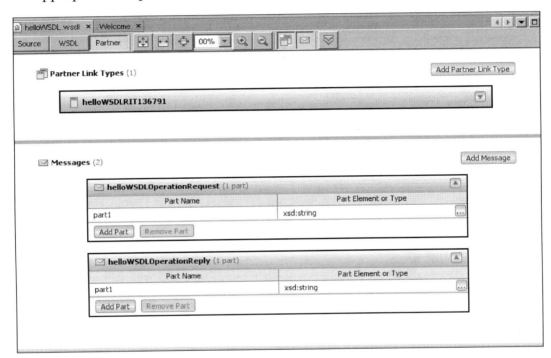

Within the Partner View, the following menu buttons provide view specific functionality:

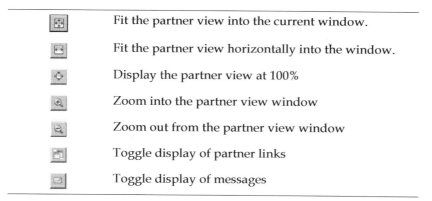

	Fit the partner view into the current window.
	Fit the partner view horizontally into the window.
	Display the partner view at 100%
	Zoom into the partner view window
	Zoom out from the partner view window
	Toggle display of partner links
	Toggle display of messages

Refactoring of WSDL Entities

To avoid any problems with accidentally deleting elements within a WSDL document, both the WSDL and Partner views provide a safe delete option. This is invoked by right-clicking on an element and choosing the **Delete** option, or by right-clicking on an element and choosing the **Refactor | Safe Delete** menu option.

Performing a safe delete causes a list of all references to the item being deleted to be shown within an IDE window. If there are no references to the specified element, then it can be deleted, however if the element being deleted is referenced elsewhere within the WSDL document, then the IDE will not allow it to be deleted.

In addition to a safe delete refactoring, the WSDL editor also provides a **Rename** refactoring. This is invoked by right-clicking on elements within the WSDL or Partner views and selecting the **Refactor | Rename** menu option.

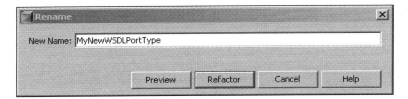

When invoking the rename refactoring, the IDE gives a view showing all the references where the element is used within a tree view as shown in the left pane of the figure below. The two panes on the right of the window show the WSDL before refactoring and what it will look like after the refactoring. When you are happy that the refactoring is correct, you can select the **Do Refactoring** button to confirm.

Building a Simple Contract First Web Service

Now that we have a good understanding of WSDL and the features that NetBeans provides for editing WSDL files, let's create a simple contract first web service. There is a lot of debate in the web services community at present as to whether contract first web services are the best way to develop interoperable web services or whether we should develop Java code first and let the WSDL be a by-product that is automatically generated for us. For our sample application, we are going to develop a simple **Hello World** web service. In this case, it's probably overkill to generate the WSDL manually (with Java EE 5 we can generate this same web service with a few annotations!), but nevertheless, the technique we are about to outline holds true for any level of complexity from simple Hello World web services to complex airline ticket booking web services. If you learn the techniques and concepts for a simple web service, it's straightforward to extend that knowledge for complex web services.

The first stage in creating our simple web service is to create a Java Web Project that can act as the service endpoint. From within NetBeans, select the **File | New Project** menu option and create a new Web Application by selecting the **Next** button.

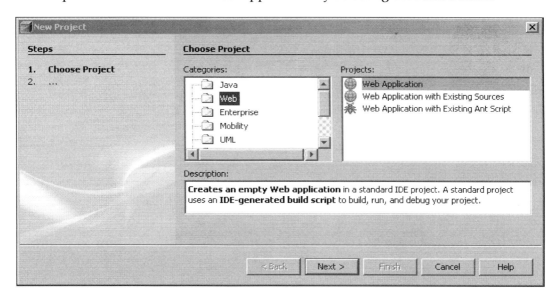

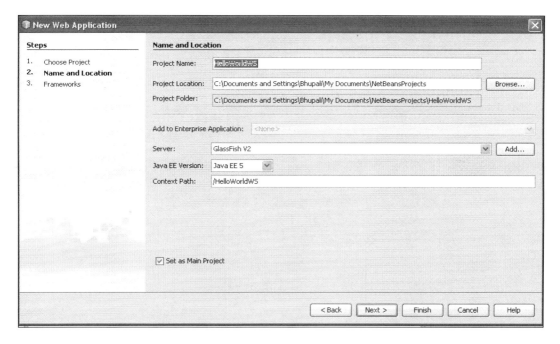

Enter the name of the project as **HelloWorldWS**. Ensure that either the Sun Java System Application Server or GlassFish **V2** (depending upon your version of NetBeans) is selected as the server and that Java EE version 5 is selected. At this point, press the **Finish** button to create the project.

Now that we have a web project to host our web service endpoint, we need to define the WSDL contract. For our simple HelloWorld web service, we are going to define one port Type (method) called sayHello. This will be a request/response web service with the request message being a single string and the response method also being a single string. We're not going to worry about what the Java code looks like yet for this service as we are defining the contract only first.

Within the **Projects** window, right-click on the **Web Pages** node for the HelloWorldWS project and select the **New | WSDL Document...** menu option. If that menu option is not available, select the **New | Other** menu option and on the resulting dialog, select the **XML** category and the **WSDL Document** file type.

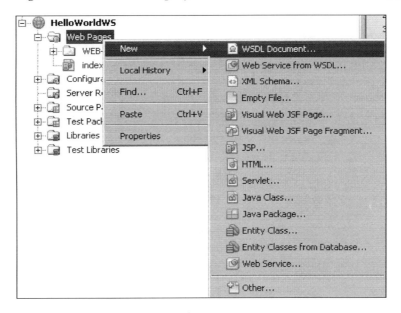

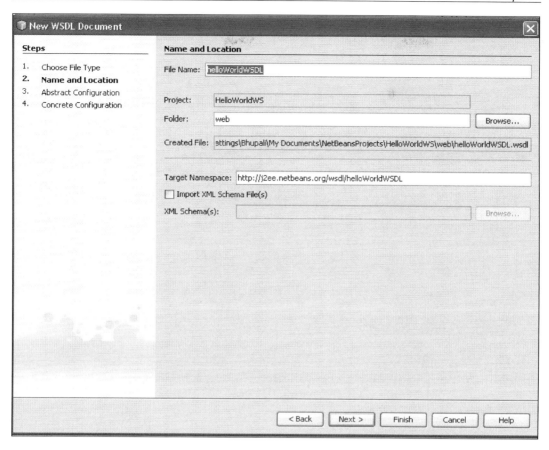

On the first page of the **New WSDL Document** wizard, enter the name of the WSDL file as **helloWorldWSDL**. Accept all the defaults for the other options. Select the **Next** button to enter the **Abstract Configuration**. On this page, change the operation name to **sayHello** and change the **Message Part Name** for the **Input** message to be **yourName** and the **Message Part Name** for the **Output** message to be **greeting**. You can see here that the message type is automatically set to request/response so we don't need to change that.

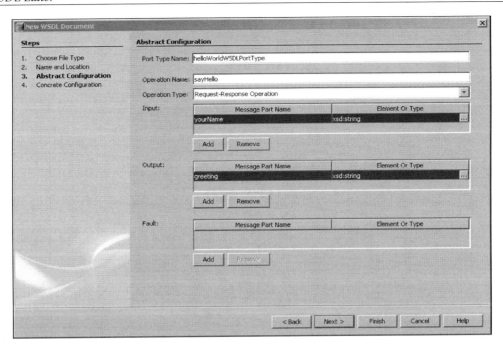

Select the **Next** button to move to the **Concrete Configuration** page of the wizard. On this page, we can see that the **Binding Type** defaults to **SOAP** so we do not need to change that for our sample web service. Select the **Finish** button to create the WSDL document.

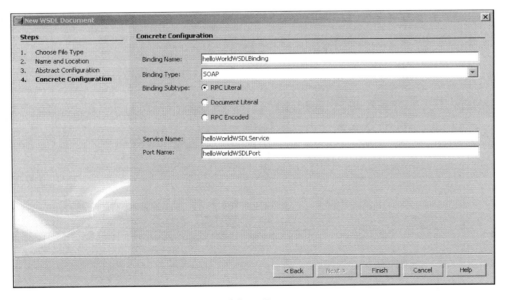

Now that we have created the contract for our web service (the WSDL document), we can use the NetBeans tools to create a web service from the WSDL. Right click on the **HelloWorldWS** project within the **Projects** window and select the **New | Web Service from WSDL...** option. If that menu option is not displayed, select the **New | Other** menu option, and then in the resulting dialog, select the **Web Services** category and **Web Service from WSDL** file type.

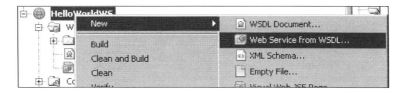

On the **New Web Service from WSDL** wizard dialog, enter the web service name as **sayHello**, the package as **soabook.ch6** and browse the file system to select the WSDL file we have just created. This WSDL file is created by default within the \Web folder of the project.

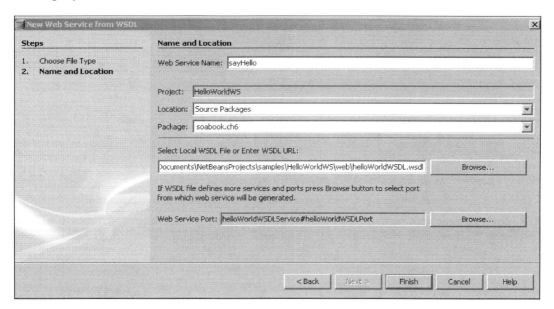

Wait a few seconds while NetBeans parses the WSDL file until the Web Services Port field is populated. At this point, select the **Finish** button to create the web service.

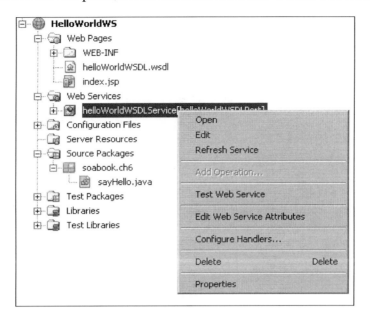

NetBeans will now analyze the WSDL document and create Java code to represent the web service we have just defined. We now need to fill in the stub code that NetBeans has generated with some business logic—our HelloWorld code. Open up the **Source Packages** node in the project explorer and open the file soabook.ch6. sayHello.java

Within that file, select the **Source** tab and locate the sayHello() method. Change the method to:

```
public java.lang.String sayHello(java.lang.String yourName) {
    return "Hello "+yourName;
}
```

Now that we have created our sample web project, lets take a look at the project structure and see what files have been created.

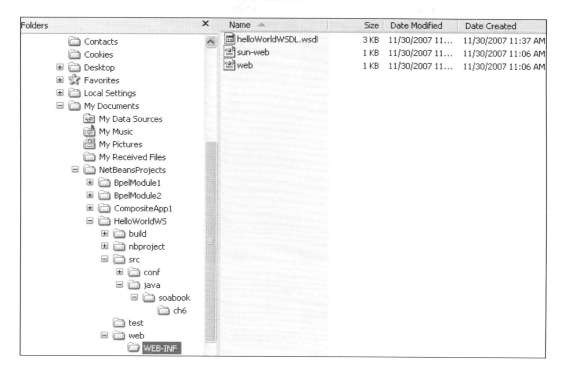

NetBeans has created a standard NetBeans Web Project directory structure with the standard **build, nbproject, src, test** and web directories. Each of these directories contains the standard files that NetBeans creates for a web project. For our sample web service project, we've not created any files in these directories. In the src/java directory however we've created a package hierarchy soabook.ch6 and included a Java file in this package called sayHello.java

Within the web/web-inf folder we can see the WSDL file we have created—helloWorldWSDL.wsdl

Now we have done all the coding necessary for our sample contract first web service—the next stage is to deploy the web service to the application server. Right-click on the project in the **Project** pane and select the **Undeploy and Deploy** option. NetBeans will now take a few seconds to deploy the web service to the application server.

To test the web service, we can use the inbuilt NetBeans web service testing tool. Expand the **Web Services** node within the project explorer, right-click on **helloWorldWSDLService** and choose the **Test Web Service** Option.

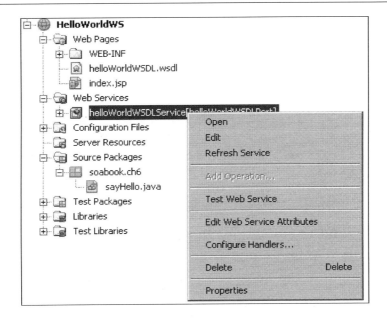

Invoking the **Test Web Service** tool causes the system default browser to be displayed running the web service test tool. This lists all the operations available to the service and allows them all to be interactively tested. Enter your name into the edit box and press the **sayHello** button to invoke the sayHello method.

If everything goes as expected, you should now see a page similar to that shown below showing the results of the web service operation and the input and output SOAP messages passed to and received from the web service.

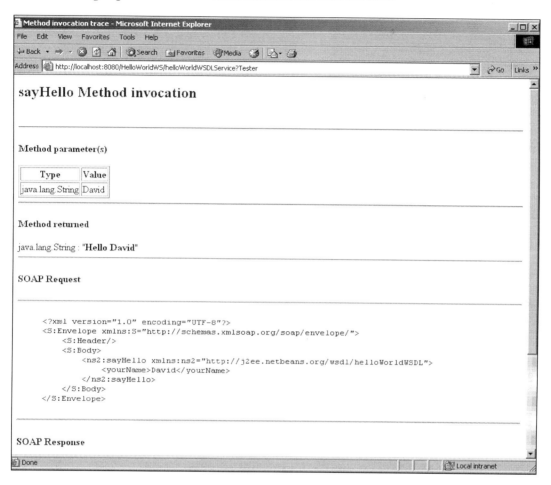

Summary

In this chapter, we have reviewed the basics of WSDL. We've learned that WSDL documents are fully-formed XML files that provide a way of describing services. They provide both an abstract and a concrete description of services with the concrete description providing details of the bindings to different protocols (such as SOAP or JMS).

We've looked at the editing support that the NetBeans IDE provides for WSDL documents and seen that NetBeans provides three different views of WSDL Documents. The **Source** view provides a raw XML editor which includes syntax highlighting and tools for checking and validating the WSDL document. The "**WSDL**" view provides 2 different graphical views (tree based and column based) of the WSDL. Each of these graphical views provides easy to use tools allowing additional components (types, imports, messages, port types, bindings and services) to be added to the WSDL document. The **Partner** view shows the messages within a WSDL document and the interactions between different partners and the messages. Messages and their interactions can be created by dragging and dropping from the palette into the Partner view.

Finally, we developed a simple contract first web service based upon a WSDL file. We showed how NetBeans provides tools to easily allow web services to be built from WSDL documents and then deployed and tested.

In the next chapter, we'll discuss the XML Schema editor within NetBeans and show how this allows us to develop complex XML schemas using graphical tools.

XML Schema Designer

7

In Chapter 6, we discussed WSDL and the WSDL editor, provided as part of the NetBeans Enterprise pack. As we saw in the previous chapter, a good knowledge of WSDL and WSDL tools is required to develop and integrate enterprise applications. We saw that WSDL documents are well formed XML documents that must follow certain guidelines to be valid. The standard mechanism for validating XML files is to use an XML schema document which describes the XML document and allows XML documents to be validated for correctness. In this chapter, we will discuss the XML Schema Designer provided as part of the NetBeans Enterprise Pack and show how this can be used to aid in the development and testing of XML Schema documents. We will start by providing an overview of XML schemas and discuss how they provide a standardized method for validating XML files. We will then continue our discussion by introducing the support that NetBeans provides for maintaining XML Schema documents and XML Schema components. Finally, we will delve into different design patterns that are supported by NetBeans for editing and refactoring XML Schema documents.

The following topics will be discussed in this chapter:

- What are XML Schemas?
- Why use XML Schemas?
- Different Views of XML Schema Documents in NetBeans
- Maintaining XML Schema Documents within NetBeans
- XML Components
- XML Schema Components
- XML Schema Design Patterns

By the end of this chapter, you should have a solid understanding of XML Schema and the support provided by the NetBeans Enterprise Pack for developers using XML Schema Language.

What are XML Schemas?

Over recent years, XML has become a dominant technology for data interchange between different systems. The advantages of XML over, say, flat files, is that the data is extensible (additional attributes or elements can be added to data structures) and self describing. Using this knowledge, we could describe an `airport`, for example, in a simple piece of XML as:

```
<?xml version="1.0"?>
<airport>
    <name>London Heathrow</name>
</airport>
```

From this XML, we can easily see that we are describing a single `airport` called `London Heathrow`. In the future, we may want to expand our simple description of Heathrow Airport by adding the Airport's IATA code and the number of major runways the airport has. In the previous paragraph we stated how XML is self describing and extensible—the key features that allow us to easily describe these new attributes in our XML sample.

```
<?xml version="1.0"?>
<airport>
    <name>London Heathrow</name>
    <iata>LHR</iata>
    <numberOfRunways>2</numberOfRunways>
</airport>
```

From the above XML samples, we can see how easy it is to extend XML and add new elements, attributes or entire structures into an XML file. Describing data structures in XML however, is only half of the problem. How do we know that the XML we have received is the XML we are expecting? What if we described our airport XML requirements as:

We need an airport element with fields for

- name
- IATA code
- number of runways

Our XML sample above meets these requirements, but so does the sample below. Which one is correct?

```
<?xml version="1.0"?>
<airport name="London Heathrow" id="LHR" numberOfRunways="two"/>
```

Given the lack of any description of our XML requirements, both XML files are completely valid, however there is no way that an application would be able to parse both of these XML files and obtain the same results. XML Schema answers our problems here by allowing us to describe how the XML should be defined. Using XML Schema, there are no ambiguities as to whether:

- *name* is an attribute
- the IATA code is an element called *iata* or an attribute called "id"
- the *numberOfRunways* is an element or attribute
- *numberOfRunways* takes an integer or a string.

XML Schema allows us to define the elements and attributes that are present within an XML file and allows the XML file to be machine validated for correctness. This second part is important, because XML schema allows us to machine validate XML files. This means that applications can check that data is valid before they attempt to process the data.

XML Schema is a W3C Recommendation which was first recommended in May 2001 (http://www.w3.org/TR/2001/REC-xmlschema-0-20010502/). The W3C describes XML Schema (http://www.w3.org/TR/NOTE-xml-schema-req) as follows:

> The XML schema language can be used to define, describe, and catalogue XML vocabularies for classes of XML documents. Any application of XML can use the Schema formalism to express syntactic, structural, and value constraints applicable to its document instances.

Given this knowledge of XML schema, we could define a simple XML schema (airport.xsd) and XML file (airport.xml) for our airport data structure as follows:

```
//airport.xsd
<?xml version="1.0" encoding="UTF-8"?>
<xsd:schema xmlns:xsd="http://www.w3.org/2001/XMLSchema"
    targetNamespace="http://xml.netbeans.org/schema/airport"
    xmlns:tns="http://xml.netbeans.org/schema/airport"
    elementFormDefault="qualified">
<xsd:element name="airport">
  <xsd:complexType>
    <xsd:sequence>
      <xsd:element name="name" type="xsd:string"/>
      <xsd:element name="iata" type="xsd:string"/>
      <xsd:element name="numberOfRunways" type="xsd:integer"/>
    </xsd:sequence>
  </xsd:complexType>
</xsd:element>
</xsd:schema>
```

```
//airport.xml
<?xml version="1.0" encoding="UTF-8"?>
<airport
  xmlns="http://xml.netbeans.org/schema/airport"
  xmlns:xsi="http://www.w3.org/2001/XMLSchema-instance"
  xsi:schemaLocation=
                "http://xml.netbeans.org/schema/airport/airport.xsd">
  <name>London Heathrow</name>
    <iata>LHR</iata>
    <numberOfRunways>2</numberOfRunways>
</airport>
```

Looking at the XML Schema definition file (`airport.xsd`), we can see several important features that allow the XML structure to be defined.

1	The .xsd file is a well formed XML document
2	The root element of any XML files conforming to this schema must be called "airport". There is only one root element allowed.
3	The root element "airport" is a complex type. In XML Schema Definitions, types are defined as either *simple* or *complex*. Simple types are types such as integers, strings, dates. Complex types are data structures built up from simple types and other complex types.
4	The complex type defines that the elements within it must appear in the order in which they are specified within the XSD file. If the elements in the XSD file are not specified in the same order, then the XML file will not validate correctly.
5	The first element in the "airport" type is the "name" which is a string.
6	The second element in the "airport" type is the "iata" code which is a string.
7	The third and final element in the "airport" type is the numberOfRunways which is an integer.

This is just a brief overview of the features of XML Schema and the benefits which it provides to applications that parse and use XML data. A complete reference of XML Schema is outside the scope of this book (there's probably enough for a book in itself), however having a solid knowledge of XML schema is very important and we recommend spending some time familiarizing yourself with XML Schema if necessary.

Now that we've seen what XML Schema is and why it's useful, let's have a look at the support that the NetBeans Enterprise pack provides developers.

NetBeans Support for XML Schema Documents

NetBeans provides both graphical and textual editing of XML Schema Definition files (*.xsd). These files can be opened using the standard **File | Open** mechanism, or can be created by selecting **File | New File** and then choosing to create an XML Schema Document from the XML category in the New File dialog shown as follows. Depending upon the type of installation of NetBeans you have, this menu option may not be available. If not, it can be easily installed from the Update Center. If XML support is not available, select the **Tools | Plugins** menu option. On the resulting dialog, select the **Available Plugins** tab and choose the **XML and Schema** plugin under the **Web & Java** EE category.

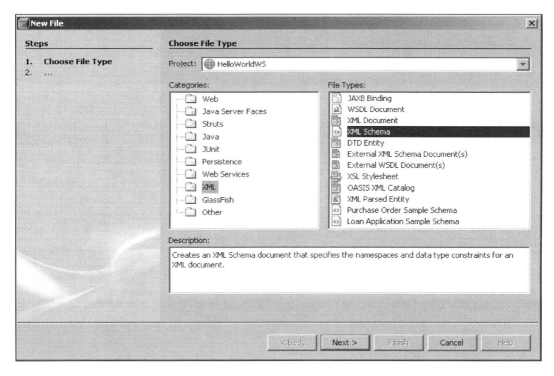

Selecting the **Next** button on this dialog invokes the **New XML Schema** wizard which allows new schema files to be defined. This wizard can also be invoked by right-clicking within the Projects explorer. In this case, a context sensitive version of this dialog shown above will be displayed showing only the categories and file types that are appropriate for the selected project type.

The wizard displays one page allowing the filename and directory to be specified for the new XSD file as shown below. If you are creating a web project and wish others to be able to access your XSD file so that they can perform their own XML validation, you would put the XSD file within the web sources folder of your project.

 Note, when creating new XSD files, it is not necessary to specify the `.xsd` file extension as NetBeans will automatically add this to the end of your file name. Specifying this will cause duplication of file extensions.

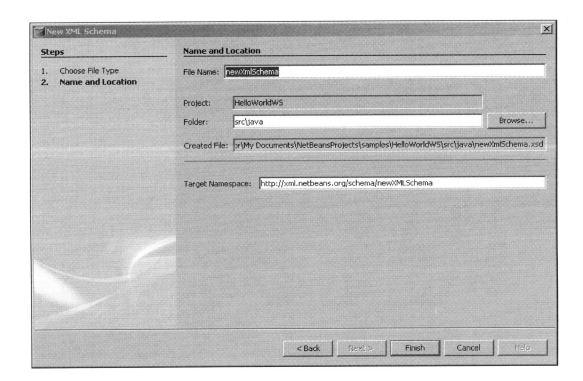

This page also allows the target namespace for the new XSD file to be specified. This defaults to `http://xml.netbeans.org/schema/fileName`, so it is recommended to change this to something more sensible for your application.

When you have created or opened an XSD file within NetBeans, you will see that NetBeans provides 3 different views of the XSD file.

- Source View
- Schema View
- Design View

The **Source** view provides a raw XML syntax highlighting editor which provides code completion tips, allowing complete control over the contents of the XSD file. The **Schema** view provides column-based editing facilities for all the different entities within the XSD file. Finally, the **Design** view provides a powerful GUI with drag and drop facilities for creating and editing XSD files. When changes are made to an XSD file in any of these views, they are automatically represented within the other views, so for example, creating a new complex type within the Design View will automatically update the XML displayed within the Source View.

Let's take each of these views in turn and discuss the features of each.

Source View

The **Source** view provides the standard XML editing facilities giving a syntax highlighted editor.

Schema View

The **Schema** view provides a column-based view of the XSD file currently being edited. The principle behind the column-based view is to allow individual categories to be **drilled down** into sub categories by clicking on an entry within a column. Clicking on an entry in a column causes the column to the right to display either all the objects of that type, or in that type. For example, selecting **Elements** in the first column will cause the second column to be populated with all the top level elements within the XSD file. Clicking on any of these elements would then cause the column to the right of that to display all the entries within that element—complex types in the case of our airport XSD file created earlier.

Within the first column all the different types of entities that can be created within the XSD file are displayed:

- Attributes
- Attribute Groups
- Complex Types
- Elements
- Groups
- Referenced Schema
- Simple Types

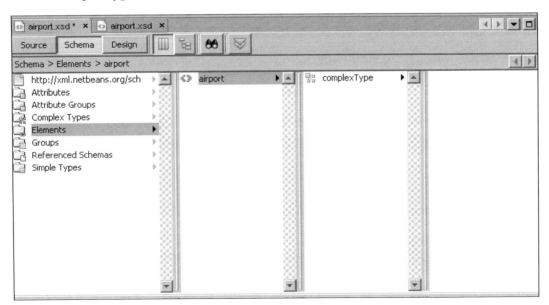

To create a new entity within the XSD file, right-click on the parent object of the new entity and select the **Add** menu option. This will cause a context sensitive menu option to be displayed allowing new entities to be added to the XSD file depending upon where is clicked. For example, right-clicking on **Elements** provides a menu option that allows only additional elements to be created whereas right-clicking on **airport** in the above example would cause a menu option to be displayed allowing attributes, elements, sequences to be added to the entity.

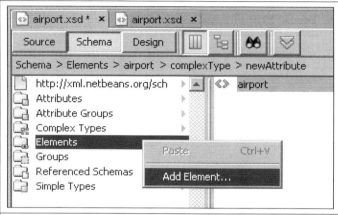	Right-clicking on a top level entity allows additional entities of the same type to be added.
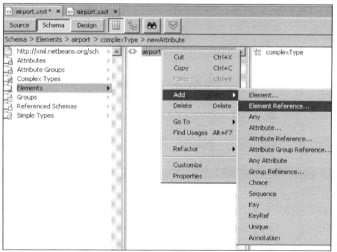	Right-clicking on other entities allows all relevant child entities to be added, not just those of the same type.

The properties of the different entities within the XSD file can be viewed and edited within the **Properties** window as shown below. In this example, we can see the properties of the **iata** element are visible. The various XSD attributes such as **Nillable, Max occurs, Min occurs,** can all be edited from within this properties window. This properties window is context sensitive and only displays the properties applicable to the entity that has been selected within the **Schema** view.

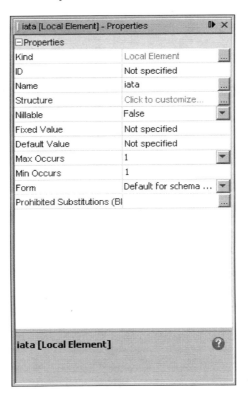

Design View

The XML Schema **Design** view provides a graphical designer, allowing complex XSD files to be easily built. We can see an example of the **Design** view below. Developers use Drag and Drop to place components from the palette into the XSD file. The **Design** view shows the **Elements** and **Complex Types** that are used to build up the XSD file. The **Elements** and **Complex Types** can be expanded and collapsed allowing all the sub components to be viewed in a tree like fashion.

In a similar fashion to the **Schema** view, selecting an entity in the **Design** view causes the entry to be selected and its properties to be displayed within the **Properties** window.

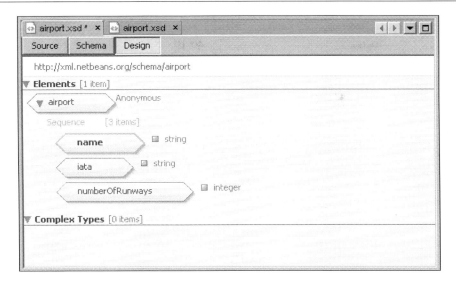

The **Palette** window is the source of all dragging and dropping to create entities within the XSD file. The palette window, as shown below, allows both **XML Components** and **XML Schema Components** to be created within an XSD file.

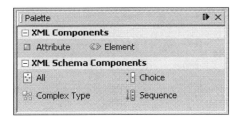

The following tables show the entities that can be created within an XSD file by dragging and dropping either **XML Components** or **XML Schema Components** into the **Design** view. An example of the type of XML that is created for each component type is also provided.

XML Components	Example
Attribute	<xsd:attribute name="isInternational" type="xsd:string"/><xsd:attribute name="isInternational" type="xsd:string"/>
Element	<xsd:element name="airport">
All	<xsd:all> <xsd:element name="name" type="xsd:string"/> <xsd:element name="iata" nillable="false"/> <xsd:element name="numberOfRunways" type="xsd:integer"/> </xsd:all>

XML Schema Components	Example

All	`<xsd:all>`
	  `<xsd:element name="name" type="xsd:string"/>`
	  `<xsd:element name="iata" nillable="false"/>`
	  `<xsd:element name="numberOfRunways" type="xsd:integer"/>`
	`</xsd:all>`

Choice	`<xsd:choice>`
	  `<xsd:element name="iata" nillable="false"/>`
	  `<xsd:element name="fullAirportName" type="xsd:string"/>`
	`</xsd:choice>`

Complex Type	`<xsd:complexType name="airportDesctiption">`
	  `<xsd:sequence>`
	    `<xsd:element name="iata" type="xsd:string"/>`
	    `<xsd:element name="fullAirportName" type="xsd:string"/>`
	    `<xsd:element name="numberOfRunways" type="xsd:integer"/>`
	  `</xsd:sequence>`
	`</xsd:complexType>`

Sequence	`<xsd:sequence>`
	  `<xsd:element name="name" type="xsd:string"/>`
	  `<xsd:element name="iata" nillable="false"/>`
	  `<xsd:element name="numberOfRunways" type="xsd:integer"/>`
	`</xsd:sequence>`

To create a new element within a XSD file you select the **Element** entry within the palette and drag it into the **Design** view. You then drop it into the location where you want the element to be placed.

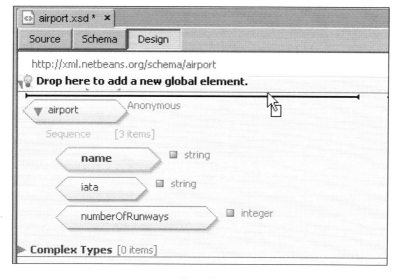

Upon dragging and dropping a new element into the **Design** View, the element is placed at the appropriate point within the designer with the default name of **newElement**. This can be changed in-place within the GUI editor or within the **Properties** window. Double clicking on any element within the GUI window will also cause the name to be editable in this fashion.

Creating attributes or XML Schema Components uses the same technique of selecting the entity in the palette and dragging it into the **Design** view. If you inadvertently attempt to drop a component into an invalid location, then NetBeans will display a warning message and will not allow the item to be dropped.

Uses of Elements

Within the **Design** view is a useful tool to allow the uses of elements and complex types within an XSD to be queried and displayed. The **Find Usages** tool is invoked by right-clicking on a complex type or element within the design view and selecting the **Find Usages** option. Invoking this option runs the tool and opens a new **Output** panel showing the usages of the selected entity in the currently open projects within NetBeans.

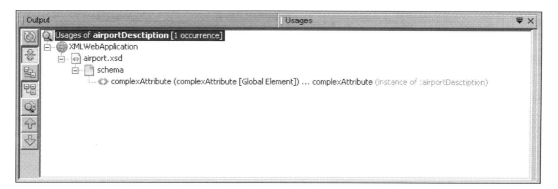

The find usages window provides several tools to help navigate around the find usages results and to change the views available.

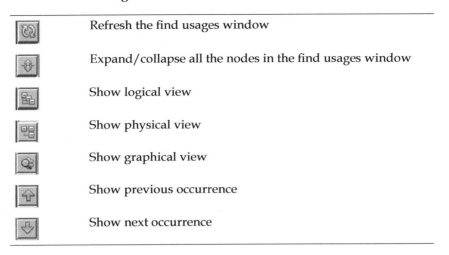

	Refresh the find usages window
	Expand/collapse all the nodes in the find usages window
	Show logical view
	Show physical view
	Show graphical view
	Show previous occurrence
	Show next occurrence

If you prefer graphical representations of data rather than the tree view type representation shown above, then the Graphical view will be useful. This view displays a usages cloud providing a pictorial representation of the entity usages.

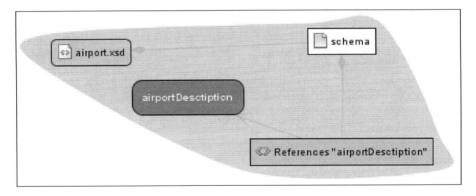

XML Schema Design Patterns

In common with other software development, XSD files can be developed to conform to certain design patterns. The NetBeans Enterprise pack provides a **refactoring** option to allow XSD files to be converted between these different design patterns. The Enterprise Pack supports 4 different design patterns: Russian Doll, Salami Slice, Garden of Eden and Venetian Blind.

Pattern	Description	Single/Multiple Global Elements	Complex Types Created?
Russian Doll	The Russian Doll pattern ensures that there is only one global element within the XSD file and all other elements are local to this global element. Complex types are created within elements and are not reused elsewhere within the XSD file.	Single	No
Salami Slice	All elements in the Salami Slice pattern are global meaning that there are no local definitions of elements and elements cannot be nested. Complex types are created within elements and are not reused elsewhere within the XSD file.	Multiple	No
Venetian Blind	The Venetian Blind pattern ensures that there is only one global element within the XSD file and all other elements are local to this global element. Complex types are created outside of elements and can be reused between elements.	Single	Yes
Garden of Eden	In the Garden of Eden pattern, all elements and complex types are created within the global namespace and and can be reused by any elements within the XSD file.	Multiple	Yes

To apply a Design pattern to a selected XSD file, right-click on the XSD file in the project explorer and select the **Apply Design Pattern...** menu option. Selecting this option causes the Apply Design Pattern dialog shown as follows:

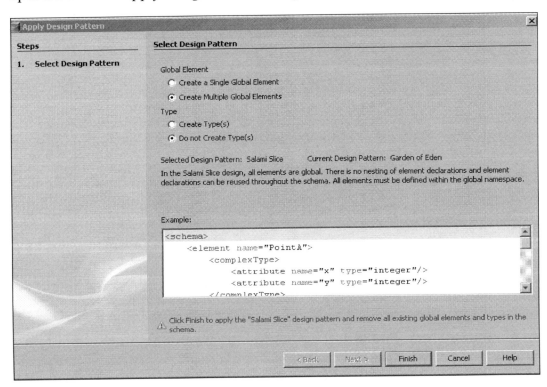

Within this dialog, you can select whether you wish to use a **Single Global Element** or **Multiple Global Elements** within your XSD file. You can also choose whether to create complex types and reuse them within the XSD file or to use local complex types for each element. For each of these options, NetBeans displays a fragment of XML code providing a preview of what the resulting XSD file will look like.

Summary

In this chapter we have reviewed the basics of XML Schema Language—a powerful way to describe XML files thus allowing machine-based validation, and therefore allowing software to validate ...XML inputs before beginning to process XML data.

We've looked at the editing support the NetBeans IDE provides for XSD documents and seen that, similar to the WSDL editor, NetBeans provides three different views to help editing. The **Source** view provides a raw XML editor which includes syntax highlighting and tools for checking and validating the XSD document. The **Schema** view provides a column-based view providing drill down support for querying parent and child relationships within XSD files. Finally, the **Design** view provides a graphical user interface with drag and drop support for adding XML and XML schema components into an XSD file. Any changes made in any of these views are automatically updated in the other views.

We also looked at XSD design patterns and how these can be applied to existing XSD files within the NetBeans editor. We discussed the Russian Doll, Salami Slice, Venetian Blind and Garden of Eden design patterns and the differences between them in terms of global elements and global complex types.

In the next chapter, we'll discuss Intelligent Event Handling and introduce the real-time business event collection and processing capabilities of NetBeans Enterprise Applications.

8

Intelligent Event Processor

We have seen enterprises struggling to identify a business process monitoring solution for their corporate solutions. Chances are very strong that your enterprise might go down, with the steady and rapid inflow of business data, when you do not have a piece of software at the doorway collecting business events and aggregate them to raise necessary notifications and triggers.

Most of the enterprise grade applications need to work with a continuous stream of data by actively monitoring the stream and filtering them based on defined business rules. They seldom work with a finite data store or database. This is because corrective actions can be performed more elegantly at the stream level than at the data store level. Hence, in the business process, the current state of data is of very less importance compared to the asynchronous and continuous data that flow through.

A business event processing tool allows business users and system integrators to put together the middleware solution, thus triggering more focused actions and enhancing automation and efficiency. There are quite a few tools in the market that do business event processing effectively. In this chapter, we will be discussing the Intelligent Event Processor (IEP) Service Engine. The IEP supports editing, deploying, and executing event processors that can work on multiple continuous data streams.

In this chapter, we will discuss the following topics:

- Need for Event Processing tools
- Introduction to IEP Service Engine
- Continuous Query Language (CQL)
- The IEP editor and palette
- Getting started
- Some examples
- Operators — input and output types

Need for Event Processing Tools

Every year, several enterprises loose business due to the fact that they fail to act on opportunities evident through monitoring and responding to critical business events. In the current time, sensitive economy is the responsibility of the enterprises. They must keenly monitor business data and events that go across their systems.

I have tested various business event processing tools available in the market today. Very few of them break away from the traditional business data processing algorithms, and provide intelligent and real time event processing which supports notifications and triggers. These tools have the capability to continuously monitor streams that propagate business data and also provide useful analytical inferences.

In our need to find an event processor, let us define the most common functionalities expected out of an event processor:

1. Continuous monitoring
2. Filtering capabilities
3. Notifications and triggers
4. Web Services support
5. Partition support
6. Seamless integration

Group of enterprise systems behaves more like a 'nervous system' that absorbe large amounts of sensory input from sources interconnected with the systems such as the stock market, news or point-of-sale transactions. In our airlines 'nervous system' there exist a business amalgamation of several partner airlines that interact with each other through data. If data is the focal point of any transaction, imagine the data flow that will happen every minute in this airlines transaction. Is performing the transaction in a fail-safe manner should be the only goal? No. This enterprise nervous system should be monitored—continuously.

What is the basic difference between traditional human monitored systems and an intelligent monitoring system? In the ordinary systems, data can be queried upon or 'pulled', but in a monitored system, data is 'pushed' to various endpoints based on some business rules. These rules govern the monitoring system as well as the enterprise nervous system.

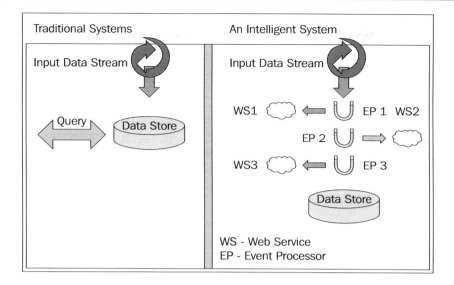

The above figure shows the traditional enterprise systems and a system designed with multiple interceptors on the input stream. Each interceptor or 'event processor' is capable of querying the stream and 'pull' data, and exposes them to other streams or web services. We can move away from a more 'reactive' system to a 'proactive' system by continuously monitoring long running business transactions.

An IEP mechanism looks for specific events across various event streams to process them into meaningful inferences. Take the case of AirAlliance, where if you need a system to filter the last three reservations of all partner alliances identified through their itinerary ID, it is possible for a filter to query this data from the stream. Note that, this will happen when the transaction is in the process and not when the transaction has finished and logged to the data store. This is important because, if duplicate reservations are processed by the system from different airlines, the error gets detected at an earlier stage.

Now, this brings us to a very interesting side effect of this whole system. IEP can be used as an efficient pre-processing mechanism for a business transaction.

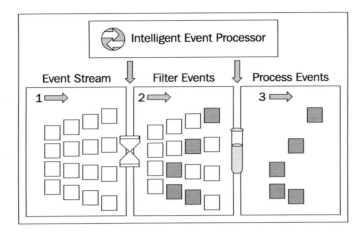

You often see today, enterprises interconnected with a large amount of events, generated through various 'emitters' like business processes. Analyzing symptoms is really critical to identify and correct errors in the system.

An ideal event processor should have all of the following facets:

- Aggregate: Ability to aggregate and filter events, based on pre-defined rules.
- Correlate: Associating events for long running business events.
- Notify: Should be 'trigger-happy' in raising alarms, in case of exceptions.
- Communicate: Ability to communicate with other processors and web services.

IEP Service Engine

The IEP Service Engine is part of the Java Business Integration (JBI) container. The JBI runtime manages the lifecycle of the Service Engine. IEP Service Engine is the backbone of the event processing system that collects, processes, and routes business events in a real time fashion. The IEP engine internally uses a database engine like Java DB for business event processing.

One of the caveats though is that the IEP Service Engine can enumerate events reaching that particular JBI container to which it is bound. In Chapter 3 on *Service Engines*, we discussed various Service Engines supported by the JBI container. IEP Service Engine, which is one among them, can work with all of the other Service Engines including BPEL Service Engine, XSLT Service Engine, and other Binding Components discussed in Chapter 4 on *Binding Components*.

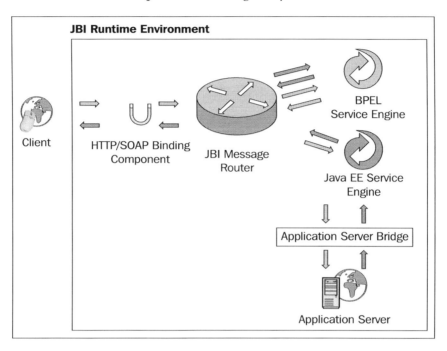

The figure above depicts the **JBI Runtime** and **IEP Service Engine** interaction. This is in no way different to how the lifecycle of the Service Engines are controlled by the JBI container (at least for the developer). The IEP runtime component obtains data via the **HTTP/SOAP Binding Component** and provides data through the File Binding Component (For more information on Binding Components, refer to Chapter 4). The IEP runtime component provides the physical connectivity between the **JBI Message Router** in the **JBI Runtime** and external SMTP clients and servers.

IEP processes inbound business events through 'windows' or data streams in units of time. Within the **JBI Runtime**, Binding Components and other Service Engines can act as containers too. Service Units (SU) can be deployed to installed Binding Components and Service Engines. The Service Unit can describe what services are provided and consumed by the component.

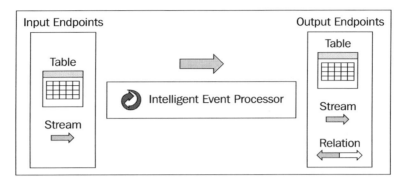

Event processors can receive events from any number of **Input Endpoints**. There are basically two kinds of **Input Endpoints**:

1. **Stream Input Endpoint**: A web service, which other applications can invoke to send events. Streams are similar to event histories.

2. **Table Input Endpoint**: Denotes a SQL database table. The event processor can read from the table, while the other applications can write to the table.

The event processors deliver events to other applications through its **Output Endpoints**. It can have multiple **Output Endpoints**. There are three kinds of **Output Endpoints**:

1. **Stream Output Endpoint**: A web service, which other applications can invoke to receive events created by the event processor.

2. **Relation Output Endpoint**: A web service, which other applications can invoke to receive updates to a relation created by the event processor.

3. **Table Output Endpoint**: Allows an event processor to provide static data output to other applications through SQL database table.

Continuous Query Language (CQL)

The Continuous Query Language is used as the language syntax of the IEP flow, and is built on SQL. CQL uses SQL for event matching, abstraction, and transformation. CQL processes events and uses a database engine to do so, minimizing possible network usage.

The IEP Service Engine supports the standard operators defined by the CQL. Apart from that, it also supports some operators like Tuple Serial Correlation and Attribute-based windows from Sun Microsystems. The IEP Service Engine is the only Service Engine that supports the JBI specification.

In NetBeans, you can design IEPs visually using the IEP editor. The flows that you define in the diagram are translated to CQLs by the Service Engine.

The IEP Editor and Palette

NetBeans's IEP Editor is the GUI for creating event processors that can be deployed to the JBI IEP Service Engine. An IEP editor helps you to create event processor schematic diagrams through a friendly interface. Typically, you would use this editor to compose event processors by drag-and-drop operators from the palette provided. The IEP editor is primarily for the following tasks:

- Create and save event processors.
- Validate event processors for Input/Output types
- Generate a WSDL interface for the event processor

The following figure shows the NetBeans IEP Editor along with the operator palette window:

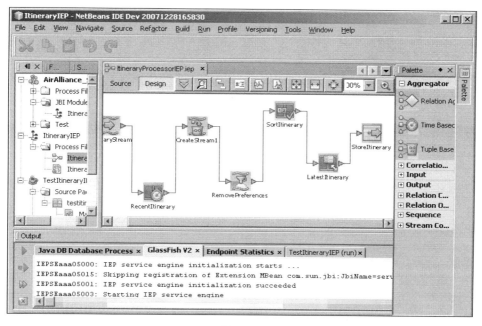

The palette window has several categories of operators that can be dragged-and-dropped into the IEP Editor window (workspace) to create rules.

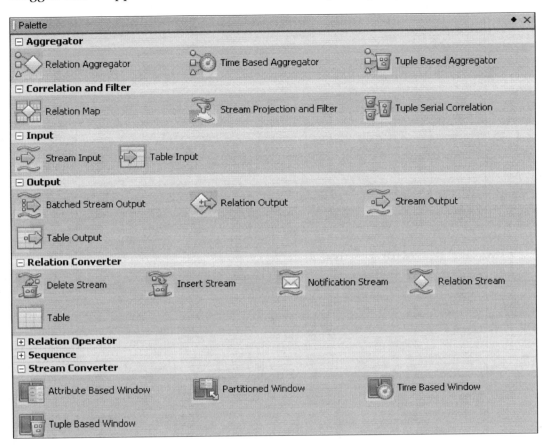

IEP project system is actually a NetBeans plug-in that comes as part of the OpenESB bundle. You can create a new **SOA | Intelligent Event Processor Module** to start with as shown in the following figure:

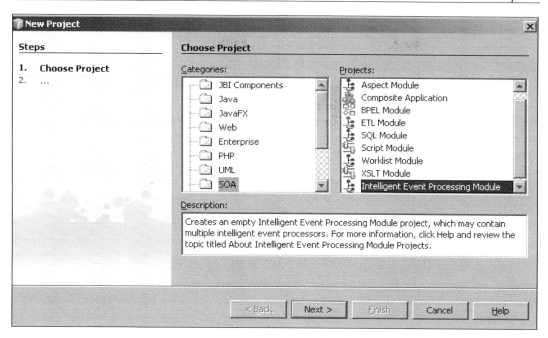

The IEP Module Projects works with **SOA | Composite-Application** project system to generate Service Engine deployment assembly for event processor deployment.

The following table briefly defines each operator and its functionality. You can create an IEP process with these operators provided that their input and output types match. For input and output types of these operators refer to the later section in this chapter.

Operator	Usage
Relation Aggregator	Enables grouping of events by a specified relation for statistical purposes.
Time-Based Aggregator	Enables grouping of events by time slots for statistical purposes.
Tuple-Based	Enables grouping of events by sequential index for statistical purposes.
Relation Map	Enables joining of multiple relations.
Stream Project and Filter	Enables filtering of events or modifying selected event attributes.
Tuple Serial Correlation	Enabling correlation of sequential events.
Steam Input	Enables event collection.
Table Input	Enables provisioning of extra event information using a relational table.
Relation Output	Enables you to define notification of changes to a relation.

Operator	Usage
Steam Output	Enables you to define event notification.
Table Output	Enables definition of relational tables for extra output data.
Delete Stream	Enables definition of monitoring event deletion from a relation.
Insert Stream	Enables monitoring of event insertion to a relation.
Relation Stream	Enables monitoring of event deletion from or insertion to a relation.
Table	Enables a snapshot of the current state of a relation.
Distinct	Enables removal of duplicate events in a relation.
Intersect	Enables definition of relation intersection.
Minus	Enables definition of difference between two relations.
Union	Enables definition of the union of unique events from multiple relations

After creating an IEP module, the first operator you need to configure is the input operator. The IEP process receives stream input containing the itinerary data of guests from different airlines. A partition-based stream converter is used to monitor the last couple of reservations from all the partner airlines.

Drag-and-drop the **Stream Input** operator into the workspace. In the **Stream Input Property Editor,** we define **Attributes, Data Type**s, and the **Size**, which will be updated in the IEP table. Enter **ItineraryStream** as the **Name** of the operator.

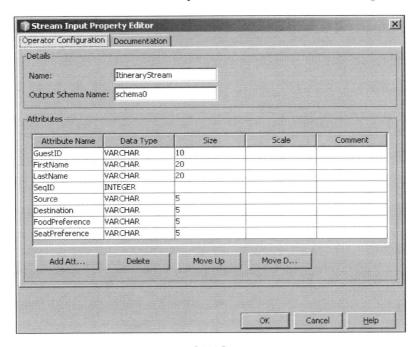

Once the input is defined, you can create a **TupleBasedWindow** stream converter that takes a pre-defined size of entries and pipe it to the stream output. Drag-and-drop the **TupleBasedWindow** stream converter into the palette. Now, drag-and-drop the arrow head from the **ItineraryStream** icon to the arrow head of the **TubleBasedWindow0** icon.

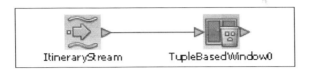

Double-click on the **TupleBasedWindow** operator. The **Attributes** are automatically populated. In the **Size** filed enter **3**. This is because, at any time, we want to process only three itineraries. This is shown in the following figure:

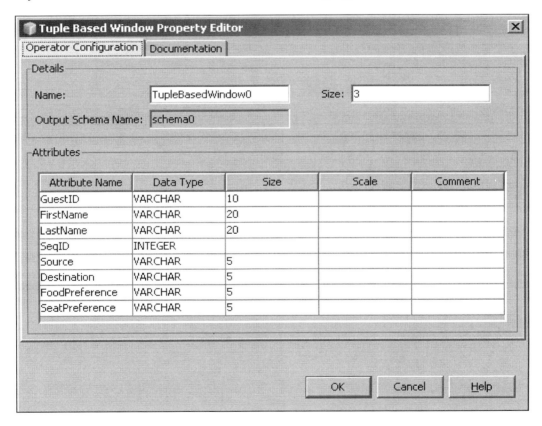

Now, drag-and-drop the **TableOutput** operator into the workspace and connect the arrow head of the **TupleBasedWindow0** icon to the arrow head of the **TableOutput0** icon as shown in the following figure:

Now, double-click on the **TableOutput** operator to view the properties dialog. Click the **IsGlobal** check box and enter the **Global ID** as **CurrentItinerary**. This will be the name of the table created by the IEP Service Engine to store the IEP processing result.

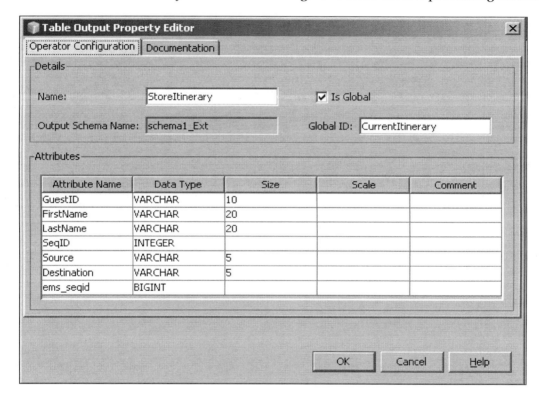

Build the IEP module and deploy the module to a composite application. For more information and some examples on an IEP based module, refer to Chapter 10 – *Building a Sample Application*.

Validating Event Processors

IEP Editor can validate `.iep` files for syntax and other errors including input/output type mismatch for the operators. You can invoke the validation operation by clicking on the **Validate** button at the top of the editor. When the validation operation is invoked, the IEP validates against some predefined rules and the errors and warnings are shown in the output windows, displayed as follows:

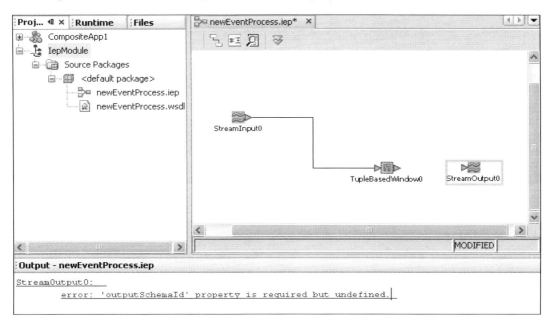

In the above mentioned IEP, the output stream is defined but not piped to the **TupleBasedWindow**.

When you save an IEP process, the IEP Editor generates a WSDL that serves as an endpoint for the IEP process. You are not supposed to change any section of the generated WSDL document.

Operators Input and Output Types

Operators can take streams or relations as input, and output streams, relations, or entire tables. Operators can be categorized by what their input and outputs consist of according to the following table:

Operator	Input Type – Output Type
Relation Aggregator	Relation - Relation
Time-Based Aggregator	Stream - Stream
Tuple-Based Aggregator	Stream - Stream
Relation Map	Relation - Relation
Stream Projection and Filter	Stream - Stream
Tuple Serial Correlation	Stream - Stream
Stream Input	None - Stream
Table Input	None - Table
Relation Output	Relation - None
Stream Output	Stream - None
Table Output	Relation - None
Insert Stream	Relation - Stream
Delete Stream	Relation - Stream
Relation Stream	Relation - Stream
Table	Relation - Table
Distinct	Relation - Relation
Intersect	Relation - Relation
Minus	Relation - Relation
Union	Relation - Relation
Union All	Relation - Relation
Attribute-Based Window	Stream - Relation
Partitioned Window	Stream - Relation
Time-Based Window	Stream - Relation
Tuple-Based Window	Stream - Relation

From the above table, you can infer some examples of valid IEP rules:

1. Stream Input (Input) -> Tuple-Based Aggregator (Stream – Stream) - > Stream Output.

2. Stream Input (Input) -> Attribute-Based Window (Stream – Relation) -> Relation Stream -> Stream Output.

3. Stream Input (Input) -> Partitioned Window (Stream – Relation) -> Union (Relation – Relation) -> Table (Relation – Table) -> Table Output

In Chapter 10 on *Building a Sample Application,* we will be creating some IEPs to monitor the airlines reservation stream.

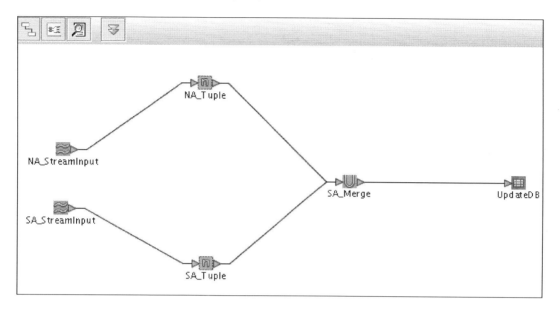

The above figure shows how you can connect operators based on the input types shown in the table.

Testing IEP Projects

When the IEP is invoked, the stream data is stored in the CURRENTITINERARY table.

The IEP example shown in this chapter needs a stream input simulator to test the IEP process. The source code bundle provided on the site has a TestItineraryIEP NetBeans project that reads an external data file and sends a data stream to the IEP module using the SheperdDriver (com.sun.jbi.engine.iep.core.runtime.client.pojo. SheperdDriver). The project is available under **src\PartG\ TestItineraryIEP**.

You can also test the project by creating a test case in the composite application.

NetBeans IDE 6.0 and above features an IEP Editor for creating IEPs that can be deployed to a **JBI** container as a composite application. Each event processor that you create can work with a single message stream. The common actions that you perform through this editor are defining actions like simple filtering, routing, and aggregations over a period of time (window). A simple example could be to create an IEP that monitors the reservation process from different airlines over a period of time.

The **JBI** container is part of the **Sun Java System / GlassFish Application Server**. In order to work with the IEP Editor, you need to start this server and also the IEP Service Engine highlighted in the following figure:

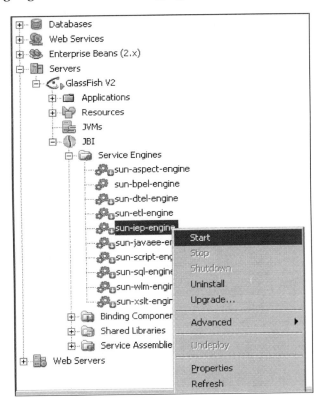

As discussed earlier, the IEP Service Engine internally uses the Java DB. Hence, make sure that the Java DB is running through NetBeans.

When you start the IEP Service Engine for the first time, it creates a set of tables that are either data tables containing data related to your IEP applications or internal tables used by the Service Engine. Do not try to alter or delete the internal tables created by the IEP Service Engine. The internal tables can include the following tables:

- EMS_PLAN: This table tracks deployment of event processors and assigns an Instance ID. Each time you deploy an IEP, an entry appears indicating the event processor has been deployed.

- EMS_OUTPUT: This table is updated every time another table is updated. Each time a specific table is updated, it will receive the same record with a new timestamp.

- EMS_PROCESSING_STATE: The IEP uses this table to restart IEP processes after an interruption.

- EMS_TABLE_USAGE: This table assists in garbage collection. For each data table, this table lists the operators that subscribe to the information.

```
IEPSEaaa05000: IEP service engine initialization starts ...
IEPSEaaa05015: Skipping registration of Extension MBean com.sun.jbi:JbiName=server
IEPSEaaa05001: IEP service engine initialization succeeded
IEPSEaaa05003: Starting IEP service engine
IEPSEaaa05005: IEP service engine started successfully
JBIFW1146: Engine sun-iep-engine has been started.
IEPSEaaa03000: Started IEP service engine heart-beat thread
IEPSEaaa04007: Started IEP service engine in-only thread
IEPSEaaa06005: Started IEP service engine out-only thread
IEPSEaaa06017: Response required: true
```

To deploy and test your IEP process, you must create a composite application project. Each composite application project instance is a container holding the deployment configuration for a collection of JBI component subprojects. Each instance maintains deployment specific data objects, such as WSDL, XSD, and JBI deployment descriptor files.

NetBeans project system generates the Service Assembly deployment package and packages Service Unit deployment jars from JBI component projects with updated deployment configuration as specified by the composite application project. Once you have created the composite application project and integrated the desired components into it (including the IEP project), by adding the IEP project as a JBI module in the composite application, you then compile it and deploy the composite application project.

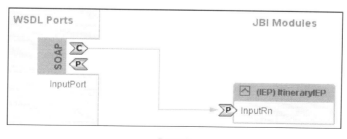

To test the output of the composite application project, from the NetBeans **Services** tab, right-click on the **Databases** and select **New Connection.** In the **New Database Connection** dialog, provide the **Database URL** as **jdbc:derby://localhost/iepseDB**, user name as **iepseDB** and password as **iepseDB** and click **OK**.

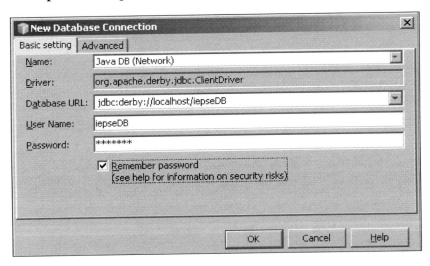

When you have connected successfully with the DB, browse the tables in **iepseDB**. All of the tables are auto-generated and you are not expected to alter or delete any of them.

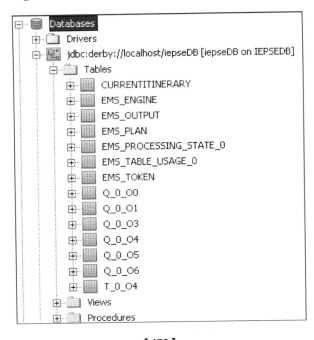

A **CURRENTITINERARY** table is also created. This is the name specified in the **Global** property field in the Table Output IEP operator.

 Note that along with the CURRENTITINERARY and EMS tables, there are other tables starting with 'Q'. They are data tables that store the current output of the operator. There are two basic types of data tables: one for output types and one for relation types. You are not expected to alter these tables.

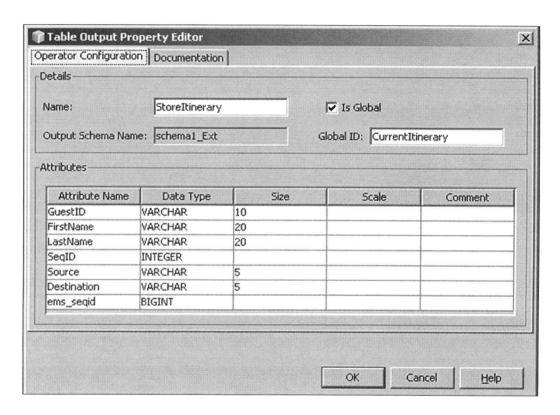

When the IEP is invoked, the stream data is stored in the **CURRENTITINERARY** table.

 The IEP example shown in this chapter needs a stream input simulator to test the IEP process. The source code bundle provided in the site has a **TestItineraryIEP** NetBeans project that reads an external data file and sends a data stream to the IEP module. The project is available under **src\PartG\TestItineraryIEP**.

Summary

This chapter has provided you an overview of the Intelligent Event Processor and the IEP Service Engine of the JBI runtime, and has also provided a summary depicting the need for an event processing tool. The IEP project system comes as a NetBeans IDE 6.0 plug-in.

9
Handling Events

In the previous chapters of this book, we saw how to use the NetBeans Enterprise Pack to build enterprise applications that can integrate with other systems. We saw how developing systems, based upon receiving and sending messages, are defined by a WSDL contract. In our approach so far, we have assumed that everything runs as expected and that no errors occur. Of course, in the real world this is not the case and so, our business processes defined by BPEL must take into account any errors that may occur. This process is called fault handling. In this chapter, we will see what support NetBeans offers to help us effectively manage fault handling within a BPEL process. NetBeans Enterprise Pack provides support for several different types of fault handlers and we will discuss each of them in this chapter.

In addition to fault handling, we will also take a look at event handling within a BPEL process and see how NetBeans can help us in this area.

Within this chapter we will discuss:

- Fault handling within WSDL documents
- BPEL handlers
    - Fault handlers
    - Event handlers
    - Compensation handlers
    - Termination handlers

At the end of this chapter, you should have an understanding of the different types of event handlers within a BPEL process and the support that NetBeans provides us for managing these events.

Fault Handling Within WSDL Documents

In Chapter 6 we discussed WSDL documents and how they define the contract
between a consumer and a service provider. Within a WSDL document, operations
are defined along with their input and output messages as shown in the
following example:

```
<?xml version="1.0" encoding="UTF-8"?>
<definitions name="HelloWSDL" targetNamespace=
                        "http://j2ee.netbeans.org/wsdl/HelloWSDL"
    xmlns="http://schemas.xmlsoap.org/wsdl/"
    xmlns:wsdl="http://schemas.xmlsoap.org/wsdl/"
    xmlns:xsd="http://www.w3.org/2001/XMLSchema"
    xmlns:plnk="http://docs.oasis-open.org/wsbpel/2.0/plnktype"
    xmlns:soap="http://schemas.xmlsoap.org/wsdl/soap/"
    xmlns:tns="http://j2ee.netbeans.org/wsdl/HelloWSDL">
    <types/>
    <message name="sayHelloRequest">                                1
        <part name="inputMessage" type="xsd:string"/>
    </message>
    <message name="sayHelloReply">                                  2
        <part name="outputMessage" type="xsd:string"/>
    </message>
    <portType name="HelloWSDLPortType">
        <operation name="sayHello">                                 3
            <input name="input1" message="tns:sayHelloRequest"/>    4
            <output name="output1" message="tns:sayHelloReply"/>    5
        </operation>
    </portType>
</definitions>
```

From a message definition point of view, we can see that this WSDL code contains
five key pieces of information.

1. message `sayHelloRequest` has been defined.

2. message `sayHelloReply` has been defined.

3. operation `sayHello` has been defined.

4. input parameter of type `sayHelloRequest` has been defined for the message
    `sayHello`.

5. output parameter of type `sayHelloReply` has been defined for the message
    `sayHello`.

The comparable Java definition of this method could be as follows:

```
public class SayHelloRequest                                    1
{

}

public class SayHelloResponse                                   2
{

}

public class SayHello
{
    public SayHelloResponse sayHello (SayHelloRequest request)
    {                                                        3, 4, 5

    }
}
```

In this Java code, points 1 to 5 represent the same items as defined in the WSDL document.

If you look carefully at this Java code, you will probably spot something missing; exceptions. If we wanted to handle errors within the sayHello method, we would need to specify on the method signature what exceptions the method throws. In the above code, if we never wanted to say hello to anyone who isn't our friend, we would define a specific exception for this case and then alter the method signature to throw the exception.

```
public class NotFriendFault extends Exception
{

}

public class SayHello
{
    public SayHelloResponse sayHello (
        SayHelloRequest resuest) throws NotFriendFault
}
```

This exception can easily be mapped within a WSDL document by specifying a new fault message and a new <fault> option within our operation. The WSDL to describe this service then becomes:

```
<?xml version="1.0" encoding="UTF-8"?>
<definitions name="HelloWSDL" targetNamespace=
                            "http://j2ee.netbeans.org/wsdl/HelloWSDL"
    xmlns="http://schemas.xmlsoap.org/wsdl/"
    xmlns:wsdl="http://schemas.xmlsoap.org/wsdl/"
    xmlns:xsd="http://www.w3.org/2001/XMLSchema"
    xmlns:plnk="http://docs.oasis-open.org/wsbpel/2.0/plnktype"
    xmlns:soap="http://schemas.xmlsoap.org/wsdl/soap/"
    xmlns:tns="http://j2ee.netbeans.org/wsdl/HelloWSDL">
    <types/>
    <message name="sayHelloRequest">
        <part name="inputMessage" type="xsd:string"/>
    </message>
    <message name="sayHelloReply">
        <part name="outputMessage" type="xsd:string"/>
    </message>
    <message name="sayHelloFault">                                      1
        <part name="faultMessage" type="xsd:string"/>
    </message>
    <portType name="HelloWSDLPortType">
        <operation name="sayHello">
            <input name="input1" message="tns:sayHelloRequest"/>
            <output name="output1" message="tns:sayHelloReply"/>
            <fault name="notFriendFault" message=
                                "tns:sayHelloFault"/>                   2
        </operation>
    </portType>
</definitions>
```

1. A new message is defined called sayHelloFault. This defines the structure of the message (in this case an xsd:string) that will be returned in the event of an error.

2. A fault called notFriendFault is defined as the fault message for the sayHello operation.

> To help when defining WSDL messages, we recommend using a naming strategy to improve readability when accessing messages within a BPEL process. For example:
> Append *Request* to input message names.
> Append *Reply* to output request names.
> Append *Fault* to fault message names.

As you would expect, when defining a new WSDL document within NetBeans, the **New WSDL Document** wizard allows faults to be defined at document creation time (see Chapter 6 for details on creating WSDL documents within NetBeans).

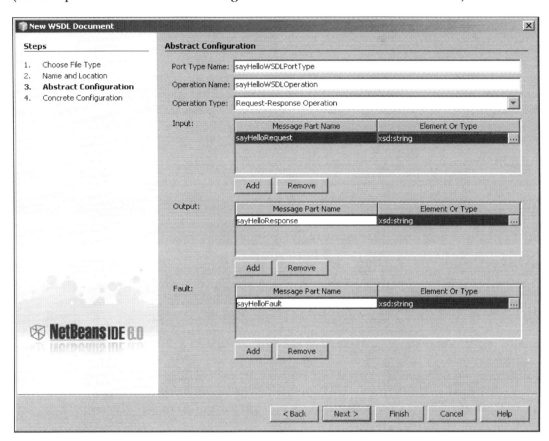

When an operation described in WSDL returns a fault both, the fault type and a description are returned to the client. In the case of a SOAP message, a returned fault code may look like the following XML fragment.

```
<SOAP-ENV:Fault>
    <faultcode>SOAP-ENV:Client</faultcode>
    <faultstring>notFriendFault</faultstring>
      <detail>
       <faultMessage>That person is not in your friend
           list.</faultMessage>
      </detail>
</SOAP-ENV:Fault>
```

Now that we have discussed how faults are specified within WSDL documents and how they are represented within XML results, let's discuss the different event handlers available to BPEL processes, and in particular fault handlers that allow developers to manage any faults that are thrown during BPEL process.

BPEL Handlers

Within NetBeans, four different types of handlers are available for use within the BPEL process designer. They are as follows:

- Fault handlers
- Event handlers
- Compensation handlers
- Termination handlers

Fault handlers allow exceptions to be caught and managed within a BPEL process. Event handlers allow events to be triggered when specified messages are retrieved within a BPEL process or when specific timed events occur. NetBeans provides GUI support for both fault handlers and event handlers allowing them to be graphically modeled as part of a BPEL process.

Compensation handlers allow business processes to be rolled back in a similar fashion to a rollback statement issued against a relational database. Termination handlers allow specific code to be executed when a BPEL process exits. Both compensation and termination handlers are defined by XML within a BPEL process. NetBeans provides editing support for these types of handlers within the **Source** tab of the BPEL designer rather than in the **Design** tab.

Let's discuss each of these handlers in turn.

Fault Handlers

Fault handlers are probably the most common type of handlers that are used within a BPEL process. The purpose of fault handlers is similar to that of **Exceptions** in the Java language, allowing fault cases to be caught and thrown and reported back to the application that invoked the BPEL process.

Within a BPEL process, we can throw faults if a particular situation occurs. These faults can be caught by a Catch handler specifically designed to catch the fault, or by a more general Catch All fault handler.

The following sample BPEL process shows how an exception can be thrown if a certain condition exists, and then how it can be caught and passed back to the calling application.

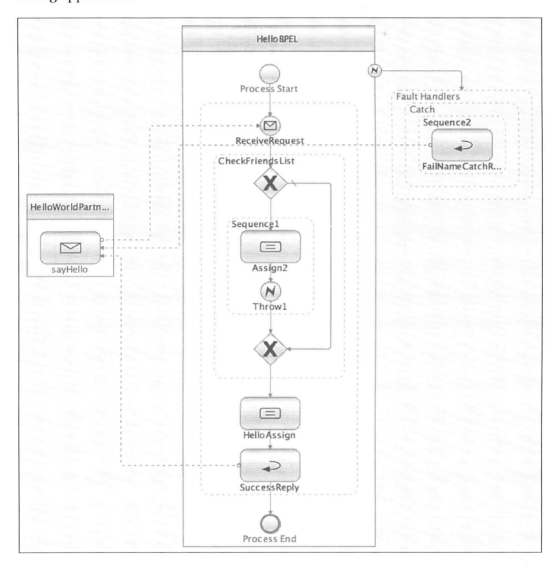

To use fault handlers within a BPEL process, the WSDL describing the operations for the partner link needs to have fault messages specified for each operation that may return a fault. After we have ensured that fault messages are defined for our operations, using a fault handler is a 3 stage process:

1. Decide when a fault needs to be thrown and assign a fault and description to return to the caller.
2. Throw the fault.
3. Catch the fault and return it to the caller.

Deciding when a fault needs to be thrown is dependent upon the business logic being performed by your application. The BPEL process designer provides lots of functionality to enable you to catch specific error cases, for example:

*   Input values are outside of specific ranges
*   Boolean operations return false
*   Processing is performed outside of a specified date range.

When you have decided to throw a fault, you will most probably want to specify an error message that can be returned to the calling application. The BPEL process designer allows you to achieve this by using the **Assign** activity.

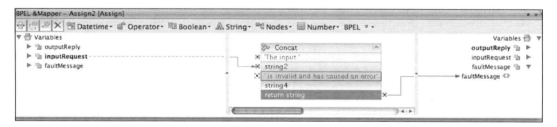

In this figure, we can see that we are using the BPEL designer's **Assign** activity to set the fault message that is going to be returned to the calling application. In this example, we are using the **Concat** construct to concatenate several strings together. The resultant string is then assigned to the **faultMessage**. In this example, the **faultMessage** is being assigned the value. The input—**inputRequest,** is invalid and has caused an error where **inputRequest** is the value of the message received by the BPEL process.

Having decided that a fault needs to be thrown and assigned a fault message, we can drag the **Throw** activity from the palette into the BPEL designer to specify that the fault should be thrown at a specific point in the process.

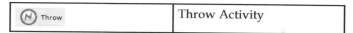

| Throw | Throw Activity |

To design the fault being thrown, we need to specify some details about the fault as shown in the following figure:

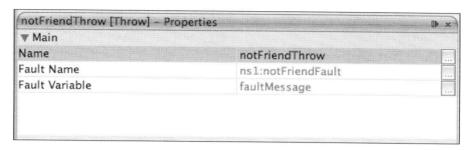

To complete the definition of the **Throw** activity, we need to specify three properties:

- **Name**
- **Fault Name**
- **Fault Variable**

The **Name** property is used purely to help us identify the throw activity within the BPEL process designer. This is used as an internal name to help us keep track of the different **Throw** activities that we may have within a process. In the sample process shown earlier in this chapter, there is only one **Throw** activity so it's not too difficult to keep track of it. In a more complex business process however, you may have several **Throw** activities and it's useful to be able to easily identify them.

Secondly, we need to specify the **Fault Name**. This is analogous to the class of an exception in Java code. The **Fault Name** can be selected from all the defined faults in the WSDL files of any partners used by the BPEL process. To select the **Fault Name**, we need to press the "**...**" button within the properties window. Selecting this causes the dialog shown below to be displayed. This dialog shows all the fault messages that are defined within the partner's **WSDL Files** in a hierarchical approach together with all the **System Faults** that can be thrown. To select a fault, select it in the tree view and press the **OK** button.

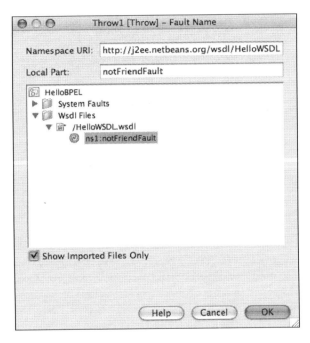

In addition to the faults defined within the partner's **WSDL Files**, the following BPEL **System Faults** can also be thrown as shown in the following table:

completionConditionFailure	Thrown if the completion condition for a "forEach" activity can never be true.
conflictingReceive	Thrown when two or more inbound message activities are enabled for the same partner link, port type and operation.
conflictingRequest	Thrown when two or more message activities are enabled for the same partner link and operation.
correlationViolation	Thrown when message contents do not match the correlation information.
invalidBranchCondition	Thrown if an invalid branch is selected within a "forEach" activity.

invalidReply	Thrown if an invalid reply is encountered.
invalidVariables	Thrown if invalid variables are encountered.
joinFailure	A joinFailure system fault occurs when the join condition in an activity is false.
mismatchedAssignmentFailure	Thrown when incompatible XML is used within an "Assign" construct.
missingReply	Thrown if an inbound message activity is completed without a corresponding reply.
missingRequest	Thrown if a "reply" activity cannot be matched with an inbound message.
scopeInitializationFailure	Thrown if an object cannot be initialized within a particular scope.
selectionFailure	Thrown when a fault occurs within a selection operation.
subLanguageExecutionFault	Thrown if an evaluated expression results in an unhandled fault.
uninitializedPartnerRole	Thrown if an activity references an uninitialized partner link.
uninitializedVariable	Thrown if an activity references an uninitialized variable.
unsupportedReference	Thrown if the BPEL engine does not recognize the XML reference-scheme attribute.

Providing a full description of these standard BPEL faults is out of scope for this book. We suggest that you consult the BPEL language specification for further details. (`http://docs.oasis-open.org/wsbpel/2.0/wsbpel-v2.0.pdf`).

Finally, after selecting a **faultMessage** to throw, we need to specify which variable holds the information or message to return to the calling application. Pressing the **Fault Variable** "..." button within the properties window displays a dialog similar to that shown below, which shows all the variables currently defined within the BPEL process. Select the appropriate variable from this list and press **OK**.

To recap, when throwing a fault we:

1. identify a situation where we want to throw the fault
2. define the message to be sent to the client along with the fault
3. define the fault that we want to send to the client

Now that we have thrown a fault within our BPEL process, we need to catch it and handle it. In its simplest case, this could be done by returning the fault message we've just generated to the client application. Alternatively, we can perform some additional BPEL processing and try to manage the fault case.

To manage thrown faults within a BPEL process, we have two options:

1. Catch a specific fault and deal with it
2. Catch any fault and deal with it

To be able to catch faults and manage them within a BPEL process, we first have to add a Fault Handler to the process. This is achieved by right-clicking on the BPEL process and selecting the **Add | Fault Handlers** menu option.

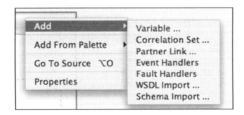

Selecting this option adds a blank fault handler to the BPEL process as shown below.

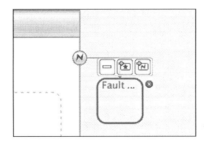

Within the empty fault handler we have three options.

*   collapse the diagrammatic representation of our fault handler
*   add a Catch handler for a specific fault
*   add a Catch-All handler for any fault.

Only one Catch All handler is allowed per process.

	Collapse the view
	Add a Catch All fault handler
	Add a Catch fault handler for a specific fault.

If we add a **Catch All** handler, there are no properties to specify. All we need to do is complete the process by specifying which actions are to be performed as a result of catching an exception. This is achieved in the same way as a BPEL process is designed, by dragging activities on to the Catch activity within the BPEL designer.

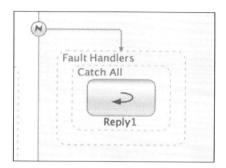

If we want to handle specific faults in different ways, we can add specific **Catch** handlers. This is analogous to having multiple catch statements within a piece of Java code. Within Java code we can catch any number of specific exceptions. The fault handlers within the BPEL process allow us to do a similar thing. BPEL runtime will attempt to match a fault to a specific **Catch** handler. If that cannot be found then a fault will be handled by the **Catch All** handler if it is present.

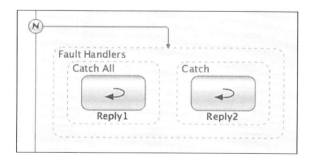

For a **Catch** handler, we need to specify the name of the fault we wish to catch within the **Catch** properties window.

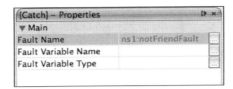

Pressing the **Fault Name** "**...**" button within the properties window causes a dialog to be displayed similar to that shown below from which the fault type can be selected.

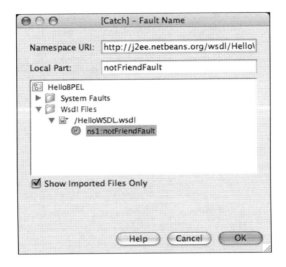

Event Handlers

A BPEL process is initiated by receiving a message from a client, for example a web service client. If the process is a synchronous process, then the client will wait for the BPEL process to complete. The process will execute without any further input from the client. This is how a typical short-lived process will execute. For more complex asynchronous processes, it often becomes necessary to send additional data to the BPEL process so that it can continue processing. BPEL mandates that a receive activity can only be used to initiate a process and cannot be used afterwards within a process. In a situation where we wish to send additional data to a running process, we must use the **OnMessage** event handler. This event handler acts in a similar fashion to a receive activity and allows a message to be received by a running process from one of the process partner links.

Within the BPEL process designer, an **OnMessage** event handler is displayed as shown in the following figure:

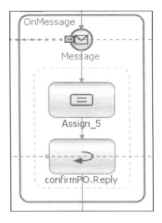

BPEL designer also supports **On Alarm** events. An **On Alarm** event is triggered at specified periods to perform certain processing. **On Alarm** events are useful for timing out a process if no response is received from a client within a specified time period. If an asynchronous process is pending information from a client, an **On Alarm** event can be used to force the process to exit if no response is received within the necessary time period.

To create an **OnMessage** or an **On Alarm** handler within the BPEL designer, we need to add a **Pick** activity to the process designer.

Pick	Pick Activity

Pick activities are added to BPEL processes by dragging the **Pick** activity icon from the palette onto the BPEL process. Right-clicking on a **Pick** activity gives you the option of adding an **OnMessage** handler or an **On Alarm** message handler. Both of these handlers allow additional actions to be performed after either the message is received or the time out occurs simply by building up the BPEL process by dragging additional actions from the palette.

With an **On Alarm** handler, the handler can be specified to wait for a given period of time before completing, or it can be specified to wait until a given date and time before completing.

Alarm Type	Description
For	Alarm waits for a specified period of time before completing.
Until	Alarm waits until a specified date and time before completing.

The properties for the alarm handler allow the Alarm type to be configured together with the corresponding timescale as shown in the following figures:

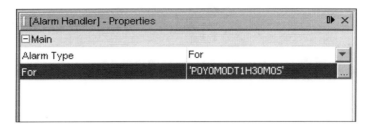

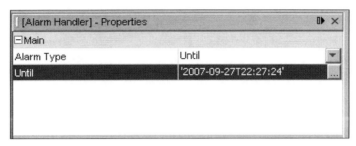

With an **OnMessage** handler, we need to specify which message the handler is going to receive and how this corresponds to the WSDL. The following properties need to be specified.

Property	Description
Partner Link	The name of the partner link that is sending the message.
Port Type	The port type defined within the WSDL document for the receiving message.
Operation	The operation, or method, that is being invoked.
Input Variable	The name of the variable within the BPEL process that will store the state of the incoming message.

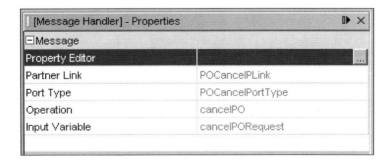

In addition to specifying these details within the properties page, they can also be specified within the **Property Editor** as shown in the figure below. The first tab on the **Property Editor** dialog allows the properties described above to be specified so you can either enter them within the dialog or directly within the Properties page.

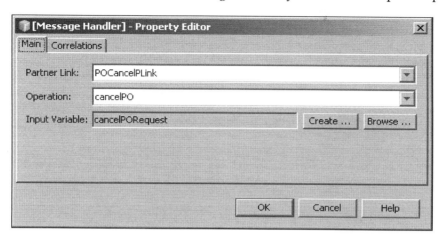

As **On Message** handlers are used within asynchronous processes, it is necessary to specify the correlations used so that the input message can be applied to the correct instance of the running BPEL process. When many instances of the same process are running within the BPEL engine, the engine uses correlations to link together messages from clients to specific instances of running processes. A correlation set is basically a unique piece of information passed from the client to the BPEL engine that can be used to uniquely tie client messages to a running process. A correlation set is rather like a prime key in a relational database. It can contain one piece of data just like the prime key of a database table, or it can consist of multiple pieces of data like a compound key. In this case, the combination of all the data within the correlation set makes up the unique identifier for the process.

Correlation sets can be created within NetBeans by right-clicking on the BPEL process within the Design view and selecting the **Add | Correlation Set...** menu option. On the resulting dialog, we can select the name we wish to give to the correlation set and define which properties from the WSDL file we wish to use to define the set.

The correlations tab of the Property Editor allows us to specify which correlation set we wish to use for the specific On Message handler.

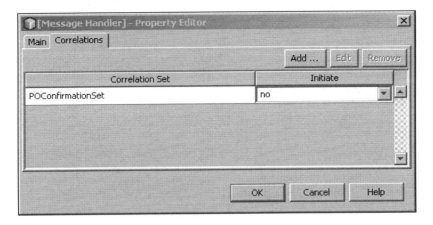

Compensation Handlers

Within BPEL processes, Compensation refers to the ability to undo or roll back activities that have occurred within a particular scope of a running process. A scope in a BPEL process is analogous to a block of Java code that starts with a '{' and ends with a '}'. Typically a scope within a BPEL process represents a particular piece of functionality that is being performed. Within the NetBeans BPEL designer, the scope of blocks of code is represented by a solid rectangle drawn around a block of activities. A Compensation Handler is a BPEL code construct that is executed when a scope is terminated unexpectedly and any processing that has been performed during that scope needs to be undone.

NetBeans does not provide any provision for graphical editing of Compensation Handlers within the BPEL designer. To add a Compensation Handler to a BPEL process, we need to switch to the **Source** view and manually enter the XML for the Compensation Handler. Right-clicking on a scope within the BPEL designer and choosing **Goto Source** will open the Source view at the beginning of the selected scope. To add a compensation handler, we need to add an XML element for the compensation handler

```
<compensationHandler/>
    <scope name="myScope">
      <compensationHandler>
         <!-- perform activities necessary to undo scope-->
      </compensationHandler>
    <!-- scope activities-->
    </scope>
```

Termination Handlers

A termination handler is in many respects similar to a compensation handler. The purpose of a termination handler is to provide code to be executed when a BPEL process is unexpectedly exited. Termination Handlers can be applied to any different scope within a process and are defined by the `<terminationHandler/>` element.

The BPEL designer provides no support for designing termination handlers, instead that must be defined within the XML for the process within the **Source** view of the BPEL designer.

The code fragment below shows how a BPEL process may have a compensation handler and a termination handler defined within a particular scope.

```
<scope name="myScope">
  <compensationHandler >
    <!-- perform activities necessary to undo scope-->
  </compensationHandler>
  <terminationHandler>
    <!-- perform activities necessary after unexpected exit-->
     <compensate />
   </terminationHandler>
     <!-- scope activities-->
</scope>
```

If no termination handler is defined for a scope then the default termination handler will be invoked. The default termination handler invokes the default compensation handler for a given scope, that is,

```
<terminationHandler>
    <compensate/>
</terminationHandler>
```

Summary

In this chapter, we've looked at the different types of event handlers that can be used within a BPEL process designed within the NetBeans BPEL designer. We've seen that there are four different types of event handlers that can be used. Fault Handlers are used for throwing and catching faults rather like the *try ... catch* and *throw* constructs within Java code. We've seen how we can throw faults and then catch them with specific fault handlers or catch-all handlers. The second type of handlers we looked at were Event Handlers and we discussed how these are used to respond to events—either specific messages or timer messages. Both Fault Handlers and Event Handlers are supported within the NetBeans BPEL designer allowing drag-and-drop of components from within the NetBeans palette into BPEL processes.

Next, we looked at compensation handlers and discussed how these are used to rollback data within a BPEL process. Finally we looked at termination handlers and saw how these are called when a BPEL process is terminated unexpectedly. We saw how the default termination handler invokes the default compensation handler within a BPEL process scope.

In the next chapter, we're going to bring all the concepts and techniques we've discussed so far together and build a real world enterprise application using NetBeans and the NetBeans Enterprise Pack.

10
Building a Sample Application

In the previous chapters, you were introduced to NetBeans IDE and the IDE's capability of designing enterprise applications using the built-in SOA tools. You also learned the usage of various editors including WSDL and XML schema editor. In addition, you were introduced to NetBeans BPEL designer and the various runtime requirements for building and running your enterprise applications.

In this chapter, let us start by designing a simple enterprise application by creating a couple of partner services and some BPEL modules and make them interact with each other to perform some basic tasks. If you have not read the previous chapters, you may not be able to understand some of the tasks that we will perform in this chapter. As a minimum requirement, read Chapter 2 – *Getting Started* and Chapter 5 – *BPEL Designer*.

This chapter also assumes that you have already configured your NetBeans IDE to reflect the following functionalities:

- Create BPEL Modules.
- Start/Stop, Sun Java System / GlassFish Application Server.
- Start and manage Java DB.

For the purpose of this sample application, we will be using NetBeans IDE, GlassFish Application Server and Java DB to build a simple application. The author recommends running the samples in NetBeans IDE that comes bundled with OpenESB components. You can download the bundle from `https://open-esb.dev.java.net/Downloads_OpenESB_Addons_NB6.html`.

About the Sample Application

The sample application we are going to develop is a simple travel reservation collaboration application called AirAlliance (AA). AirAlliance is an airlines alliance system that attempts to unify the reservation process for all its partner airline companies. The advantage of such a system having of a single interface for booking airline tickets across multiple connections and legs. Some of the design considerations for building such a system should include:

1.   Support for interacting with multiple partner systems.

2.   Ability to process itinerary event through intelligent event processors.

3.   Flight schedules are formulated to permit almost seamless travel that may include several different carriers within the alliance, on a single ticket.

Although these requirements are easy to build, one should also consider the technologies involved in creating a system that acts as an orchestration point for all the different exposed services from the airlines company.

The sample application we are developing is not an enterprise grade application. It is designed to highlight some of the features of NetBeans and the BPEL Designer. However, you can use this application to build your own full fledged application. In this chapter, we will focus only on the collaboration part of the AirAlliance application and the use of OpenESB binding components to successfully interact with partner services.

The sample application is divided into multiple parts, each highlighting a particular BPEL capability. Except the first part, each part is an incremental update of the previous part. These parts are described in the following table:

Example	Description
Part A	We will create a simple web service for NorthAir airlines from an EJB project. We will create a business process that sends guest itinerary information to the web service and receives a confirmation. Basic BPEL activities including receive, assign, invoke, and reply are depicted through this part. Whenever a request for reservation is made, the NorthAir Web Service is invoked. The NorthAir Web Service confirms the reservation with a success message.
Part B	This sample code shows how you can use the JDBC BC to update Java DB from the BPEL process. Whenever a request for reservation is made, the NorthAir Web Service is invoked and the itinerary data is updated in the SouthAir DB through the JDBC binding component.
Part C	This sample code shows how you can use the File BC along with JDBC BC to store itinerary data in Java DB and in the file system.

Example	Description
Part D	This sample code shows how you can use the JMS BC along with JDBC BC and File BC to send itinerary data to JMS Destination. Whenever a request for reservation is made, the itinerary information is updated in the file system using the JBI File BC. This file can be constantly monitored by an external process. Now, the itinerary data is send to EastAir's JMS Queue. EastAir's JMS Queue Listener can get the itinerary information for further processing.
Part E	This part introduces the sequencing and branching properties of BPEL. When a request for reservation is made, the BPEL process checks the destination sector. If the destination is set to 'SFO', then the itinerary is routed to NorthAir WS otherwise it is routed to WestAir Web Service. Since WestAir Web Service is new, we create an identical web service using NorthAir Web Service and name it WestAir Web Service. They do not do any actual itinerary processing but they send a confirmation message back to the client so we can find out which airlines service was invoked. So far through the earlier parts of this example, we have created a sequential process for invoking NorthAir Web Service, stored an itinerary and sent an itinerary to a JMS physical destination. Ideally, updating the partner airlines repository is independent of itinerary processing. In spite of failed reservations, we update the data store for the purpose of maintaining a waiting list (Of course without a confirmed reservation ID). Hence, UpdateItinerary sequence is introduced as a flow branch to process the itinerary branch, so both the sequences work in parallel. This part also shows how as part of the UpdateAirlines sequence, we send the itinerary information to the travel agent's FTP server. Uploading itinerary information to an FTP server is done through FTP BC.
Part F	The reservation process is updated to perform pre-processing before invoking the partner services. This will be useful later to build your own validation rules before invoking the partner services. A pre-processor Web Service performs a check on the sectors and sends a reply back to the process stating if the reservation could be processed. For this example, all reservation requests from 'BLR' to 'SFO' are rejected and an auto responder is sent to a predefined email address. The pre-processing also includes checking if the source and destination sectors are the same, before invoking the expensive partner service's query operations. You should have more of these checks in your real applications.

Example	Description
Part G	This part shows how you can process your data stream to do some intelligent pre-processing before performing any meaningful action on the data. In the previous parts, you used a File BC to create an XML file that contained the itinerary data. This itinerary data can be converted into a stream and can be passed through Intelligent Event Processors to project or filter the stream or to restrict the itinerary count. This part contains one intelligent event processor that does the following: • Processes all itineraries obtained from the stream for the last three seconds. • Uses stream filter to remove itinerary preferences data in order to make the itinerary data set smaller. • Contiguous ordering of itinerary data. • Stores the filtered itinerary record in database.

Source code for all of the above parts is available at http://www.packtpub.com/support/. The sources are available as NetBeans projects files. Follow the instructions provided in the Readme file in each part to set up the environment.

Getting Started

Before creating the first part of our sample application, we need to make sure that the runtime environment is set up properly. The sample comprises multiple NetBeans modules, some of which are deployable to servers. Hence, before starting with the sample, start your Application Server and BPEL Engine. For our sample, we are using Sun Java System / GlassFish Application Server, which has BPEL engine integrated. Go to the **Services** tab | **Servers** | **GlassFish V2**. Right-click on this node and click on **Start**. Refer to Chapter 2 on *Getting Started* for setting up the environment.

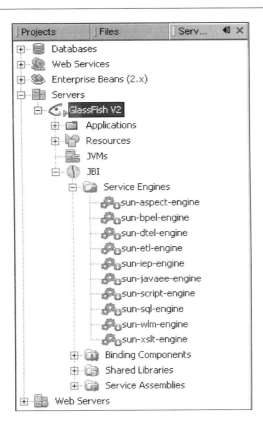

 Throughout this chapter, there are references to both GlassFish Application Server and Sun Java System Application Server. You can set up either of these servers to work with the examples given in this chapter. Sun Java System Application Server is just a supported version of the community based GlassFish Application Server and there may not be any significant differences in the way SOA applications are handled by them.

Creating Partner Services

Before building our sample application, let us understand some basics of NetBeans SOA modules and UI components. This section builds a simple application depicting how you can easily build a composite application using NetBeans.

First, we will create a web service and add an itinerary processing operation. From the **New Project** wizard select **Enterprise | EJB Module**.

The following screenshot shows the **New Project** wizard with the required project highlighted:

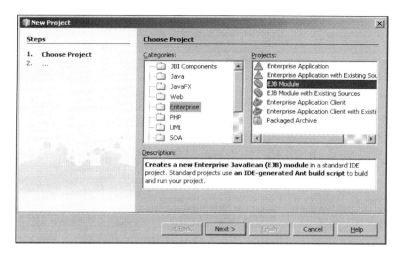

Type the **Project Name** as **NorthAirEJB**. For the first part of the demo, **NorthAirEJB** will have one web service with one operation called `processItinerary`. This method gets passenger details from BPEL implementation and sends a confirmation message back.

You need to select a target Java EE server for your EJB project. You can either select Sun Java System Application Server or the GlassFish Server.

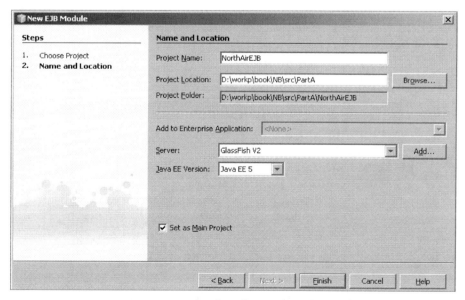

JAX-WS is an important part of the **Java EE 5** platform that simplifies the task of developing web services using Java technology. It addresses some of the issues in JAX-RPC 1.1 by providing support for multiple protocols such as SOAP 1.1, SOAP 1.2, XML, and by providing a facility for supporting additional protocols along with HTTP.

After creating an EJB module (Stateless Session Bean), let us create a web service by selecting the **Web Service** action by right-clicking the EJB Module project.

Provide the **Web Service Name** as **NorthAirWS** and provide a **Package** name. You can create an empty web service or delegate a session bean. For the purpose of this sample, we will create an empty web service.

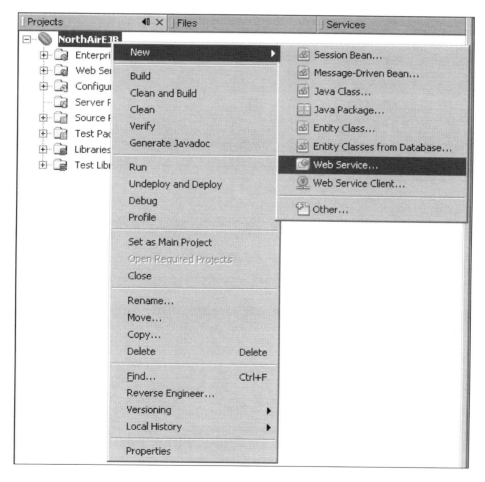

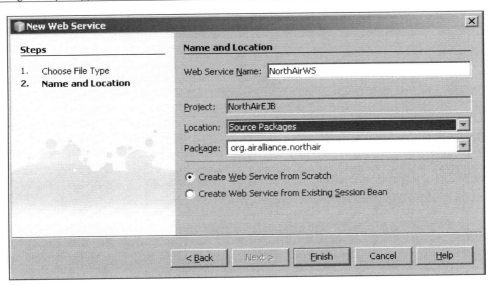

Now, right-click the **Web Service** and add a new operation as shown in the following screenshot. The purpose of any web service is to receive requests for a service, process them, and respond to the client. The operation that we are going to create accepts passenger details and sends a confirmation message back to the client.

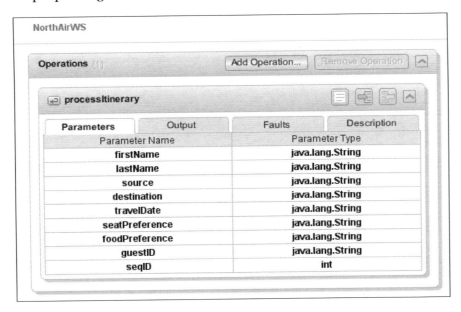

This screenshot shows the **Add Operation** dialog box. We have added one method named **processItinerary** that returns a String object and accepts passenger details like First Name, Last Name and travel information as input parameters.

At this point let us take a look at our generated Web Service code. A snippet from the file `NorthAirWS.java` is shown as follows:

```java
package org.airalliance.northair;
import javax.ejb.Stateless;
import javax.jws.WebMethod;
import javax.jws.WebParam;
import javax.jws.WebService;
@Stateless()
@WebService()
public class NorthAirWS {
/**
    * Web service operation
    */
    @WebMethod(operationName = "processItinerary")
    public String processItinerary(@WebParam(name = "firstName")
    String firstName, @WebParam(name = "lastName")
    String lastName, @WebParam(name = "source")
    String source, @WebParam(name = "destination")
    String destination, @WebParam(name = "travelDate")
    String travelDate, @WebParam(name = "seatPreference")
    String seatPreference, @WebParam(name = "foodPreference")
    String foodPreference, @WebParam(name = "guestID")
    String guestID, @WebParam(name = "seqID")
    int seqID) {
        //TODO write your implementation code here:
        return "Processed Reservation";
    }
}
```

Now we have a simple web service with one operation. In order to add this web service as a partner link, we need to deploy this web service in GlassFish Application Server. Right-click the EJB module and select **Undeploy and Deploy** to deploy the project to the default server.

When you deploy a Web Service to a web container, NetBeans IDE lets you test the web service to see if it functions as you expect. The tester application, provided by the GlassFish Application Server, is integrated into the IDE for this purpose. Right-click on the **Web Service** and select **Test Web Service** to test your **Web Service**. You can go to the **Services** tab | **Servers** | **GlassFish V2** | **Applications** | **EJB Modules** and check if your web service is deployed properly. If the **Web Service** is deployed, you can find NorthAirWS entry under **GlassFish V2** | **Applications** | **EJB Modules** | **NorthAirEJB**.

Creating the BPEL Process

Now that we have a Web Service running, let us create a business process to invoke the web service.

You have to create a **BPEL Module** and add it to a **Composite Application** in order for the business process to be deployed. From the **New Project** wizard, select **SOA | BPEL Module**.

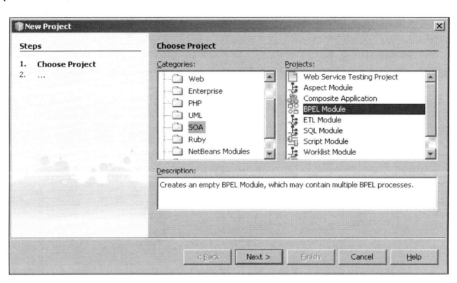

Add **BPEL_Reservation** as the **Project Name**.

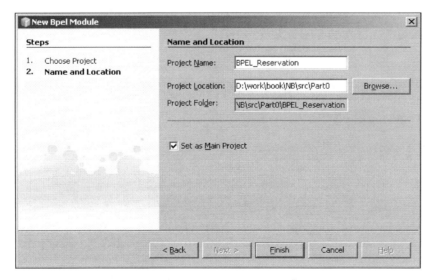

Once you have created a **BPEL Module,** it is time to create a BPEL process. Right-click on the **Process Files** and select **New | BPEL Process** to create a **New BPEL Process** as shown in the following screenshot:

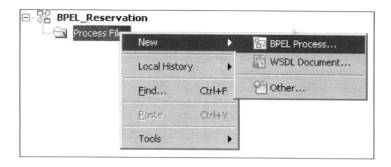

The **New BPEL Process** wizard guides you through various steps involved in creating a **BPEL Process.** Add the **Target Namespace** as `http://airalliance.org/bpel/BPEL_Reservation/BP_Reservation.`

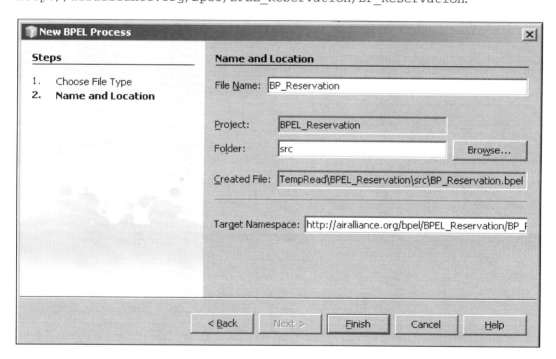

The following diagram shows a **BPEL Process** that does nothing. You cannot do much with this **BPEL Process** as it is incomplete and misses a receive activity. Note that every BPEL process should start with a receive or a pick activity.

The purpose of static analysis is to detect any undefined semantics or invalid semantics within a process definition that was not detected during the schema validation. Any process definition that fails one or more of these checks must be rejected by the WS-BPEL processor. That means, if you have invalid semantics in your BPEL process, the process header turns red.

When a BPEL process is created by the **New BPEL Process** wizard, it creates an empty activity:

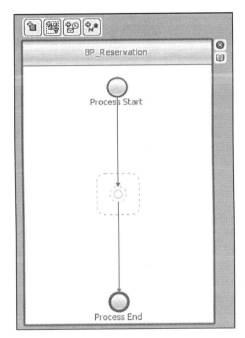

The following code shows the source of the empty BPEL process:

```xml
<?xml version="1.0" encoding="UTF-8"?>
<process
    name="BP_Reservation"
    targetNamespace=
        "http://airalliance.org/bpel/BPEL_Reservation/BP_Reservation"
    xmlns="http://docs.oasis-open.org/wsbpel/2.0/process/executable"
    xmlns:xsd="http://www.w3.org/2001/XMLSchema"
```

```
    xmlns:tns=
        "http://airalliance.org/bpel/BPEL_Reservation/BP_Reservation">
    <sequence>
    </sequence>
</process>
```

Now, drag-and-drop the NorthAir Web Service implementation from your project panel into the BPEL diagram. This action will import the public interfaces of NorthAir Web Service into the **Process Files | Partners** folder. You need to create a partner link for invoking this Web Service. When you drag-and-drop **NorthAirWS** into the BPEL diagram, the partner link property box is shown. Provide **WS_NorthAirImpl** as the partner link name and select the **WSDL File**:

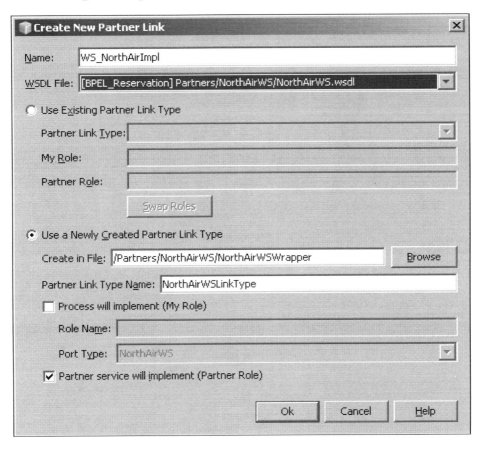

Now, right-click on **Process Files | New | WSDL Document** to create a BPEL implementation of the process.

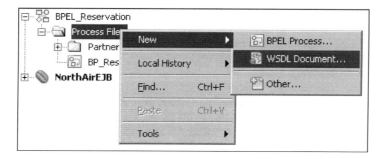

The **New WSDL Document** wizard will guide you through the process of creating a WSDL document from an existing XML schema file as shown in the following screenshot:

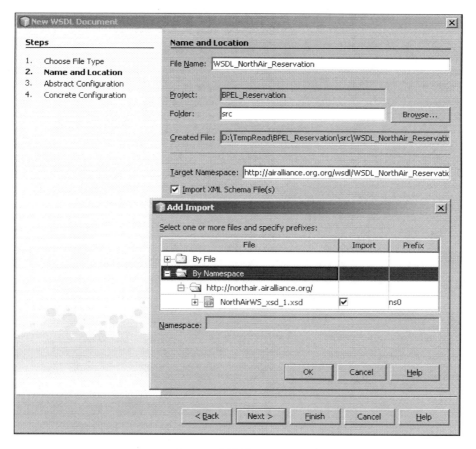

Select the auto generated `NorthAirWS_xsd_1.xsd` file. From the EJB module, when you add web services and operations, this file gets updated. You can also manually create a schema and select that file in the **Import XML Schema File** option.

After selecting the schema file, you can configure the input and output as shown in the following screenshot:

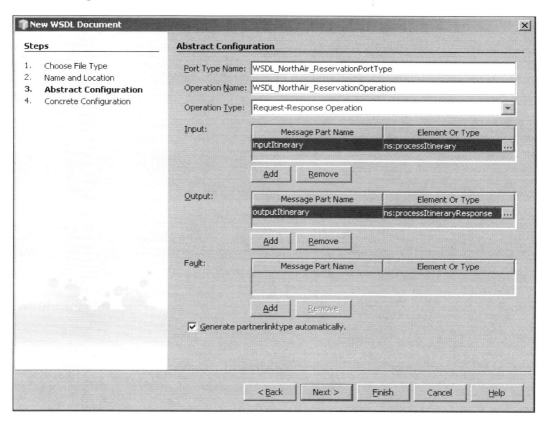

Change the **Message Part Name** for **Input** to **inputItinerary** and select the **Element** as **ns:processItinerary**. To select the element, click on the **[...]** button and select the **processItinerary** element as shown in the following screenshot:

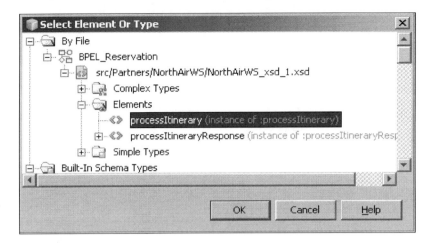

After selecting the input types, click **Next** to select the **Binding Type**. Leave the **Binding Type** as **SOAP** for now and select the **Binding Subtype** as **Document Literal** as shown in the following screenshot:

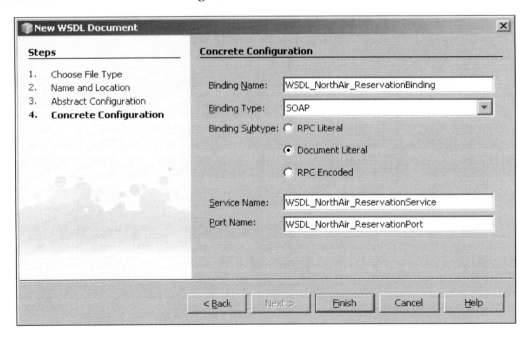

The following screenshot shows the graphical representation of the WSDL document created from the XML schema. Once you have successfully added a WSDL document, you can drag-and-drop WSDL document into BPEL diagram to create a partner service.

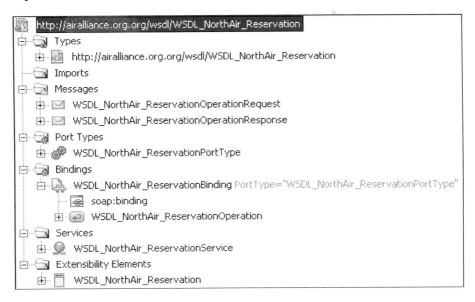

Now, you need to drag-and-drop WSDL_NorthAir_Reservation.wsdl file into the diagram to create the WSDL implementation. When you drag–and-drop the WSDL file over the BPEL diagram automatically some parts of the diagram gets highlighted as shown in the figure below. Ensure that you drop the file only on the highlighted circle.

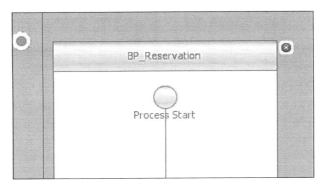

When you drop the WSDL file on the diagram, you will be prompted to enter the partner link information. Enter the partner link name as **BPEL_NorthAirReservation** and select the **WSDL File** as shown in the following screenshot:

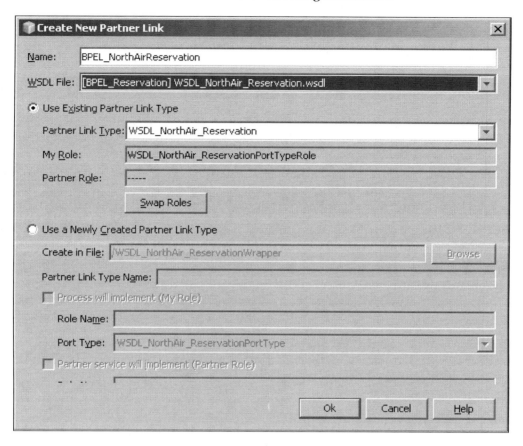

Now, let us add activities to this BPEL process to make it deployable as a JBI module. After adding receive, invoke, and reply activities, our BPEL process looks more complete. The following figure shows semantically correct business process:

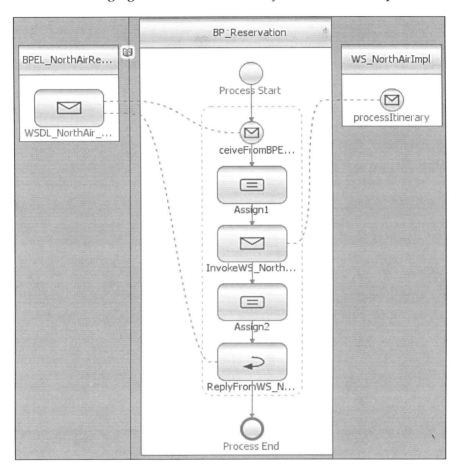

It works this way. The BPEL process receives a request for NorthAir Web Service to process a guest itinerary. The BPEL process receives the request and invokes the NorthAir Web Service operation **processItinerary** added as a partner service. Upon getting itinerary confirmation, the BPEL process replies back to the invoking service.

For more information on using the BPEL palette activities, refer to Chapter 5, which covers the BPEL Designer.

The receive activity is always mapped to the BPEL implementation of the partner service. You have the option to select the correct operation from the partner link WSDL. The invoke activity's partner link points to the EJB implementation. The following screenshots shows the **Receive, Invoke,** and **Reply** activities configuration:

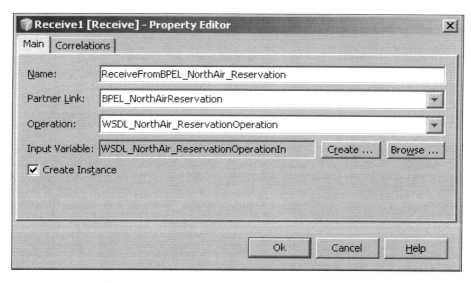

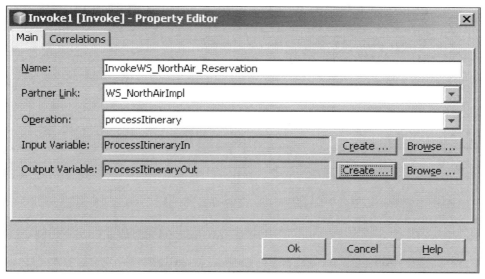

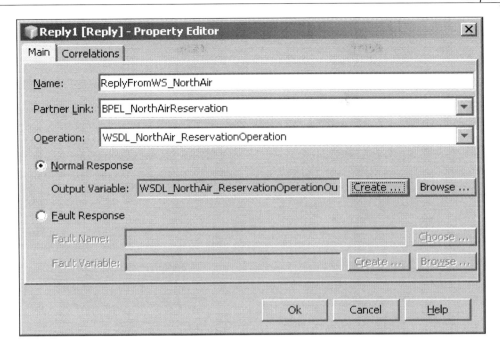

NetBeans offers an intuitive way of processing and directing BPEL process data through BPEL mapper. For more information on the BPEL, refer to Chapter 5 on BPEL Designer. The screenshot on the next page shows how we can copy the guest itinerary data across variables. Once you have successfully added **Receive**, **Invoke** and **Reply** activities as shown in the above figures, you need to assign variables. Drag-and-drop an **Assign** activity from the **Palette** between **Receive** and **Invoke** activity. Switch to **Mapper** view from **Design** View.

From **WSDL_NorthAir_ReservationOperationIn | inputItinerary,** drag-and-drop the itinerary details to the corresponding elements under **ProcessItineraryIn | parameters** as shown in the following screenshot:

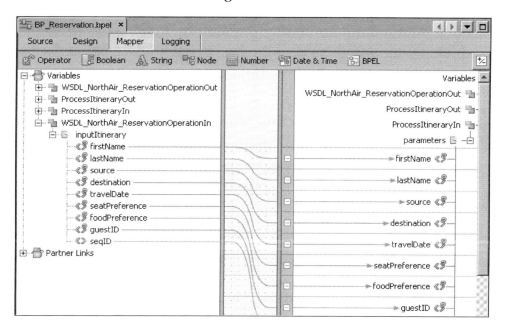

Now, when NorthAir Web Service processes the request and sends a response back, the output variable of **Invoke** activity should be copied to the variable associated with the **Reply** activity so that the invoking web clients get the appropriate message. Add one more **Assign** activity between **Invoke** activity and **Reply** activity. Now, switch to **Mapper** view and copy **ProcessItineraryOut** variable to **WSDL_NorthAir-ReservationOperationOut** as shown in the following screenshot:

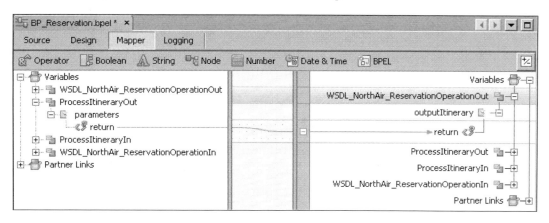

Our business process doesn't do much. It sends the guest itinerary to the NorthAir Web Service and returns the confirmation message back to the caller.

Assume, if NorthAir Web Service has the option of providing an operation, to check if there is seat availability on a particular date. Our business process should check the availability before deciding on the next action. The following diagram shows an **if** activity added to the process. The `isAvailable()` method of NorthAir Web Service returns a Boolean, based on the seat availability.

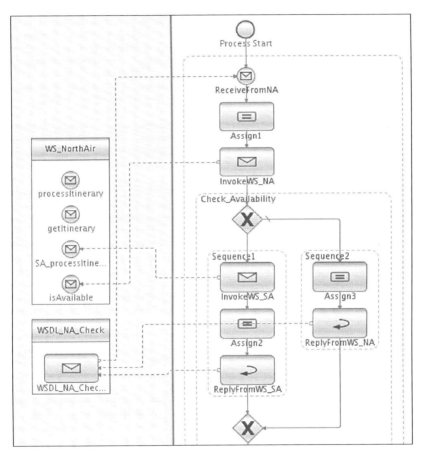

When the seat is not available, BPEL process requests the NorthAir Web Service to process the guest itinerary through another service called SouthAir and returns the confirmation back to the caller. This is transparent to the caller.

Ideally, NorthAir should not invoke SouthAir's service. In fact, NorthAir need not know about other air alliance partners. So, create another partner service called **AirAlliance** that can invoke `processItinerary` operations of other airlines.

Now, consider the following implementation. The request comes for NorthAir reservation, but upon availability check, the itinerary is routed to SouthAir reservation system.

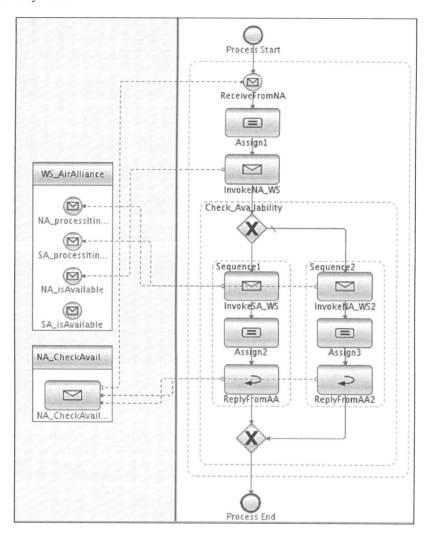

Now, look at the code showing the if activity and the condition:

```
<if name="Check_Availability">
    <condition>
        ( $NA_isAvailableOut.parameters/return = false() )
    </condition>
    <sequence name="Sequence1">
```

```
            <invoke name="InvokeSA_WS" partnerLink="WS_AirAlliance"
               operation="SA_processItinerary" portType="ns1:WS_AirAlliance"
               inputVariable="SA_processItineraryIn1"
               outputVariable="SA_processItineraryOut1"/>
         <assign name="Assign2">
            <copy>
               <from>$SA_processItineraryOut1.parameters/return</from>
               <to>$NA_CheckAvailabilityOperationOut1.part1/return</to>
            </copy>
         </assign>
         <reply name="ReplyFromAA" partnerLink="NA_CheckAvailability"
            operation="NA_CheckAvailabilityOperation"
            portType="ns2:NA_CheckAvailabilityPortType"
            variable="NA_CheckAvailabilityOperationOut1"/>
         </sequence>
   <else>
      <sequence name="Sequence2">
         <invoke name="InvokeNA_WS2" partnerLink="WS_AirAlliance"
            operation="NA_processItinerary" portType="ns1:WS_AirAlliance"
            inputVariable="NA_processItineraryIn1"
            outputVariable="NA_processItineraryOut1"/>
      <assign name="Assign3">
         <copy>
            <from>$NA_processItineraryOut1.parameters/return</from>
            <to>$NA_CheckAvailabilityOperationOut2.part1/return</to>
         </copy>
      </assign>
      <reply name="ReplyFromAA2" partnerLink="NA_CheckAvailability"
         operation="NA_CheckAvailabilityOperation"
         portType="ns2:NA_CheckAvailabilityPortType"
         variable="NA_CheckAvailabilityOperationOut2"/>
      </sequence>
   </else>
   </if>
```

A later part of this chapter develops a more complex BPEL process with `If` activities.

Creating a Composite Application

NetBeans supports combining sub-modules like **BPEL** into a **Composite Application** and deploying that **Composite Application** to **Java Business Integration (JBI)** run time. The **Composite Application** project option in NetBeans is used to create a service assembly that can be deployed to the JBI server. Within the **Composite Application** project, you can assemble an application that uses multiple project types, build JBI deployment packages, and monitor the status of JBI server components.

The JBI server can have different service engines. One of them is a BPEL service engine. In order to deploy a **Composite Application** to the BPEL runtime, it must have at least one **JBI** module.

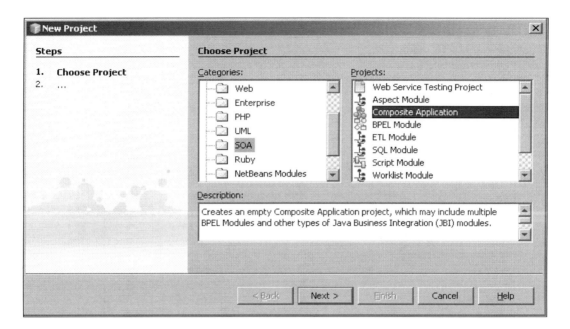

For creating a **Composite Application**, use the **New Project** wizard's **SOA | Composite Application** option. Once **Composite Application** is created, right-click on the application and select **Add JBI Module** to add the BPEL module project.

Part A - The Approach

The last section provided an overview of NetBeans capabilities for creating business processes and composite applications. In the coming sections, we'll use the above example as a background to create more complex composite applications. We will be building the sample application incrementally, so that we can thoroughly discuss the tools used during each step. For the purpose of this sample, we need to build the following components:

1. **Partner Services**: Partner services are external web services that our business process interacts with, to form an effective orchestration. From the point of view of our business process, the airline company's web services are the partner services. In our sample application, partner services are exposed as web services through two stateless session beans. Each stateless session bean representing a web service can get a passenger itinerary and process a reservation. Each partner service works with its own DB.

2. **BPEL Module**: In order to create a business process document, we need to create NetBeans' BPEL module. The BPEL module comprises of BPEL (`.bpel`) file, WSDL document derived from the partner service's XML schema, and the partner service's XML schema imported through `ws-import` command.

3. **Service Assembly**: BPEL module cannot be deployed directly to Sun Java System Application Server. Only composite applications or service assemblies having at least one JBI module can be deployed to the BPEL engine of the server. For the purpose of this sample, we'll create a Composite Application that has BPEL module deployed as JBI module. For more information on BPEL engine, JBI modules, and Service Assemblies, refer to Chapter 1.

 Our BPEL process communicates with the partner services through their public interfaces. These interfaces are defined in partner-specific WSDL files. When you drag-and-drop a partner service into a BPEL process, these interfaces are imported.

Note that our partner service implementation is minimal as it is of less interest to a BPEL developer. You can download the code and the DB scripts and work on an appropriate implementation.

The following business process diagram depicts our example:

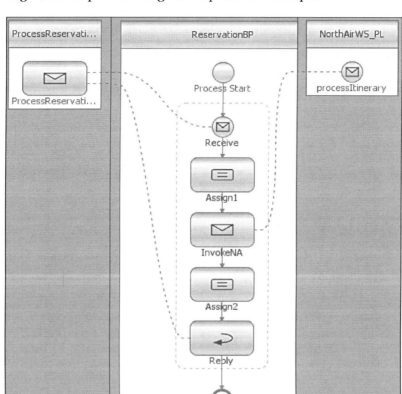

BPEL process is also a web service. Just like any other web service, BPEL process has a companion WSDL file that describes its public interfaces. This WSDL interface enumerates the operations and messages that clients can target in order to create an instance of the process.

BPEL processes are deployed to the BPEL runtime, which manages the process lifecycle. All BPEL processes start with receive or pick activity, which is responsible for initiating a process. When a **Receive** activity is invoked, BPEL runtime will create BPEL process instance and hand the message to the process instance for processing.

In the above figure, the BPEL process receives a request. To fulfill the request, it invokes the involved web service (NorthAirWS using the partner link NorthAirWS_PL) and finally responds to the original caller. Since the BPEL process communicates with another web service, it relies on the WSDL description of the web service (NorthAirWS WSDL) invoked by the process.

You now know how to create a web service from an EJB. Let us do that one more time. First we need to create an EJB project. **Select File | New Project**. Select an **EJB Module**.

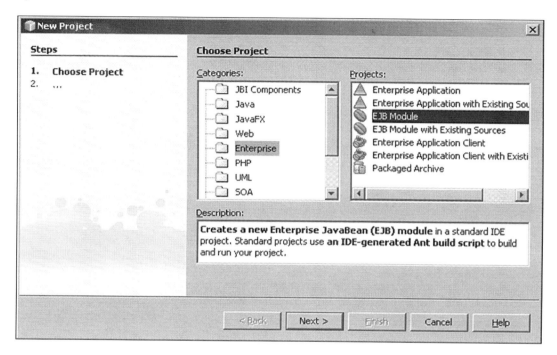

Give **NorthAirEJB** as the name for our new EJB project. You can either select **Glassfish V2** or Sun Java System Application Server as the target **Server**. You can't choose any other Java EE server you have already configured because we will be dependent on ESB components integrated with **Glassfish/Sun Java System** Application Server.

When you have the **NorthAirEJB** project ready, you have to create a Web Service (session bean) to consume requests. Right-click on **NorthAirEJB** and select **New | Web Service**.

Enter **NorthAirWS** as the name for our web service. Provide a valid **Package** name. You can either create a web service from scratch or use an existing session bean.

After creating the web service, add a web service operation in `NorthAirWS.java` as shown in the following code snippet:

```
@WebMethod(operationName = "processItinerary")
    public String processItinerary(@WebParam(name = "firstName")
    String firstName, @WebParam(name = "lastName")
```

```
String lastName, @WebParam(name = "source")
String source, @WebParam(name = "destination")
String destination, @WebParam(name = "travelDate")
String travelDate, @WebParam(name = "seatPreference")
String seatPreference, @WebParam(name = "foodPreference")
String foodPreference, @WebParam(name = "guestID")
String guestID, @WebParam(name = "seqID")
   int seqID) {
       //TODO write your implementation code here:
       return "Processed Reservation";
}
```

processItinerary operation receives itinerary information and sends a confirmation message back to the client. You can modify the code to add any specific reservation implementation. Right-click on **NorthAirEJB** module and select **Build** to compile the source file. Then right-click on **NorthAirEJB** and select **Undeploy** and **Deploy**. This action will deploy the web service in the target server.

The first section in this chapter showed you how to create a BPEL process from a BPEL module. Follow the steps to create a BPEL Process by name **ReservationBP**. This will create a ReservationBP.bpel file. You can either use the **Source** view or the **Design** view to edit the files. Create **Receive**, **Invoke**, and **Reply** activities as shown in the process diagram. Remember to assign variables using the BPEL mapper.

From the Source Code – Part A folder

Open NorthAirEJB, ReservationBPEL and AirAlliance_CA NetBeans project files and go through the code. When you open them for the first time, you will get a 'Resolve References' warning. You may need to set the correct target server for the EJB module and set the correct path to the **ReservationBPEL** jar file for the composite application. Also note ProcessReservation.wsdl. This WSDL is the Web Service that initiates the BPEL process. If you are making changes to the ReservationBP.bpel file in **ReservationBPEL** project, you need to update the JBI module again in this project. Right-click on this project and choose **Edit Application Configuration**.

You can see two WSDL ports configured with SOAP bindings.

Once you have the **BPEL** process ready, create a composite application as shown in the first section to act as a container for our **BPEL** process. Following is a simple composite application:

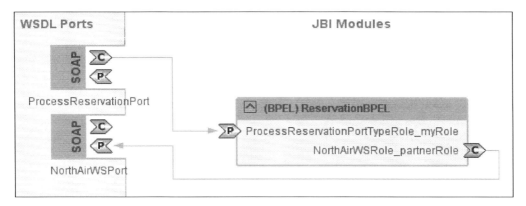

Note that our composite application has two **WSDL Ports**. Both are exposed through **SOAP** binding. This is because even though we have created an EJB, it is deployed as a web service. You can also try out the EJB binding component of OpenESB to directly invoke a session bean.

Testing Part A Source

Deploy the project AirAlliance_SA. In the AirAlliance_CA project, under **Test | TestReservation**, edit `input.xml` with some values. In the AirAlliance_CA project, execute the **TestReservation** test case under the **Test** folder. The `output.xml` under **Test | TestReservation** should be similar to the following output:

```xml
<?xml version="1.0" encoding="UTF-8"?>
<SOAP-ENV:Envelope xmlns:SOAP-ENV=
            "http://schemas.xmlsoap.org/soap/envelope/"
  xmlns:xsd="http://www.w3.org/2001/XMLSchema"
  xmlns:xsi="http://www.w3.org/2001/XMLSchema-instance"
  xsi:schemaLocation="http://schemas.xmlsoap.org/soap/envelope/
  http://schemas.xmlsoap.org/soap/envelope/">
  <SOAP-ENV:Body>
    <someNS:processItineraryResponse xmlns:someNS=
            "http://northair.airalliance.org/">
      <return xmlns:msgns="http://northair.airalliance.org/"
        xmlns:ns2=
            "http://northair.airalliance.org/" xmlns="">Processed
        Reservation</return>
    </someNS:processItineraryResponse>
  </SOAP-ENV:Body>
</SOAP-ENV:Envelope>
```

The TestReservation test case has been created for you. To create a test case, right-click and select **AirAlliance_CA | Test | New Test Case**. Provide a valid name for the **Test Case** and select the `ProcessItinerary.wsdl` document. That web service is the entry point to our BPEL process.

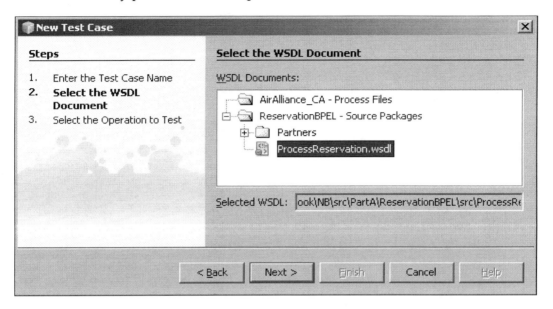

After selecting the web service, select the operation of the Web Service that we would like to test. In our case we have only one operation.

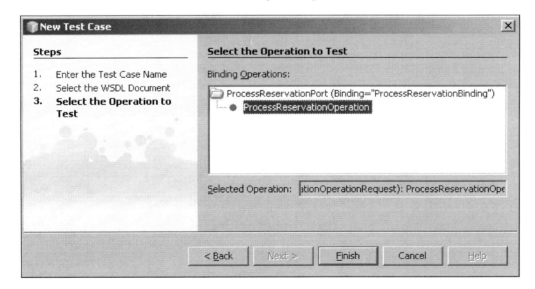

The first time you execute the test case; the test will fail as `output.xml` does not exist. Subsequent executions produce the response back from the NorthAir web service.

Part B – Using Multiple Partners

In the previous part of the example, there was only one partner service (NorthAir) that processed the itinerary requests. In this part, we will build another partner service SouthAir that can also process the request. But SouthAir is not a web service and our business process does not invoke any of SouthAir's web service. Instead, SouthAir DB is directly updated through JDBC binding component.

So whenever a request for reservation is made, the NorthAir web service is invoked and the itinerary data is updated in the SouthAir DB through the JDBC BC. This example shows you how you can use other binding components to perform non-web service calls. This is because all partner systems do not need to be based on web services. Part B source shows how you can use the JDBC BC to update Java DB from the BPEL process.

First, we will create the DB for SouthAir. While you can use any DB, this example shows how you can use Java DB that is well integrated with the NetBeans IDE. From the IDE, select **Tools | Java Database | Create Database**. Enter **SouthAirDB** as the **Database Name** and provide **User Name** and **Password**.

 If you are using the DB provided in the source code folder, set the correct path to the DB in **Database Location** field.

Create Java DB Database		
Database Name:	SouthAirDB	
User Name:	southair	
Password:	southair	
Database Location:	E:\work\AirAlliance\PartB	Settings...
	OK	Cancel

After creating the database, connect to the database by right-clicking on the **Databases** under the **Services** tab and selecting **Connect** as shown in the figure:

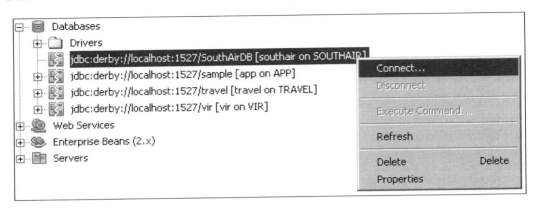

Now that our database is ready, right-click on **Tables** and select **Create Table**. The following figure shows the SouthAir database structure. This is just an example database structure. Real databases may not look like this.

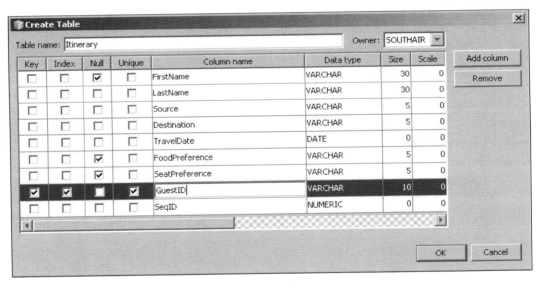

We will have some fields that match with the itinerary information that NorthAir Web Service expects.

Now SouthAirDB is ready with one table called **Itinerary** that the Reservation BPEL process updates. Unfortunately, SouthAir does not have a Web Service for our business process to interact with. So, we will create a web service that can perform the CRUD operation on SouthAir DB whenever a reservation request is made.

NetBeans provides a wizard to create a web service from a database table. The generated web service can perform the CRUD operation on the selected table. For this, right-click on **ReservationBPEL** project and select **New | Other** from the menu. In the **New File** wizard page, select **WSDL From Database** option as shown in the following screenshot:

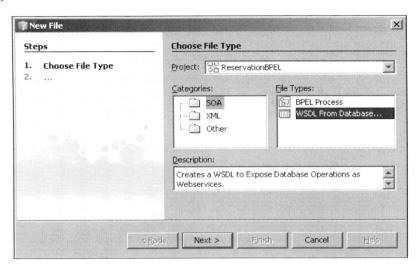

Enter the name of the WSDL.

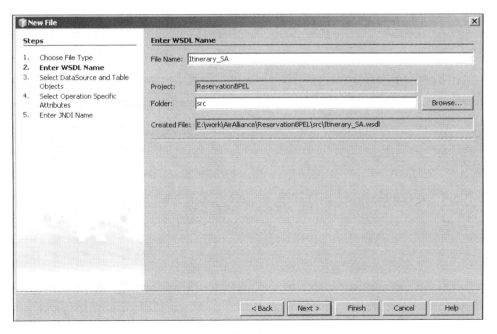

Select the **Data Source** for the wizard to connect to and retrieve the tables. Make sure that Java DB is running and you see the **ITINERARY** table. Add the table to **Selected Tables** list and click **Next**.

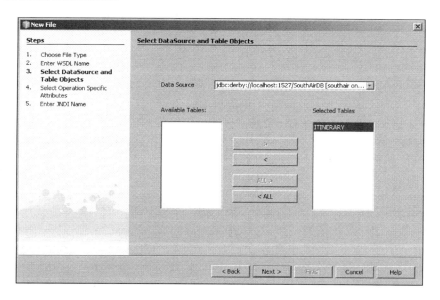

You have the option of selecting individual columns to update. Since ours is a sample, we will select all the columns to be updated.

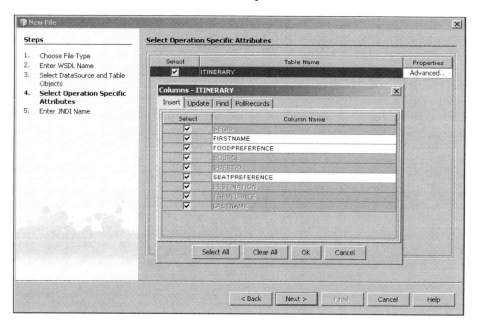

The next page will ask you about **JNDI Name** for a connection pooling that are configured to provide connections for the same database that you selected in the previous step. Type **jdbc/southair** as **JNDI Name**, we will configure **jdbc/southair** data source and the connection pooling later.

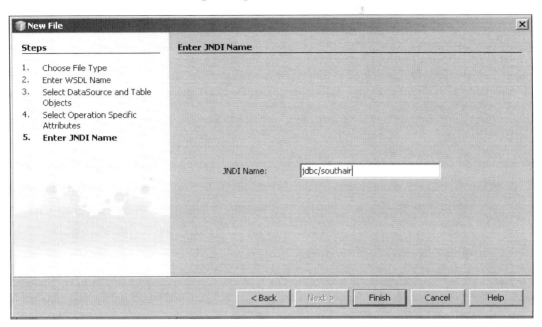

After completing the wizard, ITINERARY.xsd and Itinerary_SA.wsdl files are created automatically under ReservationBPEL project. The following is the code for ITINERARY.xsd:

```xml
<?xml version="1.0" encoding="UTF-8"?>
  <xsd:schema elementFormDefault="qualified" targetNamespace=
                        "http://j2ee.netbeans.org/xsd/tableSchema"
    xmlns="http://j2ee.netbeans.org/xsd/tableSchema"
    xmlns:xsd="http://www.w3.org/2001/XMLSchema">
    <xsd:element name="ITINERARY" type="ITINERARY">
    </xsd:element>
    <xsd:complexType name="ITINERARY">
      <xsd:sequence maxOccurs="unbounded">
        <xsd:element name="SEQID" type="xsd:decimal"></xsd:element>
        <xsd:element name="FIRSTNAME" type="xsd:string"></xsd:element>
        <xsd:element name="FOODPREFERENCE" type=
                                "xsd:string"></xsd:element>
        <xsd:element name="SOURCE" type="xsd:string"></xsd:element>
        <xsd:element name="GUESTID" type="xsd:string"></xsd:element>
```

```
            <xsd:element name="SEATPREFERENCE" type=
                                        "xsd:string"></xsd:element>
            <xsd:element name="DESTINATION" type=
                                        "xsd:string"></xsd:element>
            <xsd:element name="TRAVELDATE" type=
                                        "xsd:string"></xsd:element>
            <xsd:element name="LASTNAME" type="xsd:string"></xsd:element>
        </xsd:sequence>
    </xsd:complexType>
</xsd:schema>
```

Note that our itinerary table structure is grabbed in the schema. Now, we have a wrapper web service to update SouthAir database, but we still have not configured the JDBC resource. To create application server resources open **Services** window in IDE and expand **Servers** node and look for a green arrow near **GlassFish** server. If the green arrow is there, it means that your server is started, otherwise start the server by using the pop-up menu. After starting the server right-click on it and select **View Admin Console**. Login with your **Username** and **Password (admin/ adminadmin** by default) then from the left side navigation tree select **Resources | JDBC | Connection Pools**. When the connection pooling page is opened, click on the **New** button and fill in information as shown in the screenshot:

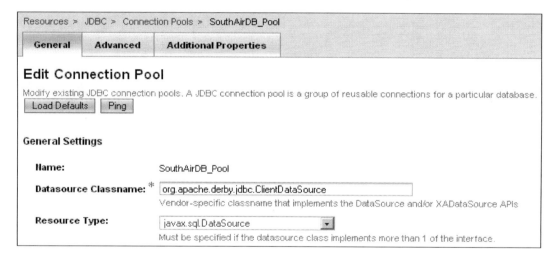

You need to add **Additional Properties** to the **Connection Pool**. Click on the **Additional Properties** tab and update the properties as shown in the screenshot. You can remove all the other properties from the table.

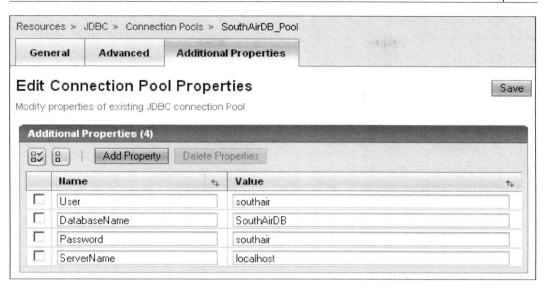

Edit Connection Pool Properties

Modify properties of existing JDBC connection Pool

Now, we have a **Connection Pool** ready to be used. Before we can use the pool, we need to define a **JNDI** entry for it. We know JNDI entry for connection pooling as data source. To define a data source for SouthAir, from the left tree navigate to **Resources | JDBC | JDBC Resources**. Click on the **New** button and enter **JNDI Name** as **jdbc/southair** and select the **Pool Name**.

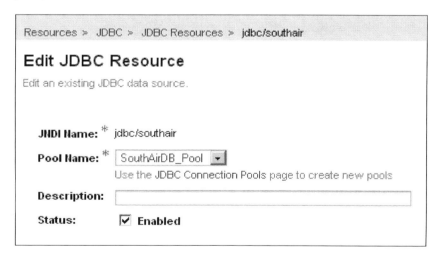

Restart the application server. Now, drag-and-drop `Itinerary_SA.wsdl` on top of the BPEL diagram. In the **Partner Link** property dialog box, enter UpdateSA_DB as the partner link name. Now, look at the following business process:

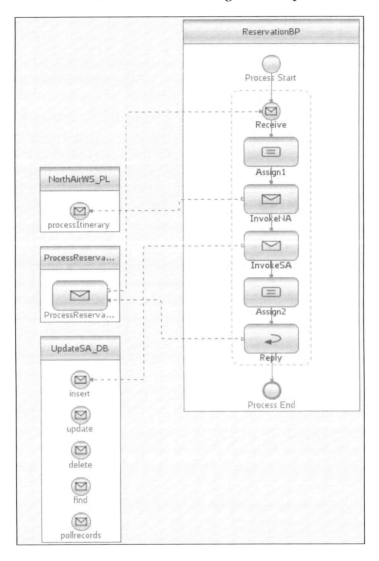

After invoking NorthAir Web Service, the itinerary information is updated in SouthAir DB through the wrapper partner service that we have created. Check out the `ReservationBP.bpel` source code in the Part B folder. For help on adding BPEL activities like **Invoke**, **Reply**, or **Assign** refer to the first section of this chapter and Chapter 5 on *BPEL Designer*.

From the Source Code – Part B folder

Open NorthAirEJB, ReservationBPEL and AirAlliance_CA NetBeans project files and go through the code. When you open them for the first time, you will get a 'Resolve References' warning. You may need to set the correct target server for the EJB module and set the correct path to the ReservationBPEL jar file for the composite application. Also note `ProcessReservation.wsdl`. This wsdl is the web service that initiates the BPEL process. If you are making changes to the `ReservationBP.bpel` file in ReservationBPEL project. If you are making changes, then you need to update the JBI module again in this project. Right-click this project and choose **Edit Application Configuration**.

You can see three WSDL ports are configured. Two ports use SOAP bindings and one port uses JDBC binding.

In NetBeans, drill down to **Services | Servers | Glassfish V[x] | JBI | Binding Components**. If you do not see **sun-jdbc-binding**, download the jar from:

```
http://download.java.net/jbi/binaries/open-jbi-components/main/
nightly/latest/ojc/
```

Then, right-click on **Services | Servers | Glassfish V[x] | JBI | Binding Components** and choose **Install New Binding Components** and select the BC jar that you downloaded from the above link.

Testing Part B Source

Deploy the project AirAlliance_CA. In the AirAlliance_CA project, under **Test | TestReservation**, edit `input.xml` with some values. In the AirAlliance_CA project, execute the **TestReservation** test case under **Test** folder

Now, check the **Itinerary** table of the SouthAirDB. Look how the DB is updated. Also check the `output.xml` file for the confirmation message from the NorthAir web service.

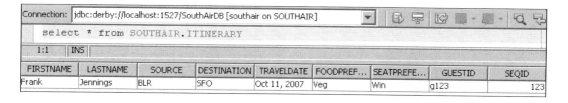

Connection:	jdbc:derby://localhost:1527/SouthAirDB [southair on SOUTHAIR]								

```
select * from SOUTHAIR.ITINERARY
```

| 1:1 | INS |

FIRSTNAME	LASTNAME	SOURCE	DESTINATION	TRAVELDATE	FOODPREF...	SEATPREFE...	GUESTID	SEQID
Frank	Jennings	BLR	SFO	Oct 11, 2007	Veg	Win	g123	123

This part introduced you to JDBC BC and showed how a BPEL process can invoke multiple web services as part of a single scope.

Part C – Writing to File

This part shows how you can use the File BC to store itinerary data in the file system. Whenever a request for reservation is made, the NorthAir web service is invoked and the itinerary data is updated in the SouthAir database. Also the itinerary information is updated in the file system using JBI file binding component. This file can be constantly monitored by an external process or an intelligent event processor shown in the later example.

File BC is a JBI BC that provides message processing capabilities over the Network File System (NFS). This component is designed to send and receive XML or text messages to or from the locally available file system. These functionalities also map to the roles file binding components play in a JBI environment—service provider and consumer, respectively. For instance, a file binding component can act as a service consumer by receiving itinerary data for logging purpose. It can also act as a service producer by providing inputs to a business process. File BC includes design-time and run-time components. The design-time component defines the set of WSDL extensions for file binding and artifacts that allow the extensions to be plugged into the NetBeans tooling system. The run-time component includes all necessary implementations and artifacts required by a JBI component.

File BC provides a set of WSDL extensions to allow a service to be bound to a file transport and thus, allows the messages to be processed by File BC. You need to download and install File BC, if you do not have it. Download File BC from `https://open-esb.dev.java.net/Components.html`.

Now, let us create a WSDL document with file binding and configure file system related properties. Create a **New WSDL Document**.

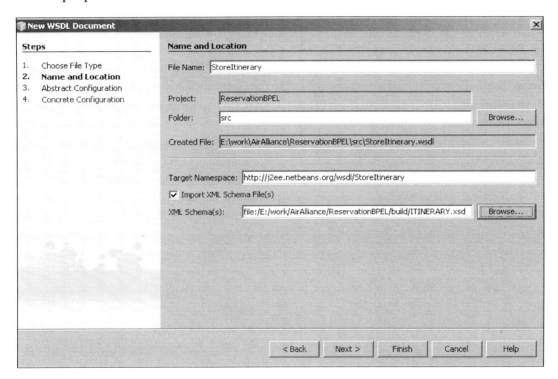

Make sure that you select a **One-way Operation,** as our BPEL process just wants to write guest itinerary information to a file and will not read from any file. In the input type, select the **ITINERARY** schema.

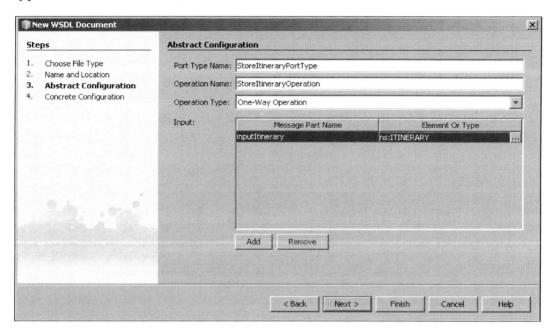

In the next screen you will need to select **File binding** as the type of binding. By default, the binding type will be **SOAP**. Now that your StoreItinerary.wsdl is ready, you need to make some changes to the WSDL as shown in the following code:

```
<?xml version="1.0" encoding="UTF-8"?>
<definitions name="StoreItinerary" targetNamespace=
                    "http://j2ee.netbeans.org/wsdl/StoreItinerary"
  xmlns="http://schemas.xmlsoap.org/wsdl/"
  xmlns:wsdl="http://schemas.xmlsoap.org/wsdl/"
  xmlns:xsd=http://www.w3.org/2001/XMLSchema
  xmlns:tns="http://j2ee.netbeans.org/wsdl/StoreItinerary"
  xmlns:ns="http://j2ee.netbeans.org/xsd/tableSchema"
  xmlns:plnk="http://docs.oasis-open.org/wsbpel/2.0/plnktype"
  xmlns:file="http://schemas.sun.com/jbi/wsdl-extensions/file/">
    <types>
      <xsd:schema targetNamespace=
                    "http://j2ee.netbeans.org/wsdl/StoreItinerary">
```

```
      <xsd:import namespace=
                       "http://j2ee.netbeans.org/xsd/tableSchema"
        schemaLocation="ITINERARY.xsd"/>
    </xsd:schema>
  </types>
  <message name="StoreItineraryOperationRequest">
    <part name="inputItinerary" element="ns:ITINERARY"/>
  </message>
  <portType name="StoreItineraryPortType">
    <operation name="StoreItineraryOperation">
      <input name="input1" message=
                          "tns:StoreItineraryOperationRequest"/>
    </operation>
  </portType>
  <binding name="StoreItineraryBinding" type=
                                    "tns:StoreItineraryPortType">
    <file:binding/>
      <operation name="StoreItineraryOperation">
    <file:operation/>
      <input name="input1">
        <file:message use="literal" fileName="GuestItinerary.xml"
          pollingInterval="1000" fileType="text" addEOL="true"
          multipleRecordsPerFile="true" recordDelimiter="\r\n"/>
      </input>
    </operation>
  </binding>
  <service name="StoreItineraryService">
    <port name="StoreItineraryPort" binding=
                                  "tns:StoreItineraryBinding">
      <file:address fileDirectory="/aademo_store"
                                          lockName="filebc.lck"
        workArea="filebc_tmp" seqName="filebc.seq"/>
    </port>
  </service>
  <plnk:partnerLinkType name="StoreItinerary1">
      <plnk:role name="StoreItineraryPortTypeRole"
        portType="tns:StoreItineraryPortType"/>
  </plnk:partnerLinkType>
</definitions>
```

Note that we have made changes to the WSDL specifying file name and directory information. Make sure that you have write permission to the directory specified. In our example, we need to have write permission to the /aademo_store directory. Now, drag-and-drop `StorItinerary.wsdl` into your BPEL diagram to create a **Partner Link**.

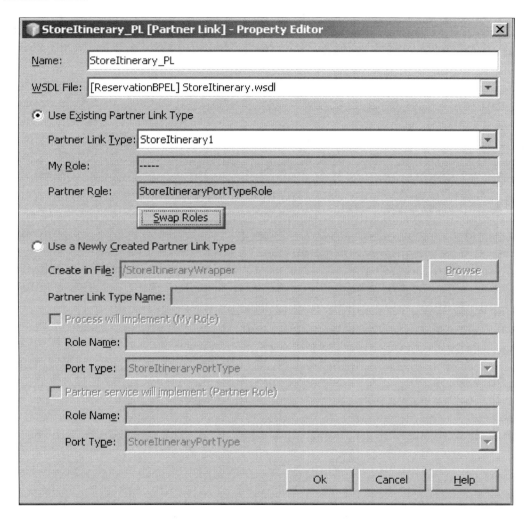

In the **Partner Link - Property Editor**, make sure that the **Partner Role** is **StoreItineraryPortTypeRole**. If **My Role** shows as **StoreItineraryPortTypeRole**, click the **Swap Roles** button. This is because the partner or the binding component takes care of storing itinerary and not the BPEL process.

Now take a look at our BPEL process:

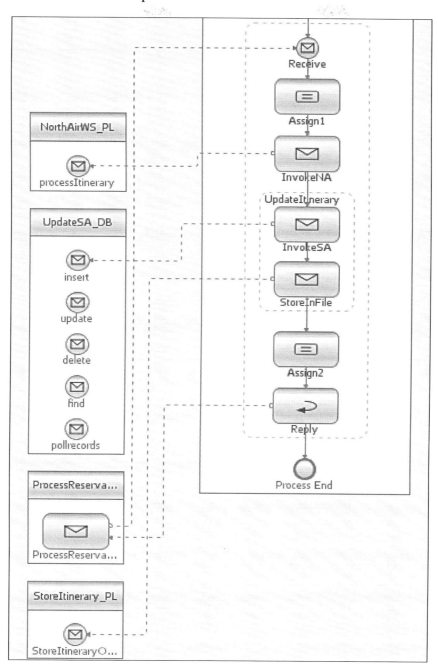

It is one sequential synchronous BPEL process. Build the BPEL module and deploy to a composite application as explained in the first section of this chapter. Now, our composite application looks like this with one additional **FILE** WSDL port:

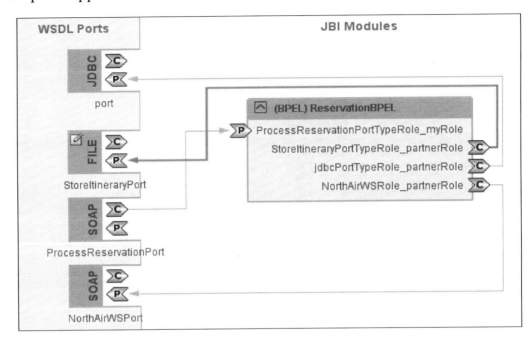

From the Source Code – Part C folder

Open NorthAirEJB, ReservationBPEL and AirAlliance_CA NetBeans project files and go through the code. When you open them for the first time, you will get a 'Resolve References' warning. You may need to set the correct target server for the EJB module and set the correct path to the ReservationBPEL jar file for the composite application. Also note `ProcessReservation.wsdl`. This wsdl is the web service that initiates the BPEL process. If you are making changes to the `ReservationBP.bpel` file in ReservationBPEL project, then you need to update the JBI module again in this project. Right-click this project and choose Edit Application Configuration.

You can see four WSDL ports are configured. Two ports use SOAP bindings, one port uses JDBC binding and one port uses File binding.

In NetBeans, drill down to **Services | Servers | Glassfish V[x] | JBI |Binding Components**. If you do not see **sun-file-binding**, download the jar from:

```
http://download.java.net/jbi/binaries/open-jbi-components/main/
nightly/latest/ojc/
```

Then right-click on **Services | Servers | Glassfish V[x] | JBI |Binding Components** and choose **Install New Binding Components** and select the binding component jar that you downloaded from the above link.

Testing Part C Source

Deploy the project AirAlliance_CA. In the AirAlliance_CA project, under **Test | TestReservation**, edit `input.xml` with some values. In the AirAlliance_CA project, execute the **TestReservation** test case under the **Test** folder.

Now, check the Itinerary table of SouthAirDB. Look how the DB is updated. Also check the `output.xml` file for the confirmation message from NorthAir web service. Additionally, check if the guest information is written to the file specified in the `StoreItinerary.wsdl` file.

Part D – Sending JMS Messages

So far, the BPEL process interacted with two different partner systems. The first system was an EJB, deployed as a web service. The second system was a wrapper service that performed CRUD operations on a partner DB. This part of the example shows how the BPEL process sends messages to EastAir's JMS Queue. The BPEL process sends Itinerary data to EastAir's JMS Queue. EastAir's JMS Queue Listener can get the itinerary information for further processing.

In the same way we created `StoreItinerary.wsdl`, create another WSDL file called `SendItinerary.wsdl` of type JMS binding. Make changes to the WSDL in order to specify connection information. Consider the following code:

```xml
<?xml version="1.0" encoding="UTF-8"?>
<definitions name="SendItinerary"
  targetNamespace="http://j2ee.netbeans.org/wsdl/SendItinerary"
  xmlns="http://schemas.xmlsoap.org/wsdl/"
  xmlns:wsdl="http://schemas.xmlsoap.org/wsdl/"
  xmlns:xsd="http://www.w3.org/2001/XMLSchema"
  xmlns:tns="http://j2ee.netbeans.org/wsdl/SendItinerary"
  xmlns:ns="http://j2ee.netbeans.org/xsd/tableSchema"
  xmlns:plnk="http://docs.oasis-open.org/wsbpel/2.0/plnktype"
  xmlns:jms="http://schemas.sun.com/jbi/wsdl-extensions/jms/">
```

```
<types>
  <xsd:schema targetNamespace=
                "http://j2ee.netbeans.org/wsdl/SendItinerary">
    <xsd:import namespace=
                "http://j2ee.netbeans.org/xsd/tableSchema"
        schemaLocation="ITINERARY.xsd"/>
  </xsd:schema>
</types>
<message name="SendItineraryOperationRequest">
  <part name="inputItinerary" element="ns:ITINERARY"/>
</message>
<portType name="SendItineraryPortType">
  <operation name="SendItineraryOperation">
    <input name="input1" message=
                        "tns:SendItineraryOperationRequest"/>
  </operation>
</portType>
<binding name="SendItineraryBinding" type=
                        "tns:SendItineraryPortType">
  <jms:binding/>
  <operation name="SendItineraryOperation">
    <jms:operation destination=
                        "EastAirQueue" destinationType="Queue"/>
    <input name="input1">
      <jms:message messageType=
                        "TextMessage" textPart="inputItinerary"/>
    </input>
  </operation>
</binding>
<service name="SendItineraryService">
  <port name="SendItineraryPort" binding=
                        "tns:SendItineraryBinding">
  <jms:address connectionURL=
                        "mq://localhost:7676" username="admin"
    password="admin"/>
  </port>
</service>
<plnk:partnerLinkType name="SendItinerary1">
  <plnk:role name="SendItineraryPortTypeRole"
    portType="tns:SendItineraryPortType"/>
</plnk:partnerLinkType>
</definitions>
```

For JMS Destination, we have mentioned the `EastAirQueue`. For the purpose of this demo, do not worry if the Queue does not exist. It will be automatically created. Just make sure GlassFish Application Server is running. Look at our new BPEL process:

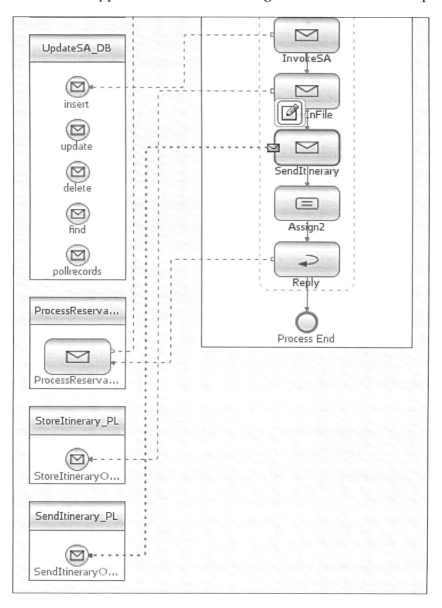

Configure the invoke activity of **SendItinerary** by double clicking on it. Create the variables as described in the previous section. While configuring the partner link, make sure that you click Swap Roles for the one way WSDL operation as shown in the earlier part. Build the BPEL module and add it to a composite application as described in the first section of this chapter. Our composite application now has five WSDL ports with an additional JMS port.

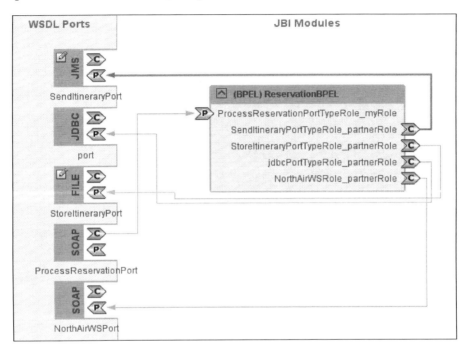

From the Source Code – Part D folder

Open NorthAirEJB, ReservationBPEL, and AirAlliance_CA NetBeans project files and go through the code. When you open them for the first time, you will get a 'Resolve References' warning. You may need to set the correct target server for the EJB module and set the correct path to the ReservationBPEL jar file for the composite application. Also note `ProcessReservation.wsdl`. This wsdl is the web service that initiates the BPEL process. If you are making changes to the `ReservationBP.bpel` file in ReservationBPEL project, then you need to update the JBI module again in this project. Right-click this project and choose Edit Application Configuration.

You can see five WSDL ports are configured. Two ports use SOAP bindings and one port uses JDBC binding, one port uses File binding and one port uses JMS binding.

In NetBeans, drill down to **Services | Servers | Glassfish V[x] | JBI |Binding Components**. If you do not see **sun-jms-binding**, download the jar from:

```
http://download.java.net/jbi/binaries/open-jbi-components/main/
nightly/latest/ojc/
```

Then right-click on **Services | Servers | Glassfish V[x] | JBI |Binding Components** and choose **Install New Binding Components** and select the binding component jar that you downloaded from the above link.

Testing Part D Source

Deploy the project AirAlliance_CA. In the AirAlliance_CA project, under **Test | TestReservation**, edit `Input.xml` with some values. In the AirAlliance_CA project, execute the **TestReservation** test case under the **Test** folder

Now, check the **Itinerary** table of the SouthAirDB. Look how the DB is updated. Also check the `Output.xml` file for the confirmation message from NorthAir Web Service. Check if the guest information is written to the file specified in `StoreItinerary.wsdl`. Now, go to the **Admin Console** of GlassFish Application Server and drill down to **Configuration | Java Message Service | Physical Destinations**. Check if **EastAirQueue** Destination is added.

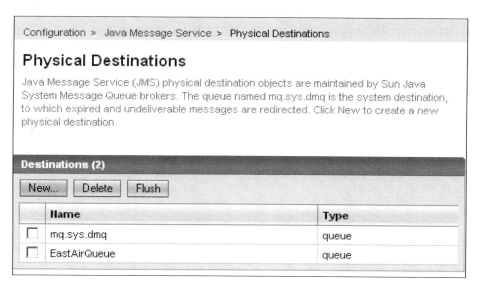

All this is achieved through JMS BC. In case of outbound message flow, where the JMS BC is being invoked by our business process, the JMS BC acts as an external JMS service provider. In this role, the JMS BC converts a normalized message that it receives as part of the message exchange from our process, to a JMS message. After the JMS message is created as a result of the message conversion, the JMS message is sent to JMS destination.

```
Successfully denormalized the NMR message to JMS message
Successfully sent JMS message to destination EastAirQueue on connection mq://localhost:7676
Set message exchange status to DONE for message exchange ID 119204025565443-56964-134150531951250004
Finished processing message exchange ID 119204025565443-56964-134150531951250004
Pattern for exchange Id 119204025565443-56964-134150531951250004 is http://www.w3.org/2004/08/wsdl/in-only
Sending Reply for MessageEx id 119204025565443-56964-134150531933590256
Pattern for exchange Id 119204025565443-56964-134150531933590256 is http://www.w3.org/2004/08/wsdl/in-out
```

The above screenshot shows the NetBeans output when the BPEL process is executed. The NMR message is converted into a valid JMS to send to the queue.

Part E – Conditions and Sequence

This part introduces the sequencing and branching properties of BPEL. When a request for a reservation is made, the BPEL process checks the destination sector. If the destination is set to 'SFO', then the itinerary is routed to NorthAirWS, otherwise the itinerary is sent to WestAir Web Service. Since WestAir Web Service is new, we create an identical web service using NorthAir Web Service and name it WestAir Web Service. They do not do any actual itinerary processing but they send a confirmation message back to the client so we can find out which airlines' web service was invoked.

So far through the earlier parts of this example, we have created a sequential process to invoke NorthAir Web Service. This process consists of storing and sending itineraries to a JMS physical destination. Ideally, updating the partner airlines repository is independent of itinerary processing. Despite of failed reservations, we update the data store for the purpose of a waiting list (Of course without a confirmed reservation ID).

UpdateItinerary sequence is introduced as a flow branch to process itinerary branch, so both the sequences work in parallel. This part also shows how as part of the UpdateAirlines sequence, we send the itinerary information to a travel agent's FTP Server. Uploading itinerary information to an FTP server is done through an FTP binding component.

Whenever a request for reservation is made, the NorthAir Web Service is invoked and the itinerary data is updated in the SouthAir database. Also, the itinerary information is updated in the file system using the JBI file binding component. This file can be constantly monitored by an external process. Now the itinerary data is sent to EastAir's JMS Queue. EastAir's JMS Queue Listener can get the itinerary information for further processing. The BPEL process also uploads the guest itinerary to a remote FTP server of a travel agent or any AirAlliance partner.

Let us create another web service WestAir_WS just like we created NorthAir_WS. Create an EJB module and create a web service from that module. Drag-and-drop WestAir_WS on the BPEL diagram to create the partner link.

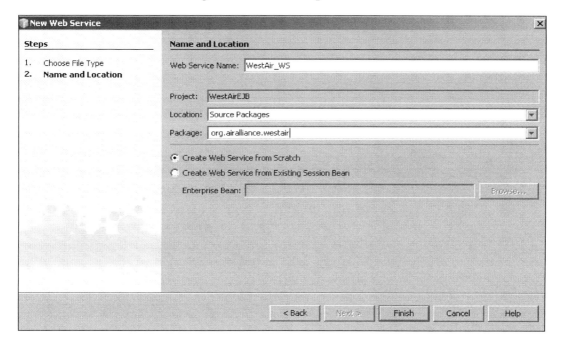

To make our example simple, let us have the same web service operation as NorthAir Web Service.

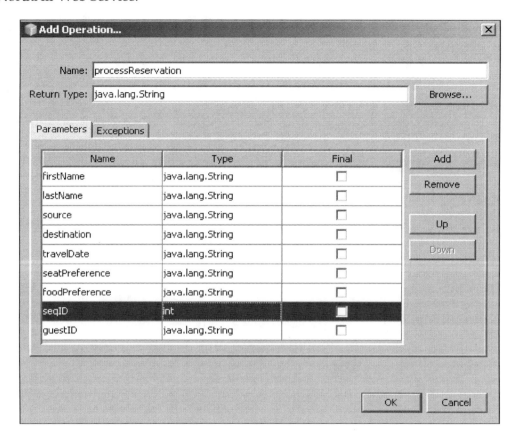

Add an If activity to the BPEL diagram and set a condition as shown in the following screenshot. In our case, the condition returns true if the destination sector matches **'SFO'**. If you are comfortable using the BPEL mapper add **Equal** operator as shown. For information on using BPEL Mapper, refer to Chapter 5 on *BPEL Designer*.

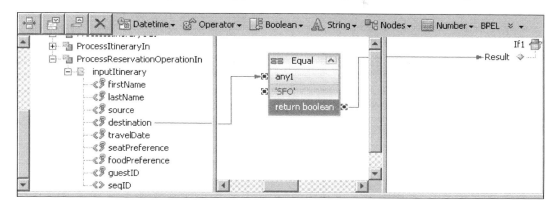

Or you can manually set the condition as shown in the following screenshot:

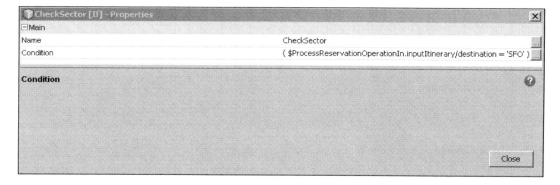

Drag-and-drop Invoke calls of both NorthAir Web Service and WestAir Web Service into the appropriate branches as shown in the following figure.

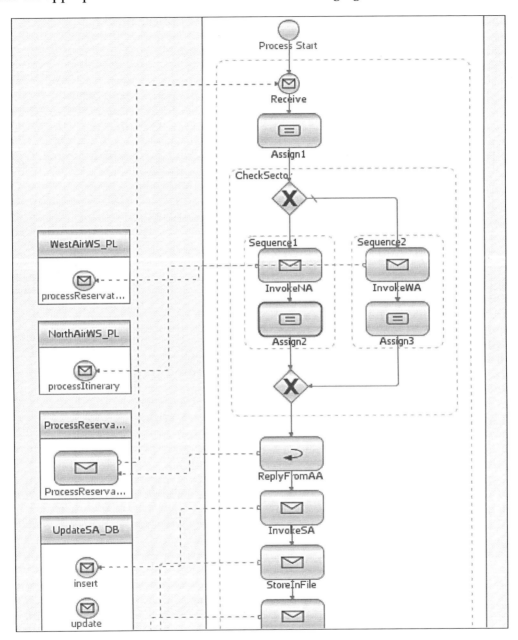

So, whenever the guest itinerary has its destination sector as 'SFO', NorthAir WS is invoked. Otherwise WestAir WS is invoked. Now, updating the SouthAir DB, storing the itinerary and sending a JMS message can happen in flow with the sector check. So, add a BPEL flow activity and drag-and-drop **InvokeSA**, **StoreInFile**, and **SendItinerary** invoke blocks to the secondary branch of the flow. Drag-and-drop the check sector block to the primary branch of the flow. Now, irrespective of who processes the request, all partner systems are updated.

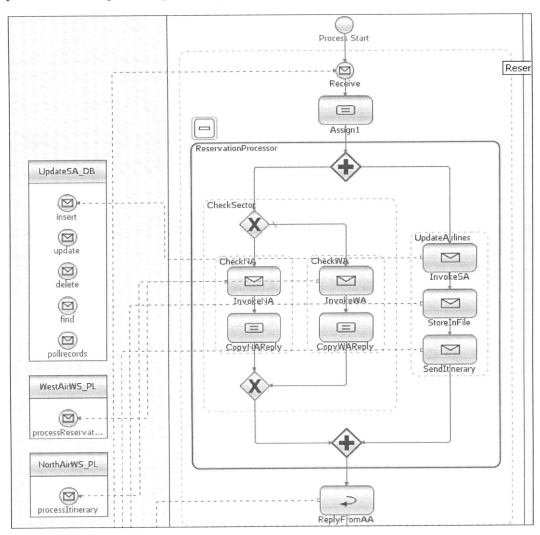

In the secondary flow branch, let us add one more invoke call that uploads the guest itinerary to a partner FTP server for further processing. For this you need to create one more WSDL file of name `UploadItinerary.wsdl`. Follow the same steps you have learnt for creating `SendItinerary.wsdl` but select FTP binding as the binding type. Now let us take a look at `UploadItinerary.wsdl`:

```xml
<?xml version="1.0" encoding="UTF-8"?>
<definitions name="UploadItinerary" targetNamespace=
                    "http://j2ee.netbeans.org/wsdl/UploadItinerary"
  xmlns="http://schemas.xmlsoap.org/wsdl/"
  xmlns:wsdl="http://schemas.xmlsoap.org/wsdl/"
  xmlns:xsd="http://www.w3.org/2001/XMLSchema"
  xmlns:tns="http://j2ee.netbeans.org/wsdl/UploadItinerary"
  xmlns:ns="http://j2ee.netbeans.org/xsd/tableSchema"
  xmlns:plnk="http://docs.oasis-open.org/wsbpel/2.0/plnktype"
  xmlns:ftp="http://schemas.sun.com/jbi/wsdl-extensions/ftp/">
  <types>
    <xsd:schema targetNamespace=
                    "http://j2ee.netbeans.org/wsdl/UploadItinerary">
      <xsd:import namespace=
                    "http://j2ee.netbeans.org/xsd/tableSchema"
        schemaLocation="ITINERARY.xsd"/>
    </xsd:schema>
  </types>
  <message name="UploadItineraryOperationRequest">
    <part name="inputItinerary" element="ns:ITINERARY"/>
  </message>
  <portType name="UploadItineraryPortType">
    <operation name="UploadItineraryOperation">
      <input name="input1" message=
                        "tns:UploadItineraryOperationRequest"/>
    </operation>
  </portType>
  <binding name="UploadItineraryBinding" type=
                        "tns:UploadItineraryPortType">
    <ftp:binding/>
    <operation name="UploadItineraryOperation">
        <ftp:operation/>
        <input name="input1">
          <ftp:message messageName="" messageNamePrefixIB=""
            messageNamePrefixOB=
                        "" pollIntervalMillis="5000" archive="true"
              protect="true" stage="true" use="literal"
                        encodingStyle="" messageCorrelate="true"
                        messageRepository="itinerary"/>
        </input>
    </operation>
  </binding>
  <service name="UploadItineraryService">
```

```
    <port name="UploadItineraryPort" binding=
                                "tns:UploadItineraryBinding">
      <ftp:address url=
            "ftp://userftp:userftp@localhost:21" dirListStyle="UNIX"
          useUserDefinedHeuristics="false" userDefDirListStyle=""
          userDefDirListHeuristics="" cmdChannelTimeout="45000"
          dataChannelTimeout="45000"/>
      </port>
    </service>
    <plnk:partnerLinkType name="UploadItinerary1">
      <plnk:role name="UploadItineraryPortTypeRole"
        portType="tns:UploadItineraryPortType"/>
    </plnk:partnerLinkType>
  </definitions>
```

As usual make changes to the binding and service parts of the WSDL document to provide your FTP server information. If you want to run this sample, set up an FTP server or provide a URL to an existing FTP server.

Now, drag-and-drop `UploadItinerary.wsdl` on BPEL diagram to create a partner link. Just as explained in the previous sections, swap roles if necessary.

Now our BPEL process diagram looks like this:

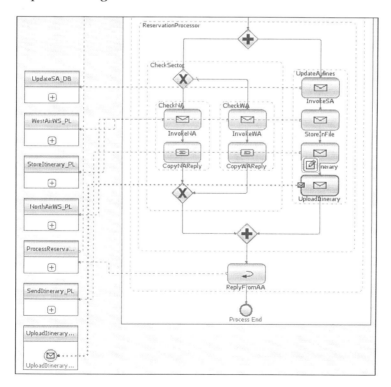

Now our composite application looks like the following figure. Note that the FTP WSDL port is highlighted.

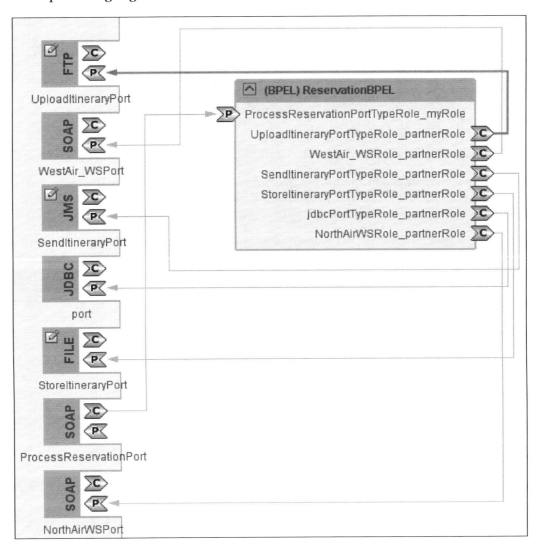

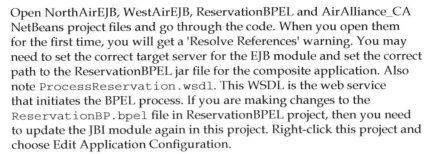

From the Source Code – Part E folder

Open NorthAirEJB, WestAirEJB, ReservationBPEL and AirAlliance_CA NetBeans project files and go through the code. When you open them for the first time, you will get a 'Resolve References' warning. You may need to set the correct target server for the EJB module and set the correct path to the ReservationBPEL jar file for the composite application. Also note `ProcessReservation.wsdl`. This WSDL is the web service that initiates the BPEL process. If you are making changes to the `ReservationBP.bpel` file in ReservationBPEL project, then you need to update the JBI module again in this project. Right-click this project and choose Edit Application Configuration.

You can see seven WSDL ports are configured. Three ports use SOAP bindings, one port uses JDBC binding, one port uses File binding, one port uses JMS binding and one port uses FTP binding.

In NetBeans, drill down to **Services | Servers | Glassfish V[x] | JBI | Binding Components**. If you do not see **sun-ftp-binding**, download the jar from:

```
http://download.java.net/jbi/binaries/open-jbi-components/main/
nightly/latest/ojc/
```

Then right-click on **Services | Servers | Glassfish V[x] | JBI | Binding Components** and choose **Install New Binding Components** and select the binding component jar that you downloaded from the above link.

Testing Part E Source

Deploy the project AirAlliance_CA. In the AirAlliance_CA project, under **Test | TestReservation**, edit `input.xml` with some values. In the AirAlliance_CA project, execute the **TestReservation** test case under the **Test** folder

Now, check the Itinerary table of SouthAirDB. Look how the DB is updated. Also, check the `output.xml` file for the confirmation message from NorthAir web service. Check if the guest information is written to the file specified in `StoreItinerary.wsdl` file. Now, go to the **Admin Console** of GlassFish Application Server and drill down to **Configuration | Java Message Service | Physical Destinations**. Check if **EastAirQueue** Destination is added. Additionally, check if the guest itinerary is uploaded to the FTP server.

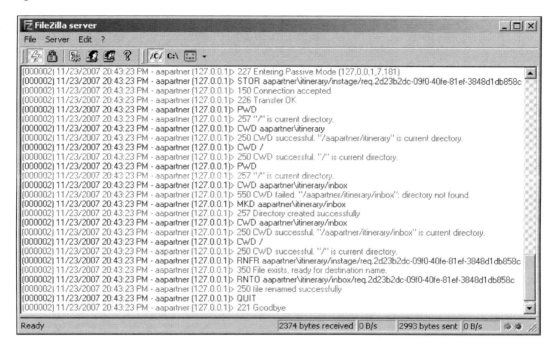

Part F – Sending Mails

The reservation process is updated to perform pre-processing before invoking the partner services. This will be useful later to build your own validation rules before invoking the partner services. AAPreProcessor Web Service performs a check on the sectors and sends a reply back to the process stating if the reservation could be processed. For this example, all reservation requests from 'BLR' to "SFO" are rejected and auto responder is sent to a predefined e-mail address.

The pre-processing also includes checking if the source and destination sectors are same before invoking the expensive partner services query operations. You should have more of these checks in your real applications.

For this purpose, we create another web service AAPreProcessor Web Service that performs the check. Create an EJB module AAPreProcessor_EJB and create a web service with just one operation. See the following code:

```
@WebMethod(operationName = "areSectorsAvailable")
  public boolean areSectorsAvailable(@WebParam(name = "source")
    String source, @WebParam(name = "destination")
    String destination)
    {
        if(source.equals("BLR") && destination.equals("SFO")){
            return false;
        }
            return true;
    }
```

It returns `true` if a particular source-destination condition is met.

The pre-processor sets a variable `AreSectorsAvailableOut` if the sectors are not available. Add an `If` activity with the following condition:

```
( $AreSectorsAvailableOut.parameters/return = false() )
```

Based on the above condition, we send auto notification mail. For this you need to install SMTP binding component.

Create `MailResponder.wsdl` file just like you created `StoreItinerary.wsdl` but select the binding type as SMTP. Now, make changes to `StoreItinerary.wsdl` to add SMTP server related information shown as follows:

```
<?xml version="1.0" encoding="UTF-8"?>
<definitions name="MailResponder" targetNamespace=
                        "http://j2ee.netbeans.org/wsdl/MailResponder"
  xmlns="http://schemas.xmlsoap.org/wsdl/"
  xmlns:wsdl="http://schemas.xmlsoap.org/wsdl/"
  xmlns:xsd="http://www.w3.org/2001/XMLSchema"
  xmlns:tns="http://j2ee.netbeans.org/wsdl/MailResponder"
  xmlns:plnk="http://docs.oasis-open.org/wsbpel/2.0/plnktype"
  xmlns:smtp="http://schemas.sun.com/jbi/wsdl-extensions/smtp/">
    <types/>
    <message name="MailResponderOperationRequest">
      <part name="bodyPart" type="xsd:string"/>
      <part name="fromPart" type="xsd:string"/>
      <part name="subjectPart" type="xsd:string"/>
    </message>
    <portType name="MailResponderPortType">
      <operation name="MailResponderOperation">
        <input name="input1" message=
                        "tns:MailResponderOperationRequest"/>
      </operation>
    </portType>
```

```
<binding name="MailResponderBinding" type=
                             "tns:MailResponderPortType">
  <smtp:binding/>
  <operation name="MailResponderOperation">
    <smtp:operation/>
    <input name="input1">
      <smtp:input message="bodyPart" subject="subjectPart"
                                        from="fromPart"/>
    </input>
  </operation>
</binding>
<service name="MailResponderService">
  <port name="MailResponderPort" binding="tns:MailResponderBinding">
    <smtp:address location="mailto:frank@jennings.in"
                  smtpserver="jennings.in" useSSL="false"
                  username="frank@jennings.in"
                  password="************"/>
  </port>
</service>
<plnk:partnerLinkType name="MailResponder1">
  <plnk:role name="MailResponderPortTypeRole"
    portType="tns:MailResponderPortType"/>
</plnk:partnerLinkType>
</definitions>
```

After creating the WSDL document, drag-and-drop `MailResponder.wsdl` on
your BPEL diagram to create the partner link. This is how your BPEL diagram will
look now:

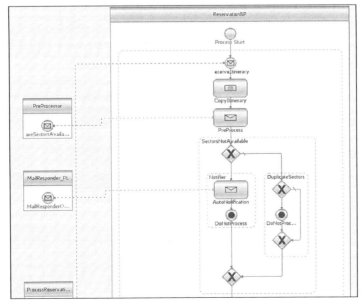

Now, if you check our sample composite application, it will look like the following figure:

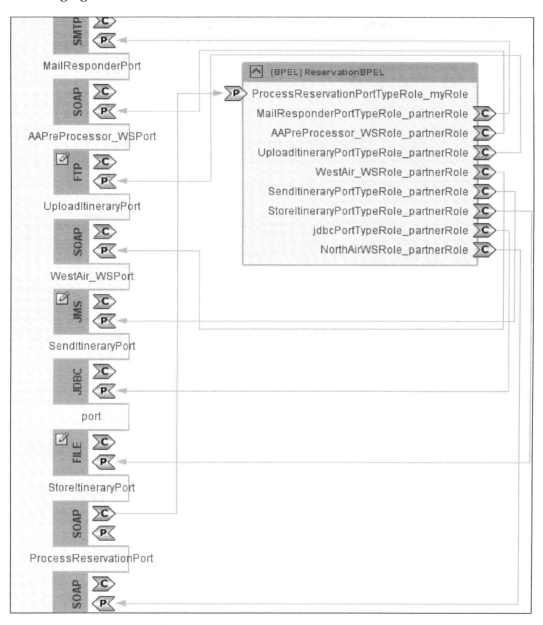

From the Source Code – Part F folder

Open NorthAirEJB, WestAirEJB, AAPreProcessorEJB, ReservationBPEL and AirAlliance_CA NetBeans project files and go through the code. When you open them for the first time, you will get a 'Resolve References' warning. You may need to set the correct target server for the EJB module and set the correct path to the ReservationBPEL jar file for the composite application. Also note `ProcessReservation.wsdl`. This WSDL is the web service that initiates the BPEL process. If you are making changes to the `ReservationBP.bpel` file in ReservationBPEL project, then you need to update the JBI module again in this project. Right-click this project and choose Edit Application Configuration.

You can see nine WSDL ports are configured. four ports use SOAP bindings, one port uses JDBC binding, one port uses File binding, one port uses JMS binding, one port uses FTP binding and one port uses SMTP binding.

In NetBeans, drill down to **Services | Servers | Glassfish V[x] | JBI | Binding Components**. If you do not see **sun-smtp-binding**, download the jar from:

```
http://download.java.net/jbi/binaries/open-jbi-components/main/
nightly/latest/ojc/
```

Then right-click on **Services | Servers | Glassfish V[x] | JBI | Binding Components** and choose **Install New Binding Components** and select the binding jar that you downloaded from the above link.

Testing Part F Source

Deploy project the **AirAlliance_CA**. In the **AirAlliance_CA** project, under **Test | TestReservation**, edit `input.xml` with some values. In the **AirAlliance_CA** project, execute the **TestReservation** test case under the **Test** folder

Now check the Itinerary table of SouthAirDB. Look how the DB is updated. Also check the `output.xml` file for the confirmation message from NorthAir Web Service. Check if the guest information is written to the file specified in `StoreItinerary.wsdl`. Now go to the Admin Console of GlassFish Application Server and drill down to **Configuration | Java Message Service | Physical Destinations**. Check if **EastAirQueue** Destination is added. Additionally check if the guest itinerary is uploaded to the FTP server.

If you enter the source as 'BLR' in `input.xml` and destination as 'SFO', then the process fails to proceed and mail will be sent to a configured Email address. Also if you have the same values for source and destination, the process stops processing the itinerary. Check if you get the reservation confirmation from NorthAir WS and if the destination is 'SFO'. If the destination is not 'SFO' the reservation confirmation comes from WestAir WS.

●	AirAlliance Auto Responder	●	postmaster@airalliance.org	●	7:48 PM

⊟	**Subject:**	**AirAlliance Auto Responder**
	From:	postmaster@airalliance.org
	Date:	7:48 PM
	To:	frank@jennings.in

```
Reservation on Hold
```

The above example shows how notification messages can be sent to partners through SMTP BC.

Part G – Event Processing

This part shows you how you can process your data stream to do some intelligent pre-processing before performing any meaningful action on the data. In the previous parts, you used a File BC to create an XML file that contained the itinerary data.

This itinerary data can be converted into a stream and can be passed through Intelligent Event Processors to project or filter the stream or to restrict the itinerary count. This part contains one intelligent event processor that does the following:

1. Processes all itineraries obtained from the stream for the last 3 seconds.
2. Uses the stream filter to remove itinerary preferences data to make the itinerary data set smaller.
3. Contiguous ordering of itinerary data.
4. Stores the filtered itinerary record in database.

Make sure that you have started the IEP service engine. Refer to the chapter on IEP for more information.

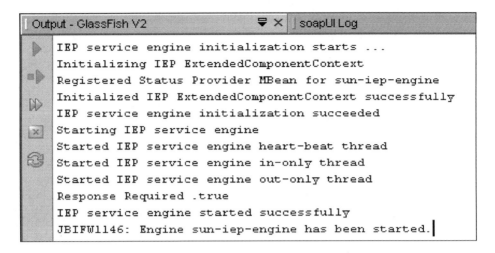

For this example, we will be creating an IEP NetBeans module and a single event processor.

From the Source Code – Part E folder

ItineraryIEP - Intelligent Event Processor NetBeans Project that contains 1 event processor by name ItineraryProcessorIEP.iep.
AirAlliance_CA – Composite application that deploys the IEP module.
TestItineraryIEP – NetBeans standalone Java application to test the event processor.

On your IEP workspace, drag-and-drop the following operators and connect them sequentially.

1. Stream Input (Input Operator)
2. Time Based Window (Stream Converter)
3. Insert Stream (Relation Converter)
4. Stream Projection and Filter (Correlation and Filter)
5. Contiguous Order (Sequence Operator)
6. Partitioned Window (Stream Converter)
7. Table Output (Table Operator)

The following figure shows how they are connected sequentially.

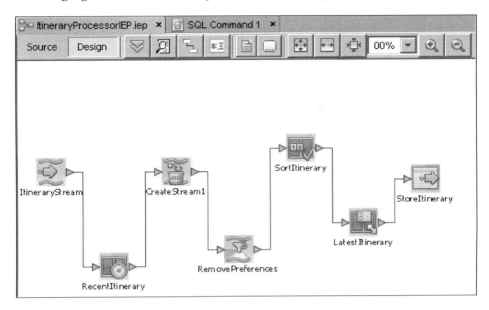

Configure the IEP to read guest itinerary information from the input stream. Specify the itinerary fields as attributes in the **Stream Input Property Editor**.

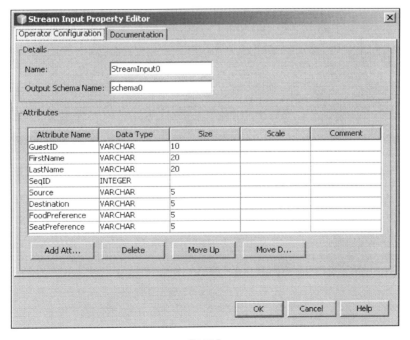

Now, we will let the IEP process only the itineraries received for the last three seconds in the stream. Double-click the **Time Based Window Property Editor** and specify the **Size** as **3** and select second from the drop-down box. Note that since you have already connected the operators, the Attributes are automatically populated from the input stream.

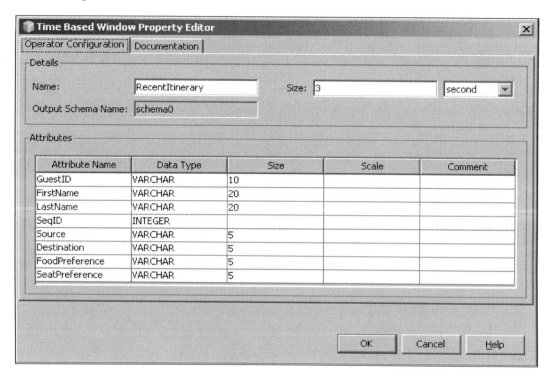

Now, if you notice the stream that we are processing also includes guest preferences like Food and Seat preference. If for some reason we want to ignore the preferences and process only the core itinerary attributes, we need to ignore these preferences. For this, we will be using the Stream Projection and Filter operator. Double-click the **Stream Projection and Filter Property Editor** and add all the attributes except **FoodPreference** and **SeatPreference**.

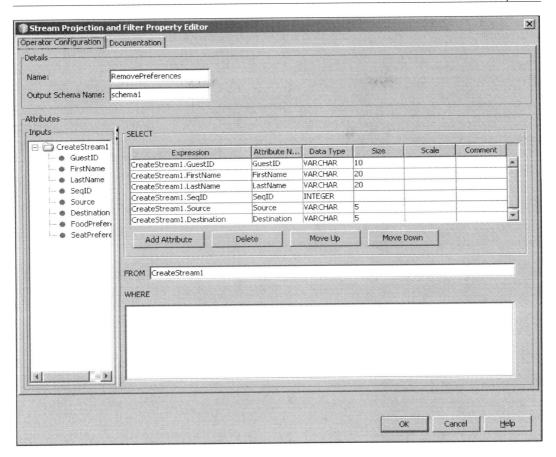

Now, we pass the stream to the Contiguous order operator to sort the stream based on the **SeqID**.

Open the **Contiguous Order Property Editor** and select **SeqID** as the **Sort by** id.

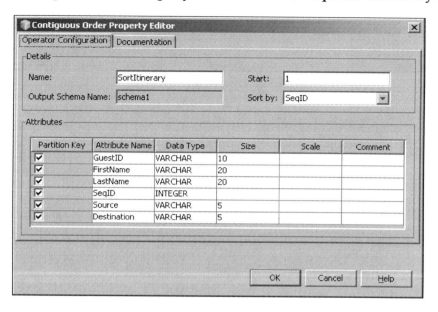

Despite of the time based filtering we did earlier, there could be several itinerary records that you may need to control processing. We can set it to process only the last four records of the itinerary using a Partitioned Window. Double-click **Partitioned Window Property Editor** and set the **Size** to **4**. Note that the preferences attributes will be missing from the list.

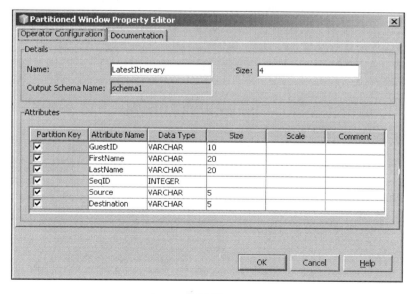

Now that our IEP is ready, we use the Table Output operator to write to a table. Double-click the **Table Output Property Editor** and select **Is Global** and give a **Global ID** name as **CurrentItinerary**.

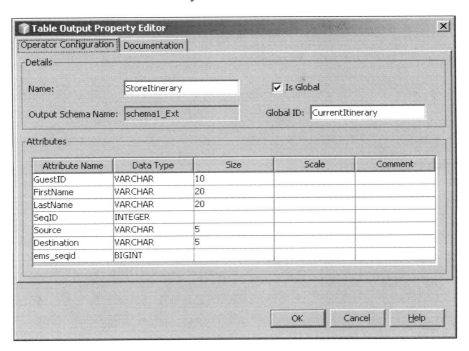

When you deploy this IEP, the IEP service engine will create a table by name **CURRENTITINERARY** as specified by the **Global ID**.

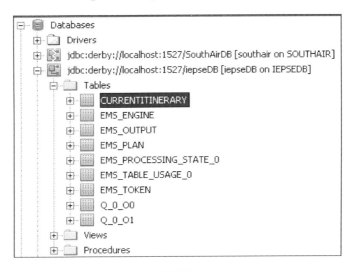

Create a composite application and add the IEP project as a JBI module and deploy the project to the GlassFish Server. At the time of deployment, the **CURRENTITINERARY** table will be created. Now to test the IEP, you need to generate a stream and pass it to the IEP. For this purpose use the **TestItineraryIEP** standalone java project. It reads the itinerary information stored in the file by the BPEL process and creates a stream and sends it to the IEP. After running the test application check the **CURRENTITINERARY** table to check the filtered itinerary output.

The idea of this part of the example is to show how you can create a very simple event processor that could be deployed as a composite application and works along with a BPEL process into intelligently process a stream of data.

Summary

This chapter showed you how you can use the NetBeans SOA tools and OpenESB components to create simple and powerful BPEL processes, all visually through wizards and property editors. Various parts of this sample showed you how to work each of the binding components and introduced branching and flow in business processes. The last part of the example showed the usage of intelligent event processors to filter and process the stream based on application preferences.

You can use these techniques and tools to build a scalable business using BPEL as the orchestration point.

11
Composite Applications

Whenever you need to deploy your BPEL process or IEP module, you have to deploy them through a service assembly or a composite application.

A composite application is a service congregation consisting of business functionality and information from disparate information sources. Composite applications are both a form of integration, as well as application development. Typically, they are created to support a company's business processes and map them to underlying information resources.

If you have done any business integration, you will be well aware that integration is a longtime messy issue for IT organizations and is the potential candidate for Web services and SOA. Composite applications are conceived as the end product for SOA. The majority of the benefits of SOA are realized when you assemble existing services into composite applications.

Role of Composite Applications

Web services uphold syntax and protocol-level communications but do not provide a way to ensure semantic interoperability. Consider, for example, how a passenger entity is defined in a system based on SAP and how a passenger entity is defined in a system based on Siebel. It could be very different. So who resolves the data disparities between these two different systems to make a meaningful business process? A composite application does that.

How does a composite application extend SOA? SOA recommends building loosely coupled applications and treating each one of them as independent 'service units'. Well-designed composite applications implement this architectural approach by providing an easy way to build business applications. They also provide integration of existing applications with other existing, as well as new applications. This SOA concept of linking together business processes is the hub of composite applications.

What essentially is a composite application?

1. A composite application is typically an application built by combining multiple services.
2. Functionality of a composite application varies based on the individual components.

In essence, a composite application is just an exposing platform for various web services.

There are many tools available today that let you create composite applications. Out of these, NetBeans SOA tools and OpenESB runtime offer an elegant and intuitive way of creating and editing composite applications.

NetBeans Project Types

NetBeans supports creating composite applications through the **Composite Application** project type. The composite application project is an Ant-based NetBeans project system. It allows users to create instances of composite application projects within the NetBeans IDE. Each composite application project instance is a container holding the deployment configuration for a collection of JBI component subprojects like BPEL, XSLT, and Java EE projects. The project system allows the user to create a Service Assembly (SA) artifact that contains all subprojects as Service Units (SUs). The SA can then be deployed to the JBI runtime on an Application Server like GlassFish Application Server or Sun Java System Application Server.

The following figure shows how you can use NetBeans' tools to create and edit composite applications:

NetBeans For Composite Applications		
Composite App.	Create ⟩	SOA > Composite Application
Service Units	Create ⟩	SOA > BPEL Module
Editors	Edit ⟩	WSDL, XDS, CASA, BPEL

First, you create a composite application and then add JBI modules to the composite application. When you build the project, Composite Application Service Assembly (CASA) file will be created. You can use the **CASA** Editor tool to edit the composite application configuration by adding WSDL ports, adding connections, and editing properties.

The main objective of the composite application project system is to provide a deployment container for various types of JBI component projects. It provides support for users to selectively include JBI component projects and deployment data. This allows one to reuse JBI component projects for different deployment scenarios. The project system provides support; allowing the user to customize the deployment configuration for different usage scenarios. This service is provided by tools that allow you to add or modify deployment specific data within a composite application project, so that JBI component projects can be designed to be more generic and reusable in multiple deployment scenarios.

Workspace

The **CASA Workspace** is a very intuitive environment. I have used many composite application editors that are not as easy to use as the workspace provided by NetBeans. The following figure shows the conceptual view of a composite application developed using NetBeans. The services interact based on a formal definition or contract implemented by WSDL. All service level communication happens through WSDL. WSDL is independent of the underlying platform and programming language so it is possible to build a composite application with heterogeneous components wrapped up by web services.

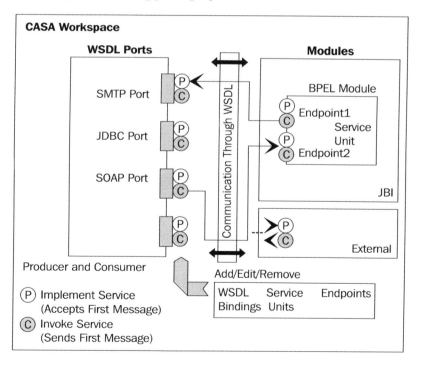

The producer endpoint accepts messages from a consumer endpoint. The producer and consumer endpoints can be in the same service assembly or different service assemblies.

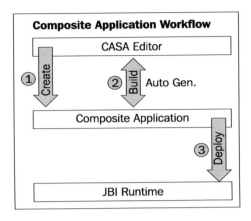

This figure shows the workflow of the **Composite Application** as applicable to NetBeans. You **Create**, **Build**, and **Deploy** composite applications in that order. **CASA Editor** lets you edit the service assembly configuration, visually. Whenever you build a project, the **CASA Editor** regenerates the view of the **Composite Application**. After building the **Composite Application** you deploy the application to a **JBI Runtime** engine provided by the application server.

Composite Application comprises of **SUs**, **End Points** and **Connections** as defined by the JBI specification.

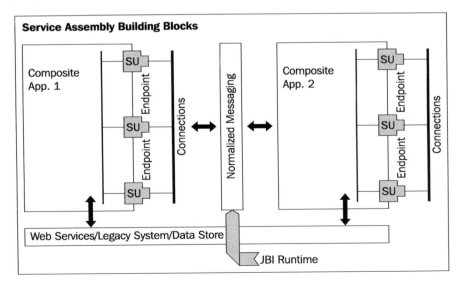

Endpoint connections are of three types:

- Connections between service units inside a service assembly. The connections are part of the same JBI platform.
- Connections between service units that are part of different service assemblies.
- Connections between service units that are part of different service platforms.

	Connection Type		
	Inter-SU	**Inter-SA**	**External**
Connection Endpoints	Services of a Service Assembly	Services of Different Service Assemblies	Services of Different Service Platforms
Service Platform	Same JBI Platform	Same JBI Platform	Maybe Different
Target Service	Early Binding (@design-time)	Late Binding (@run-time)	Late Binding (@run-time)
Message Format	JBI Normalized XML Message	JBI Normalized XML Message	WSDL Specified Message Format

Non-Hierarchical Model

A traditional enterprise application that involves web services receives a request through SOAP or other protocols, processes the request, and sends the results back to the consumer. This is often achieved through JAXP calls and JAX-WS annotations.

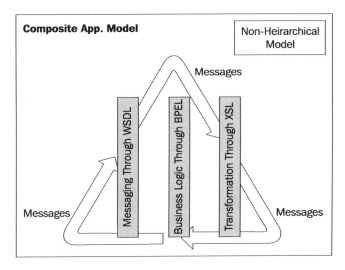

Unlike the traditional application model, which uses domain specific libraries like
Java EE, .Net, the **Composite Application Model** uses **Messages** and is based on a
Non-Hierarchical Model. This peer-to-peer nature can be used to inject aspects into
the composite applications, providing clear layers of separation.

CASA Editor

CASA editor lets you see a high-level view of how SA is connected and configured.
More importantly, users can modify connections between elements within SA. The
routing of SUs and BCs can be easily tweaked or completely redone as it provides
visual editor enriched with a component palette for all available artifacts like binding
components and service units.

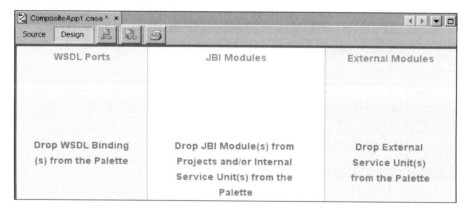

The first pane of the editor lists all the **WSDL Ports**. The second pane shows all
available **JBI Modules**. You can drag-and-drop any JBI module, including BPEL
modules, in this space. You can also add **Service Units** that are part of other service
assemblies in the third pane.

See the following figure for an example view. We have added two **WSDL Ports** of
SOAP binding. **ProcessReservationPort** consumes a BPEL process, which in turn
consumes **NorthAirWS**.

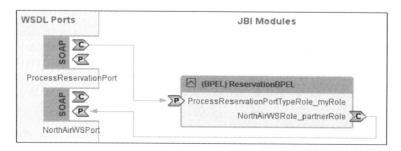

You can add more **WSDL Bindings** that may not be part of your existing BPEL module and configure the **Endpoints** graphically through the CASA Editor. If you are using OpenESB bundle, you should see many **WSDL Bindings** available in the palette as shown in the following screenshot:

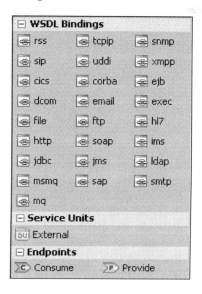

If you are using NetBeans IDE, you may not see all of the **WSDL Bindings**. In that case, you need to manually download and install the Binding Components as discussed in the previous chapters.

Summary

In this chapter, we understood the need for a composite application to build a SOA-based applications. The composite application offered by NetBeans comes with an easy to use editor. Using this editor, you can add and edit WSDL bindings, service units and end points through a graphical interface.

Index

T

termination handlers 197

W

web service activities, BPEL
  invoke 84, 85
  partner link 88-90
  receive 86
  reply 87
Web Service Definition Language.
    See WSDL
WSDL
  <definitions> element 118
  about 115
  benefits 116, 117
  documents 116
  editor 115
  entities, refactoring 129, 130
  simple web service, building 130-139
WSDL documents
  about 116
  binding types 124, 125
  creating, within NetBeans IDE 121-124
  editing, within NetBeans IDE 125-129
  fault, handling 180-183
  format 117
  Partner view 128
  Source view 126
  structure 117, 118
  views 125
  WSDL view 126
WSDL editor 115

X

XML Schema
  about 142, 143
  design patterns 154, 156
  features 144
  XML structure, defining 144
XML Schema documents
  about 145
  NetBeans support 145
XSD file
  creating, within NetBeans 146
  design patterns, applying 156
  Design view 147
  Design view, elements 153
  Design view, entities creating 151
  Design view, features 150-153
  Design view, Find Usages tool 153
  Schema view 147
  Schema view, entities creating 148-150
  Schema view, features 148-150
  Source view 147
  Source view, features 147
  views 146
XSLT Service Engine
  about 44, 45
  request reply service, creating 46
  request reply service, Service types 46
  service bridge, creating 48
  service bridge, Service types 46
  Service types 45
  XSLT modules, building 45
  XSLT modules, WSDL files 45
  XSLT modules, XML files 45

[PACKT]
PUBLISHING

Thank you for buying
Building SOA-Based Composite
Applications Using NetBeans IDE 6

Packt Open Source Project Royalties

When we sell a book written on an Open Source project, we pay a royalty directly to that project. Therefore by purchasing Building SOA-Based Composite Applications Using NetBeans IDE 6, Packt will have given some of the money received to the NetBeans project.

In the long term, we see ourselves and you — customers and readers of our books — as part of the Open Source ecosystem, providing sustainable revenue for the projects we publish on. Our aim at Packt is to establish publishing royalties as an essential part of the service and support a business model that sustains Open Source.

If you're working with an Open Source project that you would like us to publish on, and subsequently pay royalties to, please get in touch with us.

Writing for Packt

We welcome all inquiries from people who are interested in authoring. Book proposals should be sent to authors@packtpub.com. If your book idea is still at an early stage and you would like to discuss it first before writing a formal book proposal, contact us; one of our commissioning editors will get in touch with you.

We're not just looking for published authors; if you have strong technical skills but no writing experience, our experienced editors can help you develop a writing career, or simply get some additional reward for your expertise.

About Packt Publishing

Packt, pronounced 'packed', published its first book "Mastering phpMyAdmin for Effective MySQL Management" in April 2004 and subsequently continued to specialize in publishing highly focused books on specific technologies and solutions.

Our books and publications share the experiences of your fellow IT professionals in adapting and customizing today's systems, applications, and frameworks. Our solution-based books give you the knowledge and power to customize the software and technologies you're using to get the job done. Packt books are more specific and less general than the IT books you have seen in the past. Our unique business model allows us to bring you more focused information, giving you more of what you need to know, and less of what you don't.

Packt is a modern, yet unique publishing company, which focuses on producing quality, cutting-edge books for communities of developers, administrators, and newbies alike. For more information, please visit our website: www.PacktPub.com.

Service Oriented Java Business Integration

ISBN: 978-1-847194-40-4   Paperback: 350 pages

Integrating solution for Java developers

1. Enterprise Service Bus (ESB) for integrating loosely coupled, pluggable services.

2. See Enterprise Integration Patterns (EIP) in action, in code.

3. ESB integration solutions using Apache open source tools

4. JBI features explained with the help of real world examples

SOA Approach to Integration

ISBN: 978-1-904811-17-6   Paperback: 300 pages

XML, Web services, ESB, and BPEL in real-world SOA projects

1. Service-Oriented Architectures and SOA approach to integration

2. SOA architectural design and domain-specific models

3. Common Integration Patterns and how they can be best solved using Web services, BPEL and Enterprise Service Bus (ESB)

4. Concepts behind SOA standards, security, transactions, and how to efficiently work with XML

Please visit **www.PacktPub.com** for information on our titles

5042372R0

Made in the USA
Lexington, KY
28 March 2010